Anti-Arab Racism in the USA

"Steven Salaita's *Anti-Arab Racism in the USA* is an important and welcome contribution to the growing body of scholarship on the post 9/11 Arab-American experience."—**Hussein Ibish**, Vice-Chair, Progressive Muslim Union and Senior Fellow, American Task Force On Palestine

"A sobering analysis of anti-Arab racism, from neo-conservative to liberal, rooted in America's settler colonial past and seeping into every corner of our lives, especially in the universities. Steven Salaita takes the reader into the crisis of Arab-American communities in the wake of 9/11 and the emergence of what he calls the culture of imperative patriotism. Written with passion, this lucid account of the dangers of American imperialism paints a dark picture of the agenda of the Bush administration not only in the Arab world but also for people of color at home."—**Miriam Cooke**, Professor, Duke University

"*Anti-Arab Racism in the USA* offers an impassioned and deeply compelling look at the origins, evolution, manifestations and implications of anti-Arab racism today. In prose that is both scathing and theoretically and historically informed, Salaita traces anti-Arab racism from founding U.S. doctrines of manifest destiny, exceptionalism and expansionism through nineteenth-century European colonialism to contemporary political, cultural and religious discourse, both in the U.S. and internationally. A tour de force which makes it impossible to avoid grappling with the seriousness of anti-Arab racism and its implications for our times."—**Lisa Suhair Majaj**, co-editor, *Etel Adnan: Critical Reflections on the Arab-American Writer and Artist* and *Intersections: Gender, Nation, and Community in Arab Women's Novels*

"Steven Salaita dives head first into the heart of racism in America and uses his personal experiences to help readers understand the mechanics of racism as it applies to Arabs, Muslims and people who look Middle Eastern in the post-September 11 world."—**Ray Hanania**, journalist and filmmaker, author of *I'm Glad I Look Like a Terrorist: Growing up Arab in America* and *Arabs of Chicagoland*

"*Anti-Arab Racism in the USA* is a highly recommended read, not only for students of Middle East history and affairs, but for the average American who simply longs to know how we have become so intimately and yet so bitterly entwined with the people of the Middle East. Salaita does a great job of incorporating light-hearted stories of personal experience with meaty and profound concepts of great consequence. He articulates how institutions from the media to upper level government to the American people in general have been steeped in the noxious teachings of anti-Arab racism, and how those notions have readied us and dulled our sense of humanity in the face of grave injustices committed against Arabs and Muslims worldwide. Salaita has thoughtfully articulated a very regretful era of unabashed racism in American history."—**Ramzy Baroud**, Editor, *Palestine Chronicle* and author of *Searching Jenin*

Anti-Arab Racism in the USA

Where It Comes from and What It Means for Politics Today

STEVEN SALAITA

Pluto Press

LONDON • ANN ARBOR, MI

First published 2006 by Pluto Press
345 Archway Road, London N6 5AA
and 839 Greene Street, Ann Arbor, MI 48106

www.plutobooks.com

British Library Cataloguing in Publication Data
A catalogue record for this book is available from the British Library

ISBN 0 7453 2517 3 hardback
ISBN 0 7453 2516 5 paperback

Library of Congress Cataloging in Publication Data applied for

10 9 8 7 6 5 4 3 2 1

Designed and produced for Pluto Press by
Chase Publishing Services, Fortescue, Sidmouth, EX10 9QG, England
Typeset from disk by Stanford DTP Services, Northampton, England
Printed and bound in Canada by Transcontinental Printing

Contents

To all victims of racism, everywhere

Acknowledgements

Although this book was written primarily during the summer of 2004, it has been in formation for many years. During the time that I have been contemplating anti-Arab racism and its effects on the cultures and politics of the United States, I have been aided invaluably by numerous people.

I would like to thank very deeply the close group of friends with whom I was lucky enough to become involved while a doctoral student at the University of Oklahoma: Mohammad Al-Ramahi, Tariq Alzoubi, Rania Dughman, Nadim Ferzli, Ghada Janbey, Heather Janbay, Rima Najjar Kapitan, Fadi Shadfan, and Nimer Shadfan. In many ways I view this project as a collective effort between myself and these dear friends, because most of the arguments I present in *Anti-Arab Racism in the USA* grew out of our seemingly infinite conversations, our shared commitment to peace and justice in the Near East, and the work many of us did in re-forming and developing the OU Arab Student Association. The endless generosity and hospitality of this community of friends also enabled me to navigate whatever impediments arose in bringing this book into production.

I also owe a debt of gratitude to the colleagues who have supported me either by reading and commenting on the manuscript or by aiding me in my professional development: Etel Adnan, Barbara Nimri Aziz, Ramzy Baroud, Miriam Cooke, Ray Hanania, Hussein Ibish, Catherine John, Lisa Suhair Majaj, Geneva Moore, Timothy Poland, Rita Sizemore Riddle, Howard Ross, and George Savage. Roger van Zwanenberg's enthusiasm and professionalism have been integral to the publication of *Anti-Arab Racism in the USA*.

Thanks also are due to Douglas Kiel, Joseph Lubasz, and Angela Miller for extending to me an open invitation into their sweat lodge and to Luis Monterrosa for the beautiful music that often accompanied the transcription of the manuscript.

A slightly modified version of Chapter Two appeared originally in *College Literature* 32 (2005) and the section "Eulogizing Edward Said" in Chapter Three appeared in a slightly modified form in *Minnesota Review* 61–62 (2004). I thank the editors for allowing me to reprint those articles here.

I have been blessed with a continually supportive, sometimes rambunctious, always interesting, and, above all, loving family. I have learned much about the world outside of textbooks from *Amami* George, Ghaleb, Suleiman, and the late Saleem, who remains daily in my thoughts; *Amati* Fadwa, Loris, Zoyee, Zakia, and the late Cathy, who likewise is missed greatly. The same holds true for *mis tíos* Richard, Salvador, and the late Jorge, a constant inspiration; *mi tía* Marta and *mi abuelita*; and my late *abuelito*, who still visits in times of need.

For putting up with my frequent neurosis and occasional unpleasantness, I wish to offer profound appreciation to my nuclear family, which has provided me more joy than any amount of money or material possessions ever could: Nasr, Miriam, Nasri, Delia, Michael, Danya, John, and Peter—and especially my wife, Diana, who always believes in me even when I don't deserve her tremendous energy and ambition.

Introduction: The Evolution of White Supremacy

I had always pictured my paternal grandfather as a desert warrior. He was a Bedouin sheikh riding across the bronzed landscape atop a one-hump camel, his red and white *kuffiyeh* tied to his head with a black rope, the back folds flying outward as he gained speed. I would reach out to touch the golden dagger inlaid with mother-of-pearl strapped to his waist with papyrus rope. My fingers could only graze the bottom of his gray robe as he swept past, the king of the desert on a secret mission.

Yes, this was my grandfather, of the Balqa region, a Christian Bedouin of the Ma'aia tribe. ("No Whites converted us," my dad would tell me as a child. "The Salaita were baptized by Jesus.") He lived into his nineties, passing away before meeting the last of his grandchildren, with whom he could never communicate and who lived two continents away.

Yet I knew my grandfather when I was a small boy. I saw him when I went to the movies; he had his own program on television. At 6:00 pm each evening, he was on the screen, in Lebanon, Palestine, Libya, Iraq, flyting and preaching hate. He had ten or eleven starring roles in *Lawrence of Arabia*. My grandfather was a terrorist, a romance, an obedient servant.

In fact, everybody in my family, I learned at a young age, was afflicted with innately violent tendencies. The nicer ones were, TV taught me, merely irrational or voraciously promiscuous. I grew up as a first-generation Arab American hating, as do so many minority children in the United States, the essence of my very existence. That hatred has since been transformed into an intense pride. I have waited years to do whatever I can to dismantle the system that encourages Arab American children to be scared of their own names, their parents' accents, and their families' skin tones.

Unfortunately, childhood self-hatred wasn't simply reinforced in popular culture. I grew up inundated with racism. It would be dishonest for me to claim that my childhood experiences somehow represent all first-generation Arab Americans. I grew up in a different time than today's youngsters and doubtless in a much different place. In the Appalachian corridor, on the Virginia/West Virginia border, I battled an anti-Arab racism expressed with vicious sincerity. I couldn't wait to get to college, where I thought I would be freed from the small-town discrimination I so detested. I understand now, with bittersweet satisfaction, that unless I leave the United States I will never totally escape the hatred I experienced as a child. While my childhood isn't necessarily a metonym for anything, the racism of Appalachia isn't unique. It is a microcosm of a pervasive and longstanding American racism that Appalachians merely transformed to suit the cultural uniqueness of the region.

I remember every racist episode with a clarity that keeps me healthily angry. There was the time when, at age eight, I wasn't allowed into a neighbor's house to use the bathroom because "Indians don't piss." Another time, my friend's mother, an overbearing person who always wore a nightgown emblazoned with tiny green whales, demanded to know why my family "always has to do such weird shit." Perhaps nothing beats the time our bald, one-armed neighbor built a fence—only on our side of the yard. At the time, the fence amused my family, with its sheer ugliness and lopsided symbolism. Though I still remember the fence (which remains standing) with some amusement, I now view it as less benign, as it so obviously represents the same pragmatically racist attitude that has infected Israeli society in its support of the West Bank "security fence" and that inspires the omnipresent fences constructed around the United States to marginalize undesirables, who inevitably are poor or of color (usually both). Once when I was home from college for the summer, I went to my father's office at the local college to use the internet. It was right after exam week, and my father hadn't been to work since recording his grades. As I approached his office, I noticed a note taped to his door. I removed it so I could leave it on his desk, but stopped short once I saw written, with the impeccable American sense of geography: "Go home you fucking Iranian."

Things weren't much better at school. I was sensitive about my brown skin as early as I can remember because it seemed to inspire fascination among other students, who, as they became more inculcated into American exceptionalism, gradually turned the fascination into scorn. Since my mother, a Nicaraguan of Palestinian origin, taught Spanish at the local middle and high schools, I was treated to continual insults about the Rio Grande, border jumping, refried beans, and laziness. The more knowledgeable students taunted me about riding camels, fucking goats, and bombing the school. By the time I reached high school I quit trying to fight back; the foreign kid never wins crack fights in American schools.

I can't remember a single instance, from kindergarten to twelfth grade, when a teacher intervened to stop others from insulting me. In fact, at times it was teachers who articulated racism with a cruelty unsurpassed by students. A first-grade teacher once referred to the *warag dawali* (grape leaves) my mother had packed me as "little pieces of doo-doo" in front of a crowd of laughing children. Another teacher once snarled, "Don't ever do that again, you damn foreigner." Other examples are less explicit: being sent to the principal's office an extraordinary amount of times; being suspended for actions that resulted in no punishment for others; being made into the token example of everything "foreign" or "international."

Looking back, this treatment doesn't strike me as surprising anymore, something I would have realized at the time had I analyzed the schools' environments rather than vigorously ignoring them. The high school football coach, a local celebrity (and therefore a cliché), was famous for telling "nigger jokes" to every White person who frequented his office. In Civics class, we were taught that the world is unfair because of the pernicious influence of liberal media. An elementary school teacher whose husband had fought in Korea informed us that, according to her husband, the war was so difficult because "those people just didn't value life. They would send waves and waves of people to die. The Americans couldn't keep up with them." It seems so obvious now: given this environment, of course the schools were filled with racism.

The schools in my hometown haven't changed (many of the same teachers remain), but I doubt many schools in the United States are afflicted with such overt racism. I do believe, however, that tacit racism exists in schools across the country. This belief is based on the fact that tacit (and explicit) racism exists in all sectors and regions of the United States. Teachers certainly aren't immune to it. Sometimes they battle valiantly against it (at the risk of losing their jobs), but often they unwittingly reinforce it. In fact, racism is perpetually reinforced in some of the most seemingly benign institutions in the United States. Much of that racism is now directed at Arabs, although it is not exclusively devoted to them.

The Origin of White Supremacy

Much of the inspiration for the project this book represents arises from my own experience as an Arab in the United States, although I haven't penned a personal narrative. Like many academics, I became interested during university study in contextualizing my life within broader social and theoretical paradigms in order to make better sense of it. In so doing, I wanted to more thoroughly comprehend how racism functions in American society. I learned simply by existing how brutal anti-Arab racism can be, but I came to understand through intense study how anti-Arab racism is a phenomenon that, placed in the comprehensive framework of American exceptionalism, is traceable to the very origin of the United States.

Again, the experiences I describe above contribute to this understanding. Although I am a full-blooded Arab (and, on my mother's side, culturally Hispanic to some degree), I didn't always experience anti-Arab racism growing up, and I don't always experience it today. Instead, I was transformed into an Indian, both Asian and American, and treated to the full range of stereotypes about those groups. I was asked a few times whether I am "White or nigger." I've heard a frightening range of Mexican jokes. I was even once called a dago. All of these examples are the result of my moderately brown skin. In turn, I learned at a young age, without the benefit of any formal education, that it is foolish to decontextualize any potentially interrelated social phenomena, especially when they inform notions of Americanness and the peculiar modes of Othering that arose during the settlement of North America and continue in modern forms today.

Given this recognition, how is it possible to hypothesize and then delineate the existence of an anti-Arab racism? It is not an easy task. In many ways, the task is a fool's mission. Yet I see it as a necessary mission. While anti-Arab racism is linked to other forms of American racism (including anti-Semitism), it nevertheless retains specific features relating directly to the interaction of Arabism and Americana, particularly as the American capitalist system came into contact with the resources of the Arab World. The origin of American racism is a combination of European colonial values and interaction with Blacks and Indians; the racism became uniquely American as the relationship among White settlers and slaveowners and those they subjugated evolved from a seemingly one-sided display of power to a complicated (and usually discordant) discourse of oppression and resistance, capitalism and egalitarianism, stereotype and self-representation.

As the United States matured and undertook overseas military missions and absorbed more diverse waves of immigrants, American racism grew more sophisticated and increasingly contradicted its own dogmas—for example, acculturated immigrant groups assumed racist attitudes toward newcomers, while imperialist missions dictated toward whom the omnipresent, if by now ambivalent, racism was to be directed. From these contradictions grew the phenomena of essentialization, xenophobia, and bigotry, often symbiotically associated with racism but sometimes existing in their own philosophical spaces. All the while American racism could be connected to the founding narratives of the United States.

For the most part, Arabs—as compared to, say, Jews or Italians—are recent immigrants to the United States. We are still in the complex (sometimes hateful) process of acculturation, a process every ethnic group arriving in the New World underwent, some, based on their religion and skin color, with more ease than others. Moreover, the United States has for decades had political and economic interests in the Arab World, thereby complicating the positioning of Arabs in American society, which is taught by print and visual media to detest Arabs. The United States' close relationship with Israel, a society with its own tradition of anti-Arab racism, further complicates matters. The chapters that follow will examine foreign policy, capitalism, imperialism, New World settlement, xenophobia, religion, and immigration to illustrate how they created and now sustain anti-Arab racism.

Anti-Arab Racism?

It would be useful to take a moment to examine the demographics of the Arab American community and clarify how I will employ terms such as *Arab*, *anti-Arab racism*, and *Islamophobia*. Attempting to create a sociological boundary around an ethnic community and define malleable (and highly subjective) terms sometimes produces little more than uncertainty, but it will be impossible to adequately discuss anti-Arab racism if we don't theorize what it is and identify against whom it is directed. It is nevertheless wise to keep in mind that Black scholars have been defining racism for decades without agreeing on a comprehensive definition, and, after hundreds of books on the subject, the content of anti-Semitism is still under vigorous debate. Therefore, this attempt—unbelievably, the first book-length attempt—to articulate an intellectual model for highlighting and interrogating anti-Arab racism will likely be challenged and reworked frequently in the future. At least I hope my work here will be challenged and reworked, because the success of the book can only be measured by the response it generates. More important, it would mean that people are actually talking about anti-Arab racism in a systematic way rather than in isolation as individuals. Anti-Arab racism has existed in the United States since the arrival of the first Arab in North America, but since 9/11 anti-Arab racism is, to use a cliché, America's elephant in the living room—an enormous elephant, at that.

Arabs have been in the United States since at least the second half of the nineteenth century. Many of the early immigrants arrived from what is now Lebanon, particularly from the Mount Lebanon region, which until the early 1920s was part of Syria. Many of these Syro-Lebanese, as today's scholars call them, spread into rural regions of the United States and became peddlers; others congregated in urban areas in the Northeast and Midwest. The United States saw steady but never overwhelming immigration from the Near East, Lebanon particularly, throughout the first half of the twentieth century. Many Syrians and Palestinians also made the journey. (A good number of Middle Eastern immigrants in the twentieth century went to Chile, Brazil, Honduras, Mexico, and other Latin American nations.) A majority of the early Arab immigrants were Christian. Like European immigrants, they left the Near East to escape political upheaval and poverty and/or to seek their fortunes in the New World.

During this period, most Arab immigrants sought to assimilate, which met with only partial success. Assimilation is a decision one makes by examining the circumstances in which he or she lives, but it is never totally a personal affair. Assimilation occurs successfully only when the person hoping to assimilate is accepted as viable by the society he or she wishes to enter. Arab immigrants were met with discrimination by people who weren't prepared to allow them to become properly "American." Arab Muslim immigrants faced more difficulty than Arab Christians because their religion made them even more strange and threatening to wary Americans.

After the 1967 War in the Near East, however, many Arab Americans emphasized assimilation less, partly because American minority groups were underscoring ethnic pride and partly because America's support for Israel (among other policies) alienated Arab Americans and created a guarded, often unarticulated, disillusionment. Also after 1967, the demographics of Arab America began to change with the arrival of Muslims from Yemen, Egypt, Iraq, Palestine, and Lebanon. Non-Arab Muslims from Pakistan, India, Bangladesh, Iran, Indonesia, and sub-Saharan Africa also altered the nature of immigration to the United States, which in the first half of the twentieth century consisted mainly of Europeans. Although these immigrants didn't consider themselves Arab and never created any real unity with Middle Eastern immigrants, they helped buttress a general sense of pride in Islam and the East. And they became active on behalf of causes that dovetailed in some cases with those of Arabs.

The non-Arab Muslim population of the United States is important to this discussion because no clear boundaries demarcate it from the Arab American community. Furthermore, since most Arabs are Muslim (including around half of Arab Americans) we have to examine the relationship of anti-Arab racism and what in recent years has come to be known as Islamophobia. Islamophobia appears to be the equivalent to Muslims of what anti-Semitism is to Jews, at least in its current usage: at its most basic level, an inherent dislike for, or hatred toward, Islam and Muslims. The British organization Forum Against Islamophobia and Racism (FAIR) notes, "Islamophobia has now become a recognised form of racism. Furthermore, as with the inaccuracy of such terms as 'anti-Semitism' to describe the anti-Jewish hostility that developed in the late nineteenth century, 'Islamophobia' bears many similar hallmarks."[1] FAIR later claims, "This intolerance and stereotypical views of Islam manifest themselves in a number of ways from verbal/written abuse, discrimination at schools and workplaces, psychological harassment/pressure and outright violent attacks on mosques and individuals."[2] This definition of Islamophobia is comprehensive and parallels, as FAIR suggests, popular definitions of anti-Semitism. Yet the definition still leaves us with a number of slippery philosophical possibilities.

First, we have to decide whether Islamophobia exists because Islam is to many a racialized metonym of Southern/Third World savagery, or if it arose because of the Enlightenment and post-Enlightenment reordering of Christianity. Or, if both of these factors helped create Islamophobia (and here I accept the assumption that Islamophobia does exist and is a problem), how have they interacted in the past and how do they reinforce one another today? Second, the configuration of the word *Islamophobia* potentially creates ambivalence. Unlike *anti-Semitism*, which implies, or has grown to imply, intrinsic disdain, *Islamophobia* denotes fear. While fear of Muslims no doubt contributes to prejudice against them, I would argue that any serious analysis of hatred (explicit or implicit) against

Islam and its adherents must account for more than trepidation or ignorance. An interesting community to examine in this context would be the Nation of Islam, whose members likely encounter racism primarily as Blacks but also are victims of Islamophobia, an intersection of historical and modern racism that complicates any attempt to delegate racism into separate or exclusive categories and that reveals the heterogeneous nature of racism's ideological underpinnings.

Finally, it is necessary to determine against whom Islamophobia is directed. The most immediate answer, of course, is Muslims, but Islamophobia, if we strictly examine its prejudicial functions, appears at times to be directed at non-Muslims such as Arab Christians, Sikhs, Hindus, or even Hispanics—i.e., anybody perceived to be Muslim, which indicates that Islamophobia doesn't actually arise from the subject but squarely implicates the purveyor. And yet some Muslims—Fouad Ajami, Ibn Warraq, Kanan Makiya—appear themselves to engage in Islamophobia; at least they do if we isolate some of their writings and apply to them the same scrutiny that we do to, say, neoconservative Islamophobia. This fact indicates that the purveyor of Islamophobia isn't necessarily ignorant or merely indoctrinated and creates the possibility that a Muslim can direct Islamophobia at a non-Muslim. Definitions of "Muslim," therefore, are themselves slippery and inconsistent, within Muslim communities and in the United States in general.

The final observation is of greatest relevance at this point. If Islamophobia is a form of racism directed against Muslims, then what about those who are perceived to be Muslim? In turn, if we are able to detect in the United States a phenomenon we call *anti-Arab racism*, then how does that racism relate to Islamophobia? Obviously, Islamophobia—as a concept and a term—needs to be more thoroughly analyzed, especially in the United States, where its usage is common among Islamic advocacy groups but lags behind Europe (especially

Britain) in public usage.[3] Likewise, anti-Arab racism must be more carefully interrogated so we can draw out some of the assumptions and ideologies that inspire it. I hope the question of how these two terms relate—or are interchangeable—will be taken up at length by others. I suspect that at this point, *anti-Arab racism* and *Islamophobia* are generally used to describe the same thing.

I am tempted simply to subsume the term *Islamophobia* into my discussion of anti-Arab racism and let readers sort out whatever questions arise as a result. Why would I instinctively choose to subsume Islamophobia within anti-Arab racism? The answer perhaps reveals more than the question inspires. I would argue that Arab Christians (and other groups who are considered de facto if not de jure Muslims) are usually relegated into an Islamic identity in the discourse of many American racists, who often base their dislike (or fear) of Arabs on the misrepresentations of Islam pervasive in American popular culture. This dislike, however, is actually based on more than religious acrimony, whether or not those who dislike Arabs and Muslims understand the origins of their worldview (most, I would venture to guess, don't). The term *Islamophobia*, therefore, will not be comprehensive enough in a study of anti-Arab racism, even though *Islamophobia* is a valuable word that should be forced into a more common usage in the United States. *Anti-Arab racism*, I think, works better here because ultimately it contextualizes misrepresentations of Islam within a wider culture of prejudice, hatred, and oppression that continually recapitulates a modernized form of the traditional American metanarrative of racism. The word *racism* needs to be part of our vocabulary if we are to successfully juxtapose Arabs with other victims of that metanarrative. To reduce our discussion simply to distortions about Islam (an important factor, but hardly a comprehensive one), we would necessarily have to shift its focus from the United States to Europe and the theological vagrancies of industrialism and Empire.

My argument here relies on the assumption that there is something uniquely American about anti-Arab racism in the United States. By "uniquely American," I mean to say that anti-Arab racism in today's United States is organized within specific historical forces that produced racism in the New World and sustained it throughout the development of the United States. I will discuss those historical forces in more detail in Chapter Two, but for now suffice it to say that both Arabs and Muslims inherited a history when they traveled to the United States and that it would be foolish to examine the present condition of anti-Arab racism without assessing that history.

Part of the history Arabs and Muslims inherited occurred outside the United States. The inscription and evolution of racism on the North American continent have affected numerous ethnic and/or immigrant groups in the United States. Yet today Arabs and Muslims are seeing something of a rehashed geopolitical paradigm that has long influenced the image of Arabs among Americans. This geopolitical paradigm begins with Muslim piracy in the late eighteenth century off the Barbary Coast, which prompted a firestorm of vitriol among America's so-called Founding Fathers against what they deemed to be Islamic barbarians. In many ways, the engagement of the early American military with Muslims off the Barbary Coast and the insidious moralizing against supposed Arab slavetraders produced a consciousness that was reinvigorated when Arabs migrated to North America decades later. Anti-Arab racism, it might be said, has multiple origins and is both inherited and expedited geopolitically.

What, then, is anti-Arab racism? I cannot answer this question; I can only explain what I mean when I use the term in this book. I use it generally to mean acts of physical violence against Arabs based not on chance but largely (or exclusively) on the ethnicity of the victim; moments of ethnic discrimination in schools, civil institutions, and the workplace; the Othering of Arabs based on essentialized or biologically determined ideology; the totalization and dehumanization of Arabs by continually referring to them as terrorists; the marginalization of Arabs as it is informed by exclusionary conceptions of Americanness; the taunting of Arabs with epithets such as *sand nigger, dune coon, camel jockey, towelhead,* and *raghead*; the profiling of Arabs based on name, religion, or country of origin; and the elimination of civil liberties based on distrust of the entire group rather than on the individuals within that group who may merit suspicion. In short, the redirection of classic American racism at a non-White ethnic group whose origins lie in an area of the world marked for colonization by the United States and whose residents are therefore dehumanized for the sake of political expediency. Without question, some of the examples I have offered above don't at times connote racism *per se*, but I will argue later that each example is inspired to some degree by racist attitudes that cannot withstand basic scrutiny.

Anti-Arab racism, however, isn't a self-contained institution (if it can even be called an institution). It engages in a constant dialectic with other types of racism (both American and European) as well as colonialism, capitalism, nationalism, exceptionalism, and religious fundamentalism. Any definition of it must necessarily shift to account for the shifting factors that contribute to its evolution. Ultimately, though, it can be said that defining any type of racism is merely academic, because although it is difficult to define in a book or a discussion, anybody who has experienced racism knows exactly when it occurs and what it is. The recipient of racism usually undergoes a different sort of intellectual development than do White theorists: one based on the knowledge that identity does matter, and matters deeply, and that transforming anger into accessible social discourse isn't as simplistic a move as privileged academics portray it to be.

Let me digress for a moment and explain why I haven't simply endeavored to rework the term *Orientalism*, which, of course, was rendered infamous by the late Edward Said in his book of the same name. *Orientalism* has been remarkably useful as a descriptive critique of phenomena ranging from misconceptions of Arabs to foolhardy foreign policy, and has seen its use (quite justifiably) increase among Arab Americans in the post-9/11 United States. The term, however, is weighted with considerable theoretical and historical baggage, rendering it, at least in some intellectual circles, oblique or ambivalent. Given its layered connotations and the controversies over its denotation, we can sense in its usage the potential for slippage or a rhetorical imprecision born of a correspondingly ambivalent or oblique authorial/oratorical intention. Most important, though, *Orientalism* isn't entirely appropriate when we consider the effects of stereotype and bigotry on Arab Americans, who, in a much different way than their brethren in the Arab World, need to be located in a particular tradition of which they have been a partial inheritor. That tradition, uniquely American, includes the internment of Japanese Americans during World War II, institutionalized anti-Semitism until the 1960s, and a peculiarly durable xenophobia spanning decades, with, at times, acculturated immigrant groups directing it at newer arrivals. This tradition, of course, has as its partial inspiration a corresponding tradition, that of garrison settlement, slavery, and Messianic fervor, a tradition that has evolved into detectable features of modern Americana that, unlike immigrant histories, do in some way affect Middle Eastern Arabs. This corresponding tradition has inspired the premillenialist overtones so evident in American foreign policy.

Where does anti-Arab racism occur? Or, to be more precise, are we speaking of American anti-Arab racism as it occurs in, say, Iraq (in such cases as the torture of prisoners at Abu Ghraib), or only within the borders of the United States? Both.

I would argue that examples of American racism in the Arab World and instances of racism against Arabs in the United States are interchangeable. They both arise from the same intellectual framework, and when anti-Arab racism occurs in the Near East it buttresses the propensity for it to occur in the United States. In addition, I will for the most part avoid hyphenated identities throughout the book and speak of "Arabs" as Arabs, whether they live in the United States or the Arab World (although Chapter Two deals mainly with the Arab American community). I will offer numerous examples of anti-Arab racism on both continents and attach them to the same ideological dynamic.

I use the rather generic term *Arab*, then, to encompass Middle Eastern/North African Arabs, Arab Americans, and, by association, Muslims (because the majority of Arabs are Muslim and because popular discourse associates the two so interchangeably). Also included in my critique to some degree are other Easterners who usually are lumped together with Arabs as darkeyed threats to American national security: South and Central Asians, Iranians, Indonesians, and other brown-skinned peoples scattered throughout the Islamic world. We will see that the so-called interchangeability of Arabs and Muslims of all ethnic backgrounds is itself a result of anti-Arab racism. Of course, as Anouar Majid has shown us, the word *Arab* itself isn't so trenchant.[4] Nevertheless, we will base our discussion on the understanding that an Arab originates from the 22 Arabic-speaking nations of North Africa and West Asia, although anti-Arab racism is much larger than this enormous region.

The Role of Arab Americans

The Arab American community is well suited to examine anti-Arab racism because many Americans of Arab origin have experienced it and because our existence in the United

States has helped precipitate its formation. In many cases, the existence of Arabs in the United States has allowed politicians to justify draconian legislation and pursue both domestic and foreign policies that might otherwise be inconceivable. In this sense, even people concerned with the well-being of the United States are implicated in anti-Arab racism because they fail to recognize the role it plays in an array of disastrous government initiatives (the USA Patriot Act, the war on Iraq, continued support for Israeli ethnic cleansing, and so forth).

Since 9/11, the Arab American community has received considerable attention in two main forms: from neoconservatives as evidence of omnipresent danger and from ecumenical and progressive groups as evidence of the need to curtail domestic abuse and preserve civil liberties. Although Arab Americans aren't, in my opinion, afforded the necessary space in the United States to articulate our diverse cultural and political sensibilities, we are without question at the center of myriad national debates regardless of the propensity of both neoconservatives and progressives to reduce us to tropes that justify various political agendas. While anybody can certainly provide an interesting discussion of anti-Arab racism, it is my contention that only Arabs who have experienced it are qualified to demystify it with the force it demands. We should keep in mind, though, that anti-Arab racism is a national problem not simply because it denotes the continued existence of racism, but also because the racism presupposes so many policy issues of great national import.

There is no shortage of Arabs in the United States to undertake the task of dismantling anti-Arab racism. As with other minority communities, our census numbers are under considerable debate. According to the 2000 census, Arab Americans number 1.2 million, a figure that places us at less than 1 per cent of the American population. Other organizations, however, quote a much higher number based on various deficiencies in census calculations. Even though Arab Americans have been classified as African, Asian, or Other throughout our history, we are now officially classified as "White" in census documents, so numerous Arab Americans are delegated into this category because they fail to complete the section on ancestry/national origin (usually from acculturation, apprehension, indifference, or defensiveness). In addition, many Arab Americans refuse to even complete the census form because they fear being harassed or deported if they register themselves officially. (This fear was validated when the *New York Times*, in an otherwise monumentally underreported story, reported in July 2004 that the Census Bureau provides the Department of Homeland Security with detailed information about Arab Americans, a frightening development justified by a Bureau spokeswoman as a necessary means to know in which airports to post signs in Arabic.)[5] The United States also has a vested interest in undercounting Arab Americans, just as it prefers to undercount Indians.

James Zogby's Arab American Institute (AAI), one of the leading demographic institutions in the nation, claims that the Arab American population is at least 3.5 million and could be considerably larger.[6] The American–Arab Anti-Discrimination Committee (ADC), the largest Arab American advocacy organization, quotes a similar figure. Most journalists tend to follow the census numbers in reporting the demographics of the Arab American community, though many note the discrepancy between the census and the AAI numbers. I believe that if Arab students, noncitizens, and undocumented immigrants are taken into account, the Arab American community is at least 4 million. More comprehensive demographic studies in the future will show a sharp numerical increase, especially when the national environment induces less suspicion.

Arab Americans are educated to greater levels than the overall American populace. As a whole, we also earn more household and mean income, although Detroit, New York, and Chicago, among other cities, have working-class Arab

American neighborhoods. The AAI claims that only 23 per cent of Arab Americans are Muslim,[7] but I believe the proportion to be much higher, perhaps as high as 60 per cent. The majority of Arab Americans list Lebanon as their nation of origin, followed by Syria, Egypt, Palestine, Iraq, and Yemen. California has the most Arab Americans, followed by Michigan, New York, Florida, and New Jersey.[8] Wayne County (Detroit) has the highest concentration of Arab Americans; Los Angeles County has the largest Arab American population.[9]

The Arab American community is remarkably diverse. The constant reductionism with which popular media represent Arab Americans is therefore confounding and can more accurately be described as irresponsible and pernicious. While highlighting our diversity is one way for Arab Americans to counter the stereotyping that informs racism, I believe much more is necessary. Ridding the United States of anti-Arab racism would take nothing less than the elimination of all racism, a continual rewriting of mystified American history, the reordering of jingoistic foreign policy, and sweeping economic reform that privileges the human consumer over the products we consume. In short, it would take a profound reworking of all that is fundamentally American. We would need to begin with the repatriation of North America's indigenous peoples to the lands from which they were displaced and then confront the institutionalization of slavery and imperialism in the American imagination.

Are these tasks possible? Perhaps not. But for the sake of intellectual probity, that is where we will begin.

Internalizing, Ignoring, and Whitewashing Racism

In undertaking this project, we confront a variety of potential dilemmas. The first and most important is also common in anti-racist projects: self-imposed dogma. This dilemma is worth highlighting for a moment. I am wary of intellectual discourses that prescribe and then demand conformity to the dominant contemporary paradigm. For example, in analyzing anti-Semitism many Jews created a corresponding notion of Jewish self-hatred that is applied to those who reject or challenge the prevailing dogmas of Jewish self-determination as encapsulated in various strands of Zionism. Likewise, the Black American community has seen the stratification of Afrocentrists and integrationists (including neoconservatives such as Clarence Thomas and Condoleezza Rice). Although many of the debates within the Jewish and Black communities are sufficiently vibrant to strengthen the intellectual environments and political interests of those communities, the aspects of debate that inflexibly universalize the ethics of legitimacy usually are more harmful than helpful.

Take some of the popular notions of Jewishness disseminated by mainstream and rightwing Zionist groups. They place Israel at the center of Jewish consciousness, which, given their politics, is neither surprising nor especially problematic. However, in so doing they also demand that all other Jews recognize the validity of Jewishness as it is cast in their self-image. Jews who decline are called "self-hating," which implies that they have lost their right to discuss Jewish sensibilities and that their claims to Jewish identity are superficial. Gentiles who criticize Israel are simply dismissed (with moralistic vigor) as incurable anti-Semites. This sort of totalizing discourse not only precludes justice in the Near East, but also weakens legitimate claims of anti-Semitism because it amounts to crying wolf—those who have heard decent and intelligent people repeatedly called anti-Semitic for condemning Israel's ethnic cleansing become programmed into skepticism when the phrase *anti-Semitism* is uttered. Those who have vigorously battled anti-Semitism using this tactic have actually undermined their efforts to incorporate the phenomenon into the moral consciousness of the world. More important, they have constructed a discursive space in which, based on the connotative evolution of the term *anti-Semitism*, it is morally necessary for those opposed to colonization to become anti-Semitic.

Of course, the chance of this situation being repeated in the Arab American community is minimal. Anti-Arab racism is much too new a political subject to induce such internal squabbling; and besides, the moral imperative to free Palestine is considerably less questionable than the racism that underlies Zionist definitions of anti-Semitism. In other words, the Arab American community can battle anti-Arab racism with a clear conscience because our anti-racist discourse is free of the racism that permeates so many aspects of modern Zionism. We should remember, however, that notions of legitimacy usually descend into disempowering egoism. It is crucial to remain focused on the goal of eliminating a deeply rooted anti-Arab racism rather than simply on the credibility of the speaker as he or she relates to the criteria others have established to judge his or her existence. While I dislike the work of scholars such as Fouad Ajami, whose discourse ceaselessly legitimizes anti-Arab racism, I refuse to call him self-hating or deem him anything less than Arab.[10] To do so would result in a dogmatic intellectual paradigm whether or not I would actually vocalize one because the dogma would be inherent in the critique. Those who disagree with Ajami can challenge him eloquently without destroying the diversity of the Arab and Arab American communities.

I would like to note here that this is not a history book—that is, I have no attachment to any historiographical methodology. Nor is this a work of critical theory. It is, using Montaigne's conception of the word, an essay about the pervasiveness of anti-Arab racism and what might be done to counter it effectively. I will document various cases of anti-Arab racism drawn from media reports and oral testimony and theorize the existence of anti-Arab racism in discourses and institutions that most Americans normally wouldn't consider racist. The last point will be crucial in the forthcoming chapters. Racism's greatest danger is its banality. Having experienced all kinds of racism, I can say that racism is never as malicious as when it becomes insidious and in turn is presented as open-minded or enlightened.

I remember encountering a recent example of this sort of racism. I live in Madison, Wisconsin, and recently discovered Madison's wonderful radio station, WORT, of which I have become a dedicated listener. It provides a palatable alternative to the disgustingly conventional corporate stations that, beyond the occasional weather report, are totally useless. So I was a bit disappointed one afternoon driving home when I heard a guest on the local program *A Public Affair* express a position to some degree inspired by a tacit ethos of White supremacy, a position that was therefore racist in effect albeit not in intent.

He was speaking of the state of the anti-war movement in Madison and was asked in his final comments to share with listeners some of the mistakes he thought the movement had made in the months before the invasion of Iraq. After relaying some typical answers—not demonstrating enough, not successfully pressuring politicians—he suggested that the worst mistake he and others had made was not bringing Iraqi Americans into the anti-war movement. "Many people don't know this, but there are actually some Iraqis in Madison," he noted excitedly. He went on to argue that it is quite important to contact Iraqis and incorporate them into anti-war activities because, for some reason, they have been conspicuously absent, most likely because nobody took the time to reach out to them.

The guest's reasoning was spectacularly wrong. I don't claim to know why Madison's Iraqis didn't join with progressive organizations to oppose the war; only they can say, and for somebody who knows nothing about them to speculate on their behalf is, to state it politely, unsavory. I would guess that Iraqis avoided those organizations because, like most of Madison's progressive organizations, they are overwhelmingly White with exclusively White leaderships. The guest also overlooked a possibility that doesn't agree with his sensibilities: many if not most of Madison's Iraqis probably supported the war to some degree. That support was no doubt for different reasons than those of whitebread Americans and neoconservatives, but neither did it correspond with progressive opposition to the war. Numerous Iraqi Americans are political refugees. Many were tortured or harassed by Saddam Hussein's regime. Others have families in Iraq whose safety was compromised by Hussein's brutality. We must remember that before the war, Deputy Defense Secretary Paul Wolfowitz visited an Iraqi American community center in Dearborn and was encouraged to invade Iraq and remove Hussein. (Arab Americans in general, however, opposed the war, although most, myself included, tended to express their opposition in Arab American rather than White organizations.)

Obviously, I could dismiss the radio guest as ignorant, but that would be letting him off the hook—or, to be more precise, it would let the ethos that induced the ignorance off the hook, and this sort of ethos is precisely what any analyst of racism should examine. The guest's discourse was inundated with White supremacy for the following reasons:

- He wanted to incorporate Iraqis into anti-war activities not for their own benefit, but for the benefit of his legitimacy as an anti-war activist.
- Even if the point above is incorrect, the guest still expressed a patronizing philosophy framed by the belief that he and his fellow anti-war activists know what is good for Iraqis better than Iraqis do (which is the attitude that justified the war he opposes).
- He unconsciously succumbed to a longstanding White sense of entitlement by positioning himself as representing the best or only way to oppose the war.

- He assumed that Madison's Iraqis opposed the war although he (by his own admission) knows nothing about them, which squares him, whether he likes it or not, with colonizers who impose on the colonized imaginary agendas in order to advance the colonizers' own interests.

- He romanticized the Iraqis in Madison as something of an anthropological discovery with little regard for their cultural sensibilities, which, based on their nation of origin, would generally make them wary of political involvement, especially the noncitizens who have a legitimate fear of arrest and/or deportation.

The final point reminds me of an Arab Student Association (ASA) meeting some years back at the University of Oklahoma when I was in graduate school. We were a dedicated group headed by a brilliant and indefatigable Palestinian international student named Mohammad Al-Ramahi. At this meeting we were debating how we might best raise awareness on campus about Israel's devastating violence in the Occupied Territories. In attendance was a young White woman, a motivated progressive activist from an affluent family. The rest of the ASA was comprised of international students from the Near East and a few Arab Americans.

Mohammad wanted to produce a "Palestine Week" with an information booth, documentary film screenings, a community dinner, and Norman Finkelstein as the keynote speaker. (Finkelstein ended up coming and delivered a remarkable speech.) The Arab students agreed with this plan, but the young woman argued that we were being too moderate and suggested that we set up a roadblock on the busiest street on campus to illustrate the disruptiveness of Israeli checkpoints. It was a good idea in theory (and in fact was done at UC-Berkeley and a few other campuses), but immediately people in the group balked. "What if we get arrested?", one of the international students asked. "That's the point," she responded. "It'll be an amazing statement." The meeting wound down with a palpable sense of tension.

I tell this story because the White woman had no understanding of the cultural sensibilities with which she was dealing. Like the guest on WORT, she purported to know better than the Arabs what is best for them. It never occurred to her that jail has a much different connotation to the Arabs than to her, an upper-class blond American woman whose father had the influence to save her from incarceration. Nor did it occur to her that the Arab students were already evincing courage because their parents had told them repeatedly not to get involved in politics, given that political involvement in the Arab World often leads to imprisonment, torture, or even death. After 9/11, things weren't much better in the United States, particularly for Arab students, for whom civil disobedience can easily result in arrest without representation or deportation without due process. Or, as in the case of the late Farouk Abdel-Muhti, much worse (Abdel-Muhti was a secular Palestinian activist who was arrested after 9/11, tortured, and kept in solitary confinement for over eight months).[11]

Are the guest on WORT and the woman at the ASA meeting racist? *Per se*, probably not. But they do evince the classic characteristics of White supremacy, a fact that cannot be excused easily. For this reason, I place the onus of dismantling anti-Arab racism directly on Arabs. In the last four years, we have been represented by everybody with any inclination to control or romanticize us. It is therefore time for us to take the initiative in articulating our own concerns and aspirations. The lack of available media space to articulate those concerns and aspirations is connected to the sensibilities detailed above: until Whites with access to a wide range of media abandon the sense of entitlement that convinces them of how qualified they are to speak on behalf of Arabs, then it will be a difficult process. And because I have little faith in Whites to abandon that sense of entitlement, it is crucial for Arab Americans to retain our current media and work to create new publications dedicated to the elimination of anti-Arab racism (and all racism, for that matter, because racism is either eliminated altogether or all people of color will continue to suffer).

Sometimes, though, problems arise when Whites avoid any mention of Arabs in discussions of racism and thus whitewash the racism in question. Perhaps the most conspicuous whitewashing of anti-Arab racism can be found in Michael Moore's *Fahrenheit 9/11*, which generated an extraordinary buzz in the summer of 2004. A muckraking film about George W. Bush's incompetence, *Fahrenheit 9/11* drew enormous crowds at its opening weekend. So in demand was the film in Madison that my wife and I had to buy tickets on Saturday for a Monday showing. The film wasn't worth the wait. Robert Jensen has done a fine job of critiquing what he calls the documentary's "bad analysis," noting that by delegating the lion's share of blame for the state of the nation to Bush and the Republicans, Moore almost totally misses the more important point that the imperial adventurism he condemns is fundamentally a part of American politics, a reality the Democrats have played a large role in forming and supporting.[12]

Jensen also identifies what he calls a "subtle racism" in the film, evident in the nativist scenes of Costa Rican farmers on burros, and monkeys scurrying across the desert in Morocco. The more salient racism, though, arises in the brief scene in which Moore critiques the Patriot Act. In condemning the Patriot Act, Moore chose to profile a small, predominantly White group called Peace Fresno and a White male, Barry Reingold. Peace Fresno was infiltrated by law enforcement agents and Reingold was visited by FBI agents after criticizing Bush in a locker room. These are unpleasant events, to be sure, but they are needlessly docile if they are to be used in an honest critique of the Patriot Act.

Moore might have at least mentioned the anti-Arab racism that was crucial to the passage of the Patriot Act and that remains crucial to its continued existence. Watching *Fahrenheit 9/11*, one would think that only middle-class Whites are inconvenienced by it. Moore could have profiled thousands of Arabs or Muslims who have been detained on undisclosed "secret evidence," denied access to legal representation, and held for months in solitary confinement. Arabs would consider ourselves lucky if we were merely infiltrated on occasion or questioned briefly by an FBI agent. And every Arab active in politics, like most who aren't, already knows that Arab organizations, both civil and political, have been infiltrated. This section of *Fahrenheit 9/11* would be the equivalent of discussing unfair labor practices and, instead of profiling Tyson employees or migrant farmworkers, interviewing a mid-level manager who doesn't always receive overtime pay or an administrative assistant whose boss makes her fetch him coffee although it is not in her job description. I found it shocking when the overwhelmingly White theater in which I viewed the film erupted in applause after the Patriot Act section, unaware of the possibilities Moore either underestimated or overlooked.

I wouldn't argue that Moore is a racist; on the contrary, he has done well, particularly in *Bowling for Columbine*, to demythologize the fear of minorities endemic in American society. Rather, Moore either whitewashed the anti-Arab racism of the Patriot Act unintentionally, in which case he failed to produce an analysis worthy of the applause he received from liberals and progressives; or he whitewashed that racism intentionally, for the sake of rhetorical persuasiveness, in which case he pandered to an assumed ethos of White supremacy on the part of his imagined audience; an assumption, it turns out, that was totally correct. I suspect Moore avoided mentioning Arabs intentionally, because he worried that much of his mainstream audience might wonder if the Arabs he profiled were actually guilty of doing something wrong—they are

Arabs, after all, and the government wouldn't pursue them so vigorously if they didn't have enough terrorists in their community to justify the pursuit. In profiling Whites, however, he knew his critique of the Patriot Act would achieve maximal effect, because the mainstream audience would realize how ridiculous it is to interrogate and infiltrate people who are so obviously innocent. Moore, in short, pandered to the anti-Arab racism of his imagined audience, which makes him guilty of reinforcing an attitude a better film would have invoked and examined, starting with the applause for an argument that ignores its own moral underpinnings.

This pandering to the ethos of White supremacy was totally missed in most reviews of the documentary in progressive publications, including Peter Sussman in *AlterNet* and Katha Pollitt in *The Nation*.[13] All this isn't to say that *Fahrenheit 9/11* is a failure as a film; I am happy for Moore that many found it inspiring. We are tasked nonetheless with exploring why so many progressives continue to criticize policies that are predicated explicitly on anti-Arab racism without mentioning the racism. The message, at this point, seems clear: if Arabs wait for progressives like Moore to passionately denounce anti-Arab racism, we'll all have been deported before anybody says a word. We cannot rely on Whites, progressive or otherwise, to discover what we already know; it would be better to speak loudly about what we already know because those who are supposedly concerned with Arabs don't seem to understand *why* they're concerned. It appears instead that they prefer age-old American tokenism, mentioning Arabs here and there so as not to damage their credibility or compromise their bona fides as crusaders for oppressed minorities; or they reinvent the classic version of White supremacy that reduces the complex problems in minority communities to whatever they deem worthy of mention or concentrate on how those problems affect Whites.

In Conclusion: Those Goddam Arabian Children

In closing I would observe that this book—like all books, I suppose—has a beginning outside the limitations of memory. And yet a particular memory has played an important role in its formation.

I remember it as if it were this morning. Tiny glass shards glistened in the sunlight. I could hear doors slamming.

It was summer in Appalachia. I loved the summer when I was a child. My skin would tan so darkly that my friends' parents called me "nigger." I didn't care. My father taught me to be proud that I am a nigger. "They're jealous because they have money but nothing to belong to. You'll understand when you're older," he would tell me. I am older. I still don't understand.

I remember that it was hot. My thick brown glasses kept slipping down my nose as my brother and I played soccer. He kicked the ball over the neighbor's fence. I went to get it.

I remember it even more in adulthood. I remember the sun glistening from the cane raised above my head. I remember running into the house, crying. I remember my father and the bald, elderly man standing on opposite sides of a fence, screaming. I remember my father, thick lines of sweat crisscrossing his cheeks, smashing a green vase onto the garage floor.

I remember what prompted it all: "Keep those sand niggers of yours off my lawn. I don't want to see those Goddam Arabian children."

It took me years to learn how not to keep silent in these moments, and if this book somehow encourages others to condemn the dehumanization of Arabs then I will consider it one of my life's greatest successes. Although I spent much of my childhood confused and upset in the moments when I was perceived as threatening, I am not a child anymore and I have learned to fight back. Nor will I ever remain silent about racism again. For this reason, I will continue to be threatening until I am dead. I hope all Arabs say it with the dignity of our ancestors: we are human not despite our culture, but because of it, and we refuse to go anywhere. In fact, we will fight with any means at our disposal to make sure American racism, not our existence, is forced into oblivion.

1

The Perilous World of Savages and Barbarians

Nearly a year after 9/11, the *Chicago Sun-Times* ran a column by John O'Sullivan assessing post-9/11 discrimination against Arab and Muslim Americans. The column is thorough and impassioned, with a healthy undercurrent of moral indignation. It connects the backlash against Arab and Muslim Americans to the 2002 Israeli massacre in Jenin and the epidemic of Black church burnings in 1996. There is only one problem: according to O'Sullivan, the backlash was a myth.

O'Sullivan also believes, as do most supporters of Israel, that the Jenin massacre was a well-orchestrated myth. To his credit, he never disputes the fact that Black churches were burned in the United States in 1996. The physical disappearance of those churches is difficult to deny, but so is the physical disappearance of countless Palestinian civilians in Jenin, and yet O'Sullivan persists in advancing the notion, drawn from the classic discourse of ethnic cleansing, that Israel never massacres civilians. Despite the destruction of the Black churches in 1996, O'Sullivan explains that church burnings have actually decreased since 1980, as if this fact absolves the perpetrators of the 1996 crimes. He never actually presents evidence that the church burnings weren't inspired by racism; instead, he offers evidence that since 1990 "'only random links to racism' could be found in black church burnings,"[1] as if those supposedly "random" cases are benign or unimportant.

The major part of O'Sullivan's article examines what he considers a mythical backlash post-9/11 against Arab and Muslim Americans generated by a liberal media eager to sensationalize harmless minutiae as institutional racism to reinforce a pernicious multicultural agenda.[2] (In fact, the very real backlash against Arab and Muslim Americans was woefully underreported by the same media O'Sullivan criticizes.) O'Sullivan obviously failed to consult the American–Arab Anti-Discrimination Committee (ADC), the Arab American Institute (AAI), the American Civil Liberties Union (ACLU), the Arab American Action Network (AAAN), and countless other nonprofit organizations that painstakingly documented hundreds of cases of discrimination against Arab and Muslim Americans in the months following 9/11. Or he could have consulted directly with Arab and Muslim Americans, a novel idea to him, no doubt, but certainly one that might have been useful considering his article claims to represent this demographic—and in effect calls them liars.

O'Sullivan's piece is clichéd because it corresponds with a plethora of mainstream and rightwing political analysis that considers racism overexaggerated or nonexistent and construes any attempt to discuss racism as minority propaganda or an attack on American values. Today, Arabs are so frequently a subject of this argument that, despite our marginalization, we have been appropriated into the mainstream of the American consciousness. That is to say, we know we've become American because American racism has thoroughly naturalized us.

Yet O'Sullivan's article is noteworthy for two reasons: it illustrates how racism can be expressed through the denial of racism and it attaches the concerns of Arabs to those of other ethnic groups. The first point is self-evident because American racists have long articulated racism by denying the very racism they articulate, but it is noteworthy because it implicates Arabs as the mythmakers. The existence of an Arab community in the United States, then, is exploited to sustain the racist metanarrative underlying O'Sullivan's assertions. The second point is more crucial because O'Sullivan doesn't decontextualize what he calls Arab mythmaking. Instead, he places it within a tradition of anti-racism activism and hopes that readers will do the same and eventually dismiss that tradition as faulty or hysterical. Two cautions thus follow: analysts of anti-Arab racism are tasked with exploring the metanarrative O'Sullivan utilizes; and anti-racism activists would be foolish to overlook Arabs, as many do today.

I wonder sometimes how best to respond to claims like O'Sullivan's. On the one hand, many of his readers will accept those claims automatically because they fortify a preexisting ideology or ameliorate any anxiety readers may feel about the possibility of racism influencing their worldviews. On the other hand, O'Sullivan is totally wrong and the flippancy with which he dismisses a dangerous reality appears to warrant some type of response even if it won't convince O'Sullivan's target audience. If carefully researched work like David Cole's *Enemy Aliens*,[3] which documents countless cases of institutionalized discrimination, can be ignored (intentionally or not) by writers who purport to demythologize racism, then we are faced with the reality that no amount of quality journalism or scholarship can resonate effectively with a portion of the American public. This fact highlights a corresponding reality: that a large number of people in American society are unalterably racist and can be continually absolved of their racism by the fantasies peddled by O'Sullivan and others.

O'Sullivan's article provides us with a classic example of White patrimony. Because he has never experienced racism, he finds it impossible to imagine that racism actually exists, which is ironic since he illuminates one of its classic features in the article under discussion. And because he articulates racism while concurrently arguing against its existence, he must manufacture a discourse that delegitimizes those who document it empirically or through personal exposition. He thus anoints himself a spokesperson for Arabs, especially Arabs who claim to be victims of racism. O'Sullivan, in other words, attempts to control Arab discourse so he can manage the role of Arabs in American society, a technique used by Daniel Pipes, Martin Kramer, and other critics of Middle East Studies when they complain about the desire of Arabs to teach courses about their own cultures and histories. Or, to put it more thoroughly, O'Sullivan's discourse indicates that he wants himself and his colleagues to maintain their dominant position vis-à-vis Arabs in American society and simultaneously influence public opinion effectively enough to canonize their racism. This move is accomplished by dismissing legitimate Arab concerns about harassment as a tacit conspiracy arising from false ethnic verisimilitude, a move that unfairly invents and then totalizes group consciousness.

It doesn't require research expertise to uncover instances of anti-Arab racism in the United States (for Arabs it requires nothing more than being Arab). *USA Today*, for instance, reports that since 9/11 Muslim communities across the United States are having difficulty opening mosques because of local opposition. In Voorhees, New Jersey, anti-mosque advocates distributed "fliers that warned residents that extremists 'with connections to terrorists' might worship [in the proposed mosque]."[4] Agence France Presse, picking up a story from the *Detroit News*, notes that "[p]rosecutions of Arab and Muslim Americans [in Dearborn] ... have shot up since the September 11 attacks."[5] In the two years following 9/11, the number of Arab and Muslim defendants rose 9.3 per cent while the prosecution of non-Arabs dropped 6.7 per cent. In 2002, the American Jewish Committee ran television ads that dehumanized Palestinians and reduced them all to the category of terrorists.[6]

In 2004, a George Bush Jr. reelection ad focusing on terrorism displayed a swarthy Arab, something James Zogby called "a form of racial profiling."[7] In the commercial, the picture of the Arab appears when the word *terrorism* is spoken, which not only implies that all Arabs are terrorists, but also that terrorism exists exclusively in the Arab World (as opposed to, say, the White House, where Bush is responsible for more unwarranted civilian deaths than Osama bin Laden). The juxtaposition of the word *terrorism* and the stereotyped image of a bearded Arab is symbolic of how the Arab is perceived in the American consciousness. The visual reproduction of an abstract, hypothetically faceless concept (terrorism) connotes how those who manage the production of stereotype rely on caricature to reduce complex political phenomena to binaristic truths.

Young Arabs in the United States, according to the *Baltimore Sun*, are aware of how their culture is reproduced in visual caricatures. They also understand how stereotypical images affect their lives in the United States: "Arab-American students at local private schools say that after the terrorist attacks [9/11], strangers stared or made hurtful remarks when they were with their families because they spoke a foreign language, had an accent or dressed differently."[8] A student at Baltimore's Boys' Latin School, Ridwan Yaseen Tomhe, delivered a senior speech in which he claimed, "The word 'Arab' to some people is synonymous with the word 'terrorist,' implying that all Arabs are terrorists."[9] Tomhe, like most Arab American youth, knows this to be true based on experience, because Arab American youth also are included in the totalizing media and political discourse that rarely offers nuanced discussion of Arab cultures and societies. Commercials like the one Bush ran in 2004 not only reinforce that discourse, they generate it.

A Culture of Hate?

Since 1990, Iraq has been to varying degrees a topic of debate in the United States. The relationship of the American government with the Saudi ruling family has drawn much ire on both the Right and Left, particularly after 9/11, culminating with Craig Unger's *House of Bush, House of Saud*.[10] The merits and downfalls of "moderate" and "fundamentalist" Arab governments respectively are usually included in American foreign policy discussions. Human rights in the Arab World often are incorporated into deliberations on American ethics. Since 9/11, the so-called modernization of Islamic societies has assumed great importance to Americans. All of these issues contribute in some way to the proliferation of anti-Arab racism because they construe the Arab World as crucial to the well-being of the United States and usually conclude that the Arab World is a detriment to American progress. By involving itself militarily and economically in the Arab World the American government has ensured that productive intercultural dialogue and meaningful political interchange among Americans and Arabs will rarely take place.

No issue, however, has generated more anti-Arab racism than Israel's occupation of Palestine. Popular and governmental support for Israel has amplified the importance of Arabs to American foreign policy. More important, Israel's well-accepted rationalizations for occupying and settling the territories—security, terrorism, divine mandate, and so forth—necessarily subordinate Palestinians to an inferior position vis-à-vis Israeli Jews—and, by extension, Americans. Because Israel is a staunch ally of the United States and is the subject of much media coverage here, the Palestinians are represented overwhelmingly in American media. These representations, which often marginalize Palestinians by privileging Israeli narratives of suffering and American-style pioneering, produce a rhetorical framework in which anti-Arab racism flourishes. In fact, I would argue that Zionists (Christian and Jewish) in the United States are the biggest progenitors of anti-Arab racism today. This isn't necessarily to say that Zionism *per se* equals racism (a debate we will examine in Chapter Four), but Zionists without doubt have been successful in selling their settlement project to Americans—and any time a settlement project is underway, the indigenes whose land is being settled are invariably bastardized as uncivilized or savage.

For example, in an article titled "The Palestinian Culture of Hate," John Perazzo writes,

> Given the degree to which the Palestinian Authority (PA) has, for years, systematically infused its subjects' hearts with violent bigotry, there is reason to wonder whether the current Palestinian population possesses the moral or ethical foundation necessary to pursue peaceful coexistence with Israel. The generations of Palestinians already raised on this steady diet of hate may in fact be lost forever—incapable of truly accepting such coexistence even under the most favorable terms imaginable.[11]

It is, of course, problematic (and inevitably false) any time somebody denigrates an entire culture as hateful. Beyond this elemental problem, Perazzo's article is flawed for numerous reasons.

Using the traditional vocabulary of European and Euro-American colonization, Perazzo decries "the seeds of barbarism" in Palestinian society as well as their "hateful bigotry," concluding, without grammatical nuance, that they are "homicidal degenerates."[12] This homicidal degeneration, according to Perazzo, exists largely because of the textbooks used in Palestinian schools, which "turn the minds of Palestinians into reservoirs of venom."[13] Perazzo's reliance on these silly metaphors connotes a lack of intellectual authority, as does his claim about Palestinian textbooks, repeated *ad infinitum* in an assortment of Zionist publications. Are there some hateful messages about Jews in Palestinian textbooks and Arab media? Yes. Are those hateful messages as pervasive as Perazzo contends? Absolutely not. Many of the claims that Zionists and neoconservatives consider "venomous" focus on Israel's displacement of the Palestinians in 1948, 1967, and today, something Palestinian children don't need to study to understand. Settler societies never want to be reminded of the moral failings of their policies and so they mitigate their complicity in ethnic cleansing by resorting to a victimology continually informed by defensive language, which precludes any ability to recognize the dilemma of indigenes because the indigenes were dehumanized in the act of ethnic cleansing the settler society works so hard to deny.

More crucial, had Perazzo taken the time to research the problem—and it appears that neoconservatives think research is a multicultural conspiracy—he would have found at least three studies claiming that Israeli children's textbooks are filled with "venom." The first study was published by Daniel Bar-Tal of Tel Aviv University and concludes "that Israeli textbooks present the view that Jews are involved in a justified, even humanitarian, war against an Arab enemy that refuses to accept and acknowledge the existence and rights of Jews in Israel."[14] Like American textbooks in relation to Indians, "Israeli textbooks continue to present Jews as industrious, brave and determined to cope with the difficulties of 'improving the country in ways they believe the Arabs are incapable of.'"[15] Bar-Tal explains that the textbooks stereotype Arabs as "unenlightened, inferior, fatalistic, unproductive and apathetic .... 'The message was that the Palestinians were primitive and neglected the country and did not cultivate the land.'"[16] Arabs, according to the textbooks, "burn, murder, destroy, and are easily inflamed," and are described in the following terms: "tribal, vengeful, exotic, poor, sick, dirty, noisy, colored."[17]

Another study, by Eli Podeh of the Hebrew University, suggests that "while certain changes in Israeli textbooks are slowly being implemented, the discussion of Palestinian national and civil identity is never touched upon .... 'Especially evident is the lack of a discussion on the orientation of Palestinians to the [occupied] territories.'"[18] A 17-year-old Israeli high school student observes that "our books basically tell us that everything the Jews do is fine and legitimate and Arabs are wrong and violent and are trying to exterminate us."[19] The

student's observation is corroborated by Adir Cohen's 1999
An Ugly Face in the Mirror, which presents some disturbing
survey results: among fourth to sixth-grade Jewish children at
a school in Haifa "seventy five percent ... described the 'Arab'
as a murderer, one who kidnaps children, a criminal and a
terrorist. Eighty per cent said they saw the Arab as someone
dirty with a terrifying face. Ninety per cent of the students
stated they believe that Palestinians have no rights whatsoever
to the land in Israel or Palestine."[20]

Among 1,700 children's books published since 1967, Cohen
"found that 520 of [them] contained humiliating, negative
descriptions of Palestinians ... . Sixty six per cent of the 520
books refer to Arabs as violent; 52 per cent as evil; 37 per cent
as liars; 31 per cent as greedy; 28 per cent as two-faced; 27
per cent as traitors, etc."[21] Furthermore, Cohen "counted the
following descriptions used to dehumanize Arabs: murderer
was used 21 times; snake, 6 times; dirty, 9 times; vicious animal,
17 times; bloodthirsty, 21 times; warmonger, 17 times; killer,
13 times; believer in myths, 9 times; and a camel's hump, 2
times."[22] Cohen didn't complete his study in a vacuum, for it

> concludes that such descriptions of Arabs are part and parcel
> of convictions and a culture rampant in Hebrew literature and
> history books. He writes that Israeli authors and writers confess to
> deliberately portraying the Arab character in this way, particularly
> to their younger audience, in order to influence their outlook early
> on so as to prepare them to deal with Arabs.[23]

If the goal of these children's books is to prepare Israeli youth
to "deal" with Arabs, it appears to be working. Israel's brutal
occupation continues five years later, with the usual assortment
of child murders, live burials, home demolitions, crop
destruction, land expropriation, extrajudicial assassinations,
curfews, humiliation, rapes, torture, and dispossession, all of
which, no doubt, are prepared by the dehumanization of Arabs
with which Israeli children are inundated.

Perazzo finds none of these facts worth mention because one of the goals of his article is to convince Americans that Palestinians are incapable of peace; Israelis, therefore, would be free to continue their settlement of Palestinian land until the Palestinians are thoroughly subjugated or displaced. Most Americans are not only complicit in this sort of racism, they also help prepare intellectual space for its proliferation by refusing to challenge the pro-Israel perspective promulgated in nearly every corporate media report. Moreover, in justifying Israel's brutality by invoking Palestinian violence, Perazzo doesn't merely identify and condemn a real problem in Palestinian society; he exaggerates the problem as evidence of cultural inferiority and innately violent tendencies. Perazzo, in other words, does exactly the same thing he condemns in the imaginary textbooks he discusses. In any case, he didn't have to consult Bar-Tal's, Podeh's, or Cohen's studies to find evidence of a deep-seated Israeli racism he totally ignores, for that evidence was provided two years earlier by Israeli President Moshe Katsav: "There is a huge gap between us and our enemies—not just in ability but in morality, culture, sanctity of life, and conscience … . [Palestinians] are people who don't belong to our continent, to our world, but actually belong to a different galaxy."[24] Israelis, I hope, can sleep better at night knowing their children's textbooks are working.

Good v. Evil: The Trial of the New Century

Arabs are evil. Not the majority of Arabs. Not some Arabs. Not a minority of Arabs. All Arabs are evil, including the elderly, the infants, and the incapacitated. Americans, though, are good. Not a minority of Americans. Not some Americans. Not the majority of Americans. All Americans are good, including the White supremacists, backwoods militias, and corporate embezzlers. This is what all American children learn, at least those who bother to watch the news (especially Fox News) or read the editorial sections of many newspapers.

Perhaps the most interesting feature of popular American discourse today is the propensity of mainstream authors to forget adjectives and qualifiers. As a result, a handful of terrorists has come to represent 300 million Arabs. In today's America, which appears to be as stricken by religious fundamentalism as any Islamic nation but Saudi Arabia and Afghanistan (and more than the anti-Islamic regimes in Jordan, Algeria, and Egypt), public debate has become so infantile that most talk programs have resorted to booking a parade of idiots who pontificate about our moral duty to defeat evil. *Evil*, of course, means *Arabs*. Or, at the very least, it insinuates that evil is exclusive to the Islamic world while the United States has a divine monopoly on goodness.

In fact, the invasion of Iraq was predicated largely on the recapitulation of the language of nineteenth-century European colonialism. Speaking of enemies—*enemies* being anybody who might prove an impediment to the United States' appetite for foreign resources—as evil is fundamentally a part of the American vocabulary, dating back to Cotton Mather's diatribes about the evils of North America's indigenous peoples (whom he dubbed "Canaanites") and the need to do God's work by exterminating them. In addition to Iraqis, Palestinians also are cast in the role of evil ones in this neobiblical metaphor by Americans eager to impose their goodness on the less enlightened.

This sort of narrative has been expressed vigorously by American leaders since the Bush II administration came to power. In 2002, the then Attorney General John Ashcroft infamously declared, "Islam is a religion in which God requires you to send your son to die for him. Christianity is a faith in which God sends his son to die for you."[25] Ashcroft's remark, spoken in the service of removing the separation of church and state, both reinforces notions of good versus evil and prepares the discourse necessary for their existence. His diction betrays any potential claim of misquotation (something Ashcroft indeed claimed after his comments generated controversy). The word *religion* connotes rigidity, a juridical system, an ideology whose adherents are unable (or not allowed) to challenge dogma. The word *faith*, on the other hand, connotes belief in something incomprehensible but divine, something beautifully ethereal, something worth believing in.

Ashcroft isn't alone in his dangerously binaristic view of the world. Former House Majority Leader Tom DeLay, a longtime supporter of American interventionism, gave a short speech in 2004 in which he used the word *evil* nearly twenty times to describe the Arab World. Some highlights:

- "Evil will not stand."
- "This evil we face today may come in new forms, but it is not new."
- "The same evil that terrorized past generations with the Holocaust and the Gulag terrorized us with the 9/11 attacks."
- "The war on terror is a war against evil."
- "As President Bush said on 9/11, in this war on terror we now wage—this war, make no mistake, of good versus evil—we will not distinguish between the terrorists and those nations who help and harbor them."[26]

The final passage is of particular interest, for in it DeLay admits that he makes no distinction between *terrorists* and *Arabs*, thus eliminating the need for liberals to point out that neoconservatives homogenize diverse societies. DeLay tells us that he homogenizes the entire Arab World, and he gets away with it.

Although his discourse, with its premillenialist overtones, appears outrageous to the unbeliever, it is not unique. Others, including Ashcroft, Senator Rick Santorum (R-Pennsylvania), former House Majority Leader Dick Armey (R-Texas), and the President himself all evince a worldview influenced (or maintained) by the strictures of biblical literalism. All are, as a result, guilty of conceptualizing the world in Manichean terms: as a continual struggle between the forces of good and evil, with the United States permanently occupying the mistake-prone but morally infallible realm of good. It is, to put it mildly, terrifying that American foreign policy is less complex than the plot of *Rocky IV*, but we are still compelled to examine how anti-Arab racism allows this worldview to persist.

First of all, anti-Arab racism is not simply evident in neoconservative thought; it is central to it. And when Americans of any political leaning fail to recognize this fact, they are at least indirectly implicated in it because their fear of Arabs or assumptions about Arab inferiority implicitly validates policies dictated on those fears and assumptions. Second, it is useless to examine any type of racism without also analyzing its assumptions; and in the case of anti-Arab racism, its assumptions invariably lead us to the notion that anything Arab or Islamic is worthy of subordination to Western liberal values, or worthy of being replaced by them. The propensity to totalize all Arabs as "evil," even when the totalization is unintended, arises from these assumptions. Finally, the Arab-as-evil formulation has many historical antecedents. While we do well to recognize that American racism is complex and continually evolving, a common expression of American racism is to designate an entire group as "evil" when there is something to gain from that designation (Black slave laborers, for example, or Mexican farmworkers, or foreign oil producers).

Likewise, although American racism has always been articulated differently when different groups and individuals are its subject, it is ultimately, despite useful deliberations on racism like Kwame Anthony Appiah's categories of intrinsic and extrinsic racism, a dehumanizing enterprise that in some ways has remained frighteningly consistent throughout

American history.[27] That consistency is best exemplified in the word *evil*. Slaves once were evil as bearers of the mark of Cain. Indians once were evil because of their heathenry. Immigrants of all ethnicities (but particularly dark-skinned immigrants) were evil because of their strangeness. And now, Arabs are evil because they are all terrorists and because, based on their religion and geographical location, they fit perfectly into the Messianistic schema that once housed slaves and indigenes. The word *evil*, depending on the speaker, is still used sometimes to describe Blacks because they all wish to rape White women, Mexicans because they are lazy job thieves (a contradiction that nobody ever seems to notice), and Jews because they seek world domination.

DeLay has been particularly vicious in arguing that Arabs, without distinction, are evil. In 2003, during Congressional floor remarks, he described Palestinians as "violent men" who laugh when Israeli children are killed. "If this is not evil, nothing is," he concluded. Later in the speech, he remarked, "[Palestinians] are still enemies of the civilized world and must still be hunted and targeted as such." Imploring fellow Congresspersons to "join Israel's heroic stand against evil," he suggested that the only important question "is whether Palestinian leaders will stand with the civilized world in defiance of evil, or whether they will fail like their predecessors."[28] In making such remarks, DeLay inadvertently places himself in the company of slavetraders, garrison settlers, and land thieves because the venerable discourse of slavetrading, garrison settlement, and land theft pervades the ethics and assumptions of his speech. Yet the most upsetting thing about the discourse is not that it implicates DeLay as a racist because he reduces an entire people to the category of "evil," but that it implicates American society as racist because that discourse arises within the framework of acceptable debate at the highest level of government.

Obviously, the belief that Arabs must be "hunted" because they are "evil" and "uncivilized" can resonate with an audience only if that audience has already dehumanized Arabs and might therefore find it strategically viable to murder them indiscriminately. Predictably, then, we can find countless examples of the dehumanization of Arabs in neoconservative media. Writing in David Horowitz's *FrontPageMag.com*, for instance, Steven Plaut, in decrying "Palestinian barbarism," notes, "It has become vogue in many circles to represent Middle East savagery as part of some sort of 'War of Civilization.' It is not. In fact, Middle East [sic] is simply a war by barbarism against all civilization."[29] Again, we see the polarization of societies into categories of "barbaric" and "civilized," and so it appears that the United States, always the forward-looking nation, has nevertheless failed to move beyond the discursive precedent set by Cotton Mather. Those who are tempted to dismiss Plaut's argument as far-right nonsense might take a moment to recall that Democrats, from Woodrow Wilson to Lyndon Johnson to Bill Clinton, also are guilty of using the same argument dressed in less explicit language. It would be wiser to view the argument as central to the philosophy of American foreign policy (which was originally developed as a domestic policy toward indigenes).

When considering the pervasiveness of the Good v. Evil debate in the United States, I am always reminded of Bush's frequent invocation of God to help him destroy the evil in the world; DeLay's essentialization of Arabs as subhuman; the repeated calls in mainstream media to eliminate Arab barbarism; and, finally, the institutionalization of these attitudes in the American consciousness and in its language of political debate. In the battle of Good v. Evil, it appears that Evil is winning.

Tribalism and Manifest Destiny

Even if policies do not always survive generations, discourse often does. And the discourse of American exceptionalism juxtaposed with notions of foreign inferiority has survived remarkably well since the time of Euro-American settlement. The talented Palestinian American rapper The Iron Sheik has a song called "Olive Trees Remix" in which he critiques Israeli settlement and then says, "But to me that's called Manifest Destiny / I thought that went out of style in the last century." The sarcasm with which The Iron Sheik delivers these lines reveals that Manifest Destiny is in fact a living ideology, easily found not only in the Occupied Territories but also on the United States' House floor when politicians debate the merits of invading Iraq, offering increased aid to Israel, and domestic policies such as Indian affairs and immigration law. Dick Armey, after all, expressed the most fundamental premise of Manifest Destiny on the Chris Matthews Show in 2002, when he was still House Majority Leader: "I'm content to have Israel grab the entire West Bank."[30]

To further cement the American past and the American present, we can turn to the late commentator Steven Vincent, who before his death suggested that "the biggest obstacle to a peaceful, stable and democratic Iraq [is] its people's continuing allegiance to tribal customs and affiliations."[31] If this opinion sounds like nineteenth-century anthropology, that's because Vincent wanted it to. No modern, "multiculturally-minded" Anthropology professor, Vincent assured us,

> would care to live in a system that ensnares the individual in an inescapable web of kinship relations, where genealogy, rather than citizenship, defines one's place in society, and a woman's freedom, self-fulfillment and life are hostage to that most pernicious of concepts, "honor." Indeed, my two visits to Iraq convinced me that tribal blood and family ties lie at the root of nearly all the pathologies afflicting that nation—irrational violence, misogyny, religious fanaticism, and, perhaps most troubling, the inability of even educated people to fully internalize abstract principles of behavior and government.[32]

Vincent's argument is troublesome on numerous levels, but his presumptuousness is especially discomfiting. He purported to know enough about Iraqi culture, politics, and history to condemn their innate violence, misogyny, fanaticism, and lack of intellectual competence, and opined that these problems have been central to Iraqi society for centuries. The history of European and American imperialism shows us that the dehumanization of entire peoples usually precedes intervention in the Southern Hemisphere, and so Vincent's argument that Iraqis currently are hopelessly barbaric prepares a sort of discursive space in which American aspirations in Iraq can be justified on humanistic grounds.

In fact, Vincent could have turned his analysis inward. Take the following description of Iraqi social ills: "irrational violence, misogyny, religious fanaticism, and, perhaps most troubling, the inability of even educated people to fully internalize abstract principles of behavior and government." It is certainly problematic that a writer who, after two trips to a foreign nation, described the very set of social problems in that nation that he failed to recognize in the nation in which he was born, raised, and educated. Unfortunately, Vincent's style of hyperbole, articulated with lines such as "the regressive viciousness of Arab culture,"[33] is gaining credence in the United States as Americans are bombarded with a growing number of White experts on the Arab World who aren't Muslim, don't speak Arabic, and know nothing of Arab countries except perhaps what they learn during occasional visits when they spend time commiserating with American and Israeli generals.

While Vincent abandoned his neoconservative politics by having transmuted into a feminist where the Arab World was concerned, he was, down to the words he used to express his argument, implicated squarely in the classic discourse of American expansionism. This discourse has been transformed continually throughout American history based on contemporary social circumstance, but at base it has survived and is inevitably rehashed in moments when it might successfully justify a domestic injustice or a foreign intervention. In it, a critique of tribalism is used to reduce an entire people to a homogeneous lot of aggressors (or barbarians or savages) and then, following its own logical dictates, mystifies whatever crime it is invoked to rationalize. Vincent's diatribe against Arab tribalism is a textbook example of this phenomenon.

Totalization is another common practice in the lexicon of anti-Arab racism. This practice is exemplified by Andrew G. Bostom, an Associate Professor of Medicine at Brown University Medical School, in an article for *FrontPageMag. com*. Referencing the murder of Nicholas Berg in Iraq, Bostom writes, "such murders are consistent with sacred jihad practices, as well as Islamic attitudes towards all non-Muslim infidels, in particular, Jews, which date back to the 7th century, and the Prophet Muhammad's own example."[34] Bostom's reasoning, beyond its magnificent inaccuracy, tells us absolutely nothing about Arabs, Islam, Judaism, Christianity, the war in Iraq, or any other issue worth discussing. Rather, Bostom treats Berg as a straw man who is able to validate the expression of a preexisting anti-Arab racism.

Bostom's argument tells us nothing because it has been used by thousands of polemicists with myriad agendas. For instance, he claims that "for centuries, from the Iberian peninsula to the Indian subcontinent, jihad campaigns waged by Muslim armies against infidel Jews, Christians, Zoroastrians, Buddhists and Hindus, were punctuated by massacres, including mass throat slittings and beheadings."[35] One could answer Bostom by saying the following: well, yes, Islamic history is filled with examples of unjust invasions and individual cases of murder against non-Muslims. So what? All human history is filled with similar examples, as are the histories of every major religious group on the planet. Christians, for example, have no shortage of murders on their record. In fact, when one takes into account the Crusades, the Spanish Inquisition, the destruction of millions of indigenes in the New World, the Holocaust, slavery, South African apartheid, the colonization of the South Pacific, Africa, and Asia, and genocide in the Congo, Australia, and Yugoslavia, Muslims suddenly seem like model pacifists. One might argue that the perpetrators of these crimes weren't *real* Christians—quite possibly the stupidest excuse one can offer for criminality—but it doesn't matter: the perpetrators were acting as Christians and, in many cases, were able to quote Scripture to justify their behavior. It is intellectually dishonest to claim that Christian rationales for murder are decontextualized from Scripture while Muslim rationales for murder are inherent in the religion.

Likewise, one can turn to Jews and find extraordinary cases of violence. On the day that Nicholas Berg was murdered, Jewish settlers in the West Bank and Gaza Strip were squatting on expropriated land, drinking stolen water, driving on a racialized highway system, and murdering Palestinian civilians—all, of course, in the name of Judaism. Jews, for that matter, have engaged in one of the most vicious cases of ethnic cleansing in modern history for the past 60 years. And, lest we forget, they also engaged in ethnic cleansing in ancient times when God commanded Joshua to exterminate the indigenous population of the Holy Land, a command that is inscribed in the holy texts of Jews and Christians. Philosophically speaking, there is just as much (if not more) evidence to implicate Judaism and Christianity in violence as Islam.

All I have done above is carry Bostom's argument to its logical conclusion. I don't believe for a second that Jews, Christians, or Muslims are inherently violent based on their belief systems. Only fools make such arguments because anybody can find evidence of violence in any human doctrine that has actually been utilized by humans (think of Walter Benjamin's lament that "there is no document of civilization which is not at the same time a document of barbarism"). Racists, though, selectively invoke such evidence as foolproof testimony of innate barbarity. It's better to focus on institutionalized violence in the service of ending it while concurrently discussing the contributions made by religious groups to the betterment of the globe—Bostom, I imagine, probably wouldn't have acquired his medical degree without the mathematical genius of Muslims and he certainly wouldn't have acquired it without the brilliant medical contributions of Avicenna.

Bostom, however, focuses only on individual acts of Muslim violence because it suits an agenda that is racist by virtue of its certainty of the superiority of Westerners over Arabs, an undemonstrable point developed unsurprisingly without any analytical nuance. Bostom proves yet again that objectivity is a subjective phenomenon because he says nothing about the current surge of Christian fundamentalism that has pervaded the United States, especially its President and Attorney General, which is at least partly responsible for the unprovoked invasion of a sovereign nation, leading to thousands of civilian deaths and billions in property damage, and that in the future will surely be the cause of innumerable cancer cases. Of course, Bostom says nothing about these things because he has an ideological interest in supporting that invasion by dehumanizing the people American soldiers are killing, a rather tired approach perfected much earlier in the United States during its westward expansion.

Terrorist Connections

My Amo Saleem died in 2004. He was a wonderful man who knew no English besides the words *sit* and *drink*. Amo was of the old school. Until his death, he retained his Bedouin culture and wore a grey *dishdasha* with a black and white *kuffiyeh*. I stayed in his house two different summers in Madaba, Jordan, an Old Testament town about 20 miles south of Amman. The last time I stayed with him, in the summer of 2003, Amo, a gentle person who never spanked any of his six children, was in poor health. A cancer survivor, he was afflicted with diabetes and arthritis. Yet every day he shuffled up the hill to the tiny cubby he owned, where he sold everything from cooking pans to goat cheese. I walked with him one morning and commented on the weather every few moments when he stopped to rest, the dignity of his culture not allowing him to acknowledge that he couldn't, as he'd done every day the past 60 years, walk up the hill and open his shop. I still have a *kuffiyeh* he gave me the first time I met him many years ago; it smells of cigarette smoke and his wife's perfume.

Amo died a few months after I returned to the United States. When I heard the news, I mourned silently for days, remembering more than once what he had told me before I left: "Your heart and your history are here. We love you like you love us." He bore out this sentiment repeatedly by providing me, in the best tradition of Arab hospitality, everything I needed to continue loving my origin. You can imagine, then, the heartbreak I felt upon returning to the United States and being reminded of a fundamental truth about Amo: that he was a terrorist.

Amo never blew up buses or kidnapped tourists. He owned no Katyushas or bombmaking equipment. By all accounts, in fact, he was the best type of pacifist, one who didn't proselytize about nonviolence but never engaged in a violent act during his life. According to many of my American peers, however, Amo was still a terrorist because he was an Arab.

I should make a confession before I continue with a discussion of how the word *terrorism* functions today in American society. I despise the word. I think the word is overused zealously and carries with it a racist undertone and a startling ability to dehumanize those at whom it is directed (which has a lot to do with its current overuse in the United States). In turn I suspect that, like *anti-Semitism*, the word is now so overused that it might come to describe nothing rather than a deadly phenomenon existing in different forms around the world.

I should also take this opportunity to announce that nowhere in this section will I denounce *terrorism*, an injunction often imposed on public Arabs, which, once its implied descriptors are included, means *Arab* terrorism or *Islamic* terrorism. I can think of few contexts in the United States in which *terrorism* is used to describe, as it should, American politicians, multinational corporations, or Israeli settlers. This reality, though, isn't necessarily why I refuse to denounce terrorism, nor is my refusal the result of a belief that Arabs don't commit terrorism. Some Arabs, unfortunately, commit plenty. I refuse to denounce terrorism on principle.

The ethics of this refusal are worth examining, for they certainly aren't exclusively mine. I know many Arabs who refuse to denounce terrorism publicly and in their refusal we have much to learn about the ethics of diction and the antagonism of representation in the United States. How could somebody possibly refuse to denounce terrorism on principle? I would argue that it is easy to refuse ethically because in the United States the word *terrorism* is more prejudicial than descriptive. That is to say, there is no proportionality in its usage and so the word has come to be synonymous with Arab politics, culture, and psychology, thus precluding any application to the thousands of other movements around the globe that could be considered terrorist if consistent criteria were used.

Moreover, the injunction on Arabs to denounce terrorism results in what I call the prerequisite to speaking. The prerequisite to speaking is simple: the ability of Arabs in the United States to articulate our political sensibilities is limited by the continuous juxtaposition of those politics with terrorism; in corporate media, therefore, Arabs are either expected to immediately denounce terrorism or they are asked immediately to do so. The prerequisite to speaking is disturbing because it assumes (not so tacitly) that Arabs only have agency in the context of American morality. It also assumes that Arabs are mendacious intellectually unless we acknowledge our own shortcomings (to an audience, incidentally, that uses those shortcomings as a pretext to invade Arab nations) before speculating on the possibility of shortcomings in American foreign policy. Ultimately, the prerequisite to speaking is, for Arabs, an uncritical capitulation to those who believe we are inferior to Americans (read: Whites) and subsequently expect that inferiority to be reflected in any Arab–American interchange. (This situation isn't totally different from the refusal on principle of some Blacks to condemn so-called Black anti-Semitism.)

Finally, because the word *terrorism* has come to be synonymous with Arab culture, denouncing Arab terrorism is, in many contexts, a denouncement of Arab culture, if not on the part of the speaker then to at least some of the audience. In many cases, when an Arab in the United States denounces terrorism simply to fulfill his or her audience's expectations, then the speaker has done nothing more than validate to that audience his or her cultural inferiority. Terrorism, like every human action, has a context; analyzing the context of terrorism is not the same as justifying it. In the case of Arab terrorism, context is rarely offered. Consequently, Arab cultures and politics are inevitably reduced to simplistic phenomena that demonstrate the existence of violent tendencies in Arab tribalism, Arab family structures, the Arab mind, or whatever facile descriptor is employed to totalize Arabs as subhuman.

Suicide bombings, for instance, are invoked repeatedly in corporate media to demonstrate that Palestinians are mindless terrorists, but the brutal occupation to which suicide bombings are directly related is usually whitewashed or ignored. Palestinians, then, become purveyors of horrid violence because they are inherently bloodthirsty and not because they have long been victims of the same type of terrorism for which Saddam

Hussein was ousted. And while Arab charities, activists, and academics are probed constantly by the FBI for terrorist links, or accused flippantly by media figures such as Bill O'Reilly of supporting terrorism, I have heard nothing in corporate media of the many Zionist groups in the United States that work openly to mystify and rationalize Israeli violence. These groups include the America Israel Public Affairs Committee (AIPAC), the Jewish Defense League, Americans for a Safe Israel, Friends of Israel, the Christian Coalition, and Christians for Israel. Also included are the majority of the American Congress and Senate. Of course, these groups and individuals aren't implicated for supporting terrorism because, in a troublesome moral inversion, the same commentators who so flippantly accuse Arabs of terrorist sympathies because they oppose Israeli settlement don't consider the possibility that the settlement is, by any honest criteria, a terrorist enterprise.

Terrorism, then, is a highly subjective term and its subjectivity has been used to highlight Arab violence disproportionately while comparable American and Israeli violence is disregarded (or celebrated). A recent letter to *USA Today* demonstrates how Arabs have, without distinction, become synonymous with terrorism. Angry about the murder of Nicholas Berg, a reader predicted, "I doubt there will be an apology coming from the terrorists."[36] An underlying suggestion here is that the United States shouldn't have apologized for the Abu Ghraib torture scandal, or that in doing so the United States is morally superior to the Iraqis who murdered Berg. The letter writer (or the editors at *USA Today*) failed to alter his grammar so that *terrorists* would modify only those who committed the murder. In the letter, *terrorists* signifies all Iraqis, Arabs, and Muslims. Even if this grammatical signifier was unintended, it reveals much about the way *terrorism* has come to describe national and cultural phenomena as much as political ones.

Moving beyond grammatical quarrels, we might ask why the letter writer is so confident that Berg's murderers are terrorists

while the torturers and murderers of Iraqi prisoners—whose
actions are described by the writer as "prison incidents"—are
merely derelicts whose abuse is indicative of nothing beyond
their momentary lapse of judgment. The answer, in a word:
racism. Like most Americans, the letter writer cannot imagine
that violence is in any way endemic to American institutions,
even the military, while it appears natural to him that Arabs,
even outside the military, would engage in mindless violence.
Is not the torture of civilians across Latin America a form of
terrorism? Or the unnecessary invasion of Panama in 1989
in which 3,000 civilians were murdered and thousands more
dispossessed? Or the sanctions on Iraq throughout the 1990s
that, according to many observers, resulted in the deaths of
half a million Iraqi children? These actions aren't terrorism
if they are voraciously rationalized as the good work of a
nation interested only in liberating others from their barbarity.
In contrast, the culture of the barbarians needing liberation
is necessarily terroristic if the rationalization for torture
and intervention is to succeed. (Chapter Six will explore the
discourse of the Abu Ghraib torture in more detail.)

After 9/11 the word *terrorism* wasn't simply called into
service as a pretext to fulfill a longstanding plan to invade
Iraq. It was also employed to mystify rabid xenophobia. As
Terrence P. Jeffrey explains in an article portentously titled,
"Illegal Immigration: the Terrorist Connection," "If [political
leaders] don't secure our borders against illegal immigration,
how can they secure our country against Hizballah?".[37] No
matter their political sensibilities, Jeffrey's readers won't have
to analyze his argument too thoroughly to understand that he
wants no Arabs in the United States whether they arrived here
legally or not. His repeated use of the word *terrorist* is intended
to attach itself to a preexisting fear in American society and in
turn rationalize a proposal—removing Arabs from the United
States—that might widely be identified as excessive if many
Americans weren't preoccupied with the omnipresent threat

of terrorism, a threat that, based on *terrorism*'s connotations, only includes Arabs.

Lawrence Auster provides a more explicit case of xenophobia, using, like Jeffrey, a pragmatic title that reduces an entire people to warlike descriptors, "How to Defeat Jihad in America." He writes, "*The sole source of the growth of jihadism and terrorism in the West is Moslem immigration*" (italics his).[38] His logic bespeaks racism because it evokes an earlier period in American history in which people of color openly were considered to be unalterably different and thus should be managed with a sort of pessimistic wariness:

> To assimilate means to make similar or the same; and the American Creed teaches us that all people in the world are basically the same as *us* [sic], or can readily be *made* the same as us [sic]. The problem, of course, is that Moslems by and large are *not* the same as us [sic], nor can they be made the same as us [sic], for the simple reason that they adhere to a religion and a set of beliefs that are radically incompatible with—and indeed hostile to—our culture and our very being as Westerners. (italics his)[39]

Auster later proposes to "*remove the citizenship of and deport all naturalized and native-born citizens who are supporters of jihad*" (italics his), a proposal that arises because Auster is dedicated to stopping and reversing "the Islamicization of America."[40]

I suppose it would be easy simply to dismiss Auster as unrealistic, but such a dismissal would miss the larger point that, according to the contemporary American ethos, his article is only slightly radical. I would venture to guess that, with only small variations, the majority of Bush's supporters agree with Auster, as do many liberals who prefer to outfit the argument with more euphemistic language. Auster's wariness about a darker-skinned minority has been a part of the American rhetorical tradition since before the United States became a nation. There is nothing original in his argument, only a reiteration of a dangerous ideology that came into existence with the removal of Indians and that was bolstered further in a variety of oppositions: to abolition, to full citizenship for Blacks, to removing immigration quotas, to women's suffrage, to desegregation, to Indian repatriation, to Mexican farmworker unionization, and so forth. One could say, in fact, that Auster draws from the most American of traditions, which is summed up well by his colleague David Horowitz, who writes, "Of course we have to live by a higher standard than the barbarians we are fighting."[41]

American language has always conformed to suit the needs of this tradition. At present, *terrorism* is the most effective, and most widely used, term to effect the disenfranchisement of Arabs in the United States and abroad. As Robert Fisk observes, "[Westerners] now depict Arabs in our films as the Nazis once depicted Jews. But Arabs are fair game. Potential terrorists to a man—and a woman—they must be softened up, 'prepared', humiliated, beaten, tortured."[42] So, no, I won't ever acquiesce to requests to denounce terrorism, only to requests to denounce the totalizing influence of *terrorism* as a racist word. For if I denounce terrorism on the terms of those who request the denouncement, I will have validated the racism they so often express; and I will have, simply by virtue of speaking, classified my Amo Saleem and all my family as barbarians who deserve to be civilized through invasion, occupation, torture, and death. It is my hope that all Arabs in the United States avoid this injunction and instead honor the brilliance of their cultures.

Liberal Racism

The major part of this chapter has quoted from neoconservatives to provide evidence of racism, but we would be remiss not to highlight examples of liberal anti-Arab racism, which also is rampant in the United States. Some of the most virulently anti-Arab periodicals and organizations in the country, such as the Anti-Defamation League (ADL), the Simon Wiesenthal Center, *Dissent*, the *New York Times*, the *New Republic*, and the Democratic Party, bill themselves to varying degrees as liberal. The language of liberal anti-Arab racism, as we shall see, is markedly different than the apocalyptic vocabulary employed by religious fundamentalists and neoconservatives, but this difference doesn't mean that liberal anti-Arab racism is more benign or less extensive. Liberal anti-Arab racism exists within the same historical framework and is too embedded in the traditional American metanarrative of expansionism and White supremacy to avoid racist assumptions in analyzing the Arab World. This fact holds true even when some liberals would otherwise claim to oppose those assumptions—and at times when they purport to dismantle them.

Perhaps no liberal (or semi-liberal, depending on his mood) is as patronizing to Arabs as *New York Times* columnist Thomas Friedman. At base, Friedman's politics aren't anything noteworthy. Sometimes he reluctantly calls on Israel to withdraw from the Occupied Territories, but only in the framework of impossible Palestinian concessions (such as the ubiquitous "stop terrorism" injunction). More often he lectures Arabs about their need for enlightenment and modernization (or he asks American leaders to force Arabs into enlightenment and modernization). Friedman's politics regarding the Israel–Palestine conflict can thus be described as centrist, as he rarely engages in the partisan rhetoric on behalf of Israel so endemic among his peers George Will, William Safire, and Charles Krauthammer.

Why, then, might Friedman be implicated in a study of anti-Arab racism? The answer can be found in the ethics of his rhetoric, which inevitably subordinates Arabs to the whims of their more tolerant American patriarchs. At times, Friedman assumes rightwing positions, as when he writes, "Attorney General John Ashcroft is not completely crazy in his impulse to adopt unprecedented, draconian measures and military courts to deal with suspected terrorists."[43] Although Friedman notes that he is "glad critics are in Mr. Ashcroft's face," he finds himself "with some sympathy for Mr. Ashcroft's moves."[44] If this is the case, then Friedman finds himself, whether he likes it or not, with some sympathy for unconstitutional imperatives that rely on the degradation of Arabs to generate a moral appeal. These imperatives rely generally on the reduction of all Arabs to aggressors, which in an ontological sense differs little from biological determinism, a mentality Friedman reinforces when he says, "And let's not forget how long they lived among us and how little they absorbed—how they went to their deaths believing that American laws were only something to be eluded, American citizens only targets to be killed and American society only something to be destroyed."[45] It is disappointing to find Friedman eliciting fear in order to rally support for a reduction of civil liberties (Friedman's civil liberties, of course, are safe, and he knows it). His shaky diction aside, the more compelling feature of his argument proclaims that American exceptionalism is to be preserved at any expense, even that of the elimination of the legal institutions that make the United States exceptional. In this morality play, Arabs occupy the role of, to use Friedman's words, "radical evil."

Friedman also offers similar arguments in the context of what may be his biggest intellectual weakness: the romanticization of American foreign policy and the United States' role in the world. He suggests that "for America to stay America, a free and open society, intimately connected to the world, the world has to become a much more ordered and controlled place."[46] I wouldn't necessarily call this suggestion racist, but I would argue without hesitation that it unconsciously extols the values of White supremacy. It does so by assuming that the United States is ordered while the majority of the world is chaotic, a highly questionable point given that five days earlier Friedman had argued for the implementation of "draconian measures and military courts." Moreover, Friedman, through either willful or actual ignorance, seems to believe that the United States wants to create order in the world, when all evidence suggests that instead it desires the sort of disorder that will create larger corporate profits. That disorder includes unwarranted overseas intervention, the monopolization of domestic politics by business interests, the retention or implementation of friendly dictatorial regimes, the destruction of the environment, and the militarization of both earth and space.

Apparently, none of these issues matters to Friedman, and in his romanticization of America's global influence he privileges the right of the wealthy to impose order on the rest of the world, a capitalist premise that has never in recorded history served the interests of the poor or disenfranchised. Friedman's notion that the United States is well-ordered is equally problematic. It is well-ordered to those in positions of authority, but not to the migrant workers who are exploited as virtual sweat-shop labor, the Indians whose reservations are dumping grounds for the majority of America's toxic waste, and the hundreds of Arabs and Muslims who, as per Friedman's sense of justice, languish in solitary confinement without due process or legal representation. Friedman, in short, invents a humane ethics for the United States while simultaneously urging the United States to export those ethics to an inhumane world. It never occurs to him that the exportation of American values is a huge reason why the world is so inhumane in the first place.

Friedman might be dismissed as overoptimistic, but another liberal heavyweight, Alan Dershowitz, offers more trenchant examples of tacit racism. Dershowitz sees no contradiction in being dubbed a "civil libertarian" and "torture advocate" in the same sentence, because he frames his argument in the context of a humane altruism that purports to be concerned ultimately with the safety of Israelis and Americans. I argued in the introduction and in earlier portions of this chapter that numerous discourses in the United States, focused somehow on the dialectics of intervention in the Arab World, render—

either intentionally or, more often, unconsciously—the colonial agent the subject through which the colonized object can be defined. This discursive tradition generally results in concern for the safety and the interests of the colonizer by reducing the colonized population to the status of an omnipresent threat or danger. Racism is inscribed at least implicitly in this sort of reductionism because its progenitors expunge the agency and thus the humanity of those whose behavior is judged outside the framework of foreign encroachment and liberationist aspirations, usually resulting in a circumscribed intellectual morality and misrepresentation of the colonized population. Dershowitz's advocacy of Israel's torture of supposed Palestinian terrorists plainly renders his morality questionable, and, given the context in which this advocacy arises, opens him to charges of totalizing and dehumanizing Arabs, Palestinians especially.[47] More important, Dershowitz's apologia for Israel's occupation, displayed in popular books like *The Case for Israel*,[48] also situates his discourse in the aforementioned tradition because to support Israel's presence in the Occupied Territories and deny the excesses of its military are to essentially advocate a geopolitical status quo in which the Palestinians are rendered without dignity and expendable. I bring him up here, however, not simply to highlight the assumptions that might lead readers to infer that Dershowitz construes Palestinians as collectively hostile.[49] Rather, I am interested in a particular claim Dershowitz is fond of making, that the Palestinians are racist. In a piece titled "The Palestinians' Genocide Campaign," for example, Dershowitz writes,

> It should not be surprising that Palestinian terrorists employ racist criteria in selecting their civilian targets, since the entire goal of Palestinian terrorism is racist to its core. It seeks to deny the Jewish people the right to self-determination. Under their version of Islamic law, it is impermissible for Jews to govern any land that was once under Muslim control, and it is equally impermissible for a Jewish majority to govern a Muslim minority, namely Israeli Arabs.[50]

Dershowitz leaves us with a quandary. If Israel's occupation is racist and Palestinian resistance to it is also racist then we must confront competing claims that, as a result of their rhetorical interplay, both lose moral credibility.

We should begin, therefore, with an assessment of Dershowitz's criteria for *racism*: denying the right of others to self-determination; refusing to live as a minority; selecting targets of attack based solely on their ethnicity; and invoking religious law to justify violence. With some variations, I would agree with these criteria, and that is why I believe Israel's occupation is racist, because each criterion describes a hallmark of Israel's presence in the Occupied Territories. In other words, Dershowitz is in general accurate philosophically when he condemns as racist the targeting of civilians and the denial of self-determination to a people based on their ethnicity; the problem is, he has an inverted understanding of the Israeli–Palestinian conflict.

Sometimes, people employ a questionable methodology to transform the objects of their racism into racists in order to mystify a violent and unjust worldview. Dershowitz personifies this strategy. While there certainly are elements of anti-Semitism (not racism) in Palestinian society, their resistance to Israel's occupation, including suicide bombings, cannot reasonably be considered anti-Semitic. Dershowitz seems to forget that Israelis, not Palestinians, have self-determination; that Israelis, not Palestinians, construct institutions intended to exclude others based on their ethnicity; that Israelis, not Palestinians, work vigorously to deny others self-determination; that Israelis, not Palestinians, use religion as the basis of juridical reasoning; that Israelis, not Palestinians, have displaced an indigenous population in order to create an ethnonationalistic state; and that Israelis, not Palestinians, continue to displace indigenes according to the dictates of their ethnonationalism.

Although elements of Palestinian resistance present us with profound ethical questions, I will have to argue, as did a range of anti-colonialists from Aimé Cesare to Frantz Fanon to Edward Said, that the work of decolonization, while at times morally questionable, is never racist. The work of colonization, on the other hand, almost always is. Dershowitz might agree, but because of his moral imperative or political agenda or whatever one wishes to call it, he seems to believe that Israelis, not Palestinians, are engaged in the work of decolonization. The quandary of moral equivalency he offered us earlier therefore becomes moot because debates over moral equivalency disappear in the presence of pervasive inaccuracy.

We should examine here another well-known commentator who subordinates the Palestinians into a space in which their agency is compromised, the Tikkun Community leader, Rabbi Michael Lerner, who has gained some notoriety among American Jews for his opposition to Israel's occupation. Lerner is more progressive than liberal and has earned his recognition as a peace activist by criticizing Israeli leaders for refusing to pursue a realistic settlement with Palestinians. His personal messages via email to the Tikkun Community (many of whose recipients never asked to be on the list, myself included) display remarkable ambivalence, as Lerner reserves harsh criticism for Palestinians who attack Israelis, both civilians and settlers. At the same time, the messages usually condemn the occupation and the misery it induces. One can detect Lerner struggling through this contradiction while trying his best to decontextualize both Jewish and Palestinian violence from sociopolitical phenomena and retain an ethic of immoral equivalency—i.e., equal disdain for any violence no matter who commits it.[51]

Lerner's nonviolent indignation and his desire for a just peace accord have no chance of symbiosis. It is with great sadness that I offer this point, but as anybody who has spent time in the Occupied Territories knows, one cannot expect strict nonviolence based on the political and economic conditions in which Palestinians live. In turn, when people like Lerner condemn Palestinian violence with more passion than they generally reserve for Israel's ethnic cleansing, the Palestinians are yet again reduced to irrational aggressors. In addition, Lerner's sense of historical accuracy is entirely whitewashed, thus augmenting his inability to accept Palestinians' liberation on the terms they have created for it, as only they have the right to do. Furthermore, when Lerner denounces peace groups for their "one-dimensional stupidity" and their "anti-Semitic and anti-Israel feelings," it might appear to many that, as American liberals have long been wont to do regarding criticism of the United States, he is not so much interested in an organic decolonial movement but is merely shielding Israel from the sort of criticism that falls outside the purview of his limited engagement with Palestinian imperatives for liberation.[52] This sort of timidity is one reason why I believe very strongly that Arab Americans interested in politics are impelled to involve themselves in any public discourse that arises about the Arab World.

In Lerner's introduction to *Healing Israel/Palestine* he notes, "In the long history of propaganda battles between Zionists and Palestinians, each side has at times told the story to make it seem as if the other side was consistently doing bad things for bad reasons. In fact, both sides have made and continue to make terrible mistakes. Yet it is also true that both sides can make a reasonable case for their choices."[53] His short history of the Zionist colonization of Palestine follows:

> The Palestinians and the Arab people of the Middle East were in the midst of a struggle to free themselves from colonial powers, and were afraid of the Zionist dream of the creation of a Jewish state right on top of their own fledgling Palestinian society. They viewed the Jews who came to Palestine not as desperate refugees but as Europeans introducing European cultural assumptions, economic and political arrangements, and thereby extending the dynamics of European domination. So the Arabs in general, and those who lived in Palestine in particular, were unwilling to give Jews a safe place to land.

The Palestinians used acts of violence and the influence of Arab states with the British to deny Jews a refuge. Their insensitivity to the Jewish people and our needs helped create a dynamic in which Jews actually became what the Palestinians had feared: a group that would cause Palestinians to become refugees. Years later, Jews responded in kind when we refused to provide Palestinians with a way to return to their homes when it was we who had power.[54]

Lerner's analysis betrays an implicit anti-Arab racism because he fails to consider that Palestinian historical narratives, which are quite a lot more unkind than his, have any veracity whatever, and he thus engages in the technique of ethnocentrism. The logic of his history lesson is confounding: foreign Jews who colonized Palestine weren't colonizers; Palestinians should have given Jews their land to become a third-class minority to atone for a genocide they didn't commit; the European Jews who settled Palestine didn't have European sensibilities; Palestinian insensitivity led to the Jews' decision to dispossess Palestinians; Jews didn't displace Palestinians but later refused to allow Palestinians to return to their homes.

But Lerner is a progressive activist, so we should give him the benefit of the doubt and assume that he hasn't gotten around to reading Vladimir Jabotinsky, the famous revisionist intellectual who played an enormous role in the formation of settlement policy: "Zionist colonization, even the most restricted, must either be terminated or carried out in defiance of the will of the native population."[55] Nor, apparently, has Lerner found the line where Jabotinsky described Arabs and Muslims as a "yelling rabble dressed up in gaudy, savage rags" and opined that they are "beasts of the desert, not a legitimate people."[56] And perhaps Lerner can be forgiven for not yet reading David Ben-Gurion's announcement that "we must expel Arabs and take their places" and "I favour compulsory transfer—I see nothing unethical in it."[57] Or Theodor Herzl's plan: "We shall try to spirit the penniless [Arab] population across the border."[58]

Surely, because Lerner actually likes Palestinians, we might wait for him to peruse Avi Shlaim's seminal *The Iron Wall*, in which Shlaim observes,

> Jabotinsky's strong pro-Western orientation stemmed from his distinctive worldview. He rejected the romantic view of the East and believed in the cultural superiority of Western civilization. "We Jews have nothing in common with what is denoted 'the East' and we thank God for that," he declared. The East, in his view, represented psychological passivity, social and cultural stagnation, and political despotism … . Zionism was conceived by Jabotinsky not as the return of the Jews to their spiritual homeland but as an offshoot or implant of Western civilization in the East.[59]

In the same book, Lerner will find that two rabbis who traveled to Palestine on a fact-finding mission for Herzl cabled him, "The bride is beautiful, but she is married to another man."[60] He will also find that Shlaim notes of Herzl, "He viewed the natives as primitive and backward, and his attitude toward them was rather patronizing. He thought that as individuals they should enjoy full civil rights in a Jewish state but he did not consider them a society with collective political rights over the land in which they formed the overwhelming majority."[61] Herzl, evidently, influenced Jabotinsky: "As the bearers of all the benefits of Western civilization, the Jews, he thought, might be welcomed by the residents of the backward East."[62] World Zionist Organization President Chaim Watzman, Lerner will discover from reading Shlaim, also held no illusions about Zionist settlement: "About the moral superiority of the Jewish claim over the Arab claim to a homeland in Palestine, he never entertained any doubt."[63]

Lerner's storybook version of Zionism, then, holds no sway. He wants to believe that Jews did nothing wrong in displacing Palestinians, but were simply victims of circumstance and were compelled to ethnically cleanse the Palestinians based on Arab intractability. His prescriptions for a peace settlement are thus voraciously skewed and so I sometimes find his romanticization of Israeli history even more disturbing than the ruminations of hardliners like Alan Dershowitz or Daniel Pipes. Lerner is interested solely in saving Israel from the charge of its inhumanity. The Palestinians are only accidentally involved in this quest for redemption. Although others might forgive him for failing to read the parts of the Zionist narrative he finds disagreeable to his fantasy of benevolent settlement, I am not so willing. After all, without liberal apologia, colonization wouldn't have lasted one month anywhere it occurred.

Institutionalized Liberal Racism

Racism in the form of support for Israel's ethnic cleansing has long been institutionalized in American governance, and the Democrats have largely affected that institutionalization. The 2004 Democratic presidential candidate John Kerry, for example, wrote a brief piece in 2001 titled "The Cause of Israel is the Cause of America" in which he proclaims, "In this difficult time we must again reaffirm we are enlisted for the duration—and reaffirm our belief that the cause of Israel must be the cause of America—and the cause of people of conscience everywhere."[64] Kerry forgot to mention that insofar as the United States is committed to preemptive intervention, military occupation, and racist foreign policy, Israel's and America's cause already are the same. Israel's cause, in any case, would be impossible if it weren't for the roughly $5.5 billion in aid Israel receives each year from the United States, aid that has transformed more politicians into hypocrites than any other action, including adultery.

Kerry's liberalism has never stopped him from helping bankroll Israeli expansionism. His legislative record on the Near East is dismal, as he has supported or co-sponsored pro-Israel positions in the Senate over 95 per cent of the time. Nor has it stopped other liberal Congresspersons from legitimizing Israeli colonization. House Resolution 294 (2003), a piece of legislation that institutionalized anti-Arab racism of the most vicious sort, passed the House with 399 yeas to 5 nays, with 7 voting present and 23 not voting. As Howard Berman (D-California) noted in his floor comments, "The reason that the Israelis have the courage to move forward, notwithstanding the continued terrorist attacks, is because they know that the United States Government and particularly that the Congress stands with them in this conflict."[65] According to *The Washington Report on Middle East Affairs*, of the top ten career recipients of pro-Israel PAC funds in the House and the Senate respectively, in the House nine are Democrats and in the Senate eight are Democrats. For the 2004 contribution cycle, six of the top ten were Democrats in both the House and the Senate.

This support for Israel, against not only international law but the world's consciousness from China to South America, testifies to the pervasiveness of anti-Arab racism in the United States. Numerous people of conscience in the United States support worthy causes but put no pressure on their representatives, as would be in their power, to force Israel into a peace settlement based on the international agreements to which it is party. Likewise, in 2004 Kerry's repeated exaltation of Israel didn't seem to bother the majority of progressives, who were willing to embrace his candidacy despite the fact that his platform included assistance for settler colonialism. Those who argued that Palestine is only a minor issue and unimportant in the face of more pressing domestic problems were not only rationalizing a brutal form of violence, they also were reinforcing a consciousness that plays an instrumental role in creating many of the problems they hoped to eliminate. If not for the United States' own history of settlement and ethnic cleansing, many of the profound domestic problems with which liberals and progressives are so concerned might not be pervasive (or dismissed as the minor flaws of national destiny). I can't say how the United States might eliminate these domestic problems, but I am certain more settler colonialism isn't the answer.

In any event, liberal support for Israel actually does affect domestic politics in the United States. On 17 September 2003, the House Subcommittee on Select Education unanimously approved HR-3077, a bill to create a federal tribunal to monitor criticism of Israel on American college campuses. Offending professors will now be subject to investigation. On 21 October 2003, the bill was passed by the full House. The bill will set up a seven-member advisory board that has the ability to recommend cutting federal funding to universities harboring academics accused of endangering Israel's interests. University of Michigan history professor Juan Cole explains,

> What they mean ... if you pin them down is ambivalence about the Iraq war, or dislike of Israeli colonization of the West Bank, or recognition that the U.S. government has sometimes in the past been in bed with present enemies like al-Qaeda or Saddam. None of these positions is "anti-American," and any attempt by a congressionally appointed body to tell university professors they cannot say these things—or that if they say them they must hire somebody who will say the opposite—is a contravention of the First Amendment of the U.S. Constitution.[66]

For all their rhetoric about justice and civil liberties, then, liberal Democrat American politicians are as implicated in anti-Arab racism as their Republican counterparts. And by failing to hold their representatives accountable, much of the liberal American population supports legislation imbued with anti-Arab racism, whether or not they actually know it. This situation, in my opinion, illustrates dramatically why any desire to eliminate the American system of racism by working within the framework of that same system is not only destined to fail, but will also unwittingly buttress the racism most liberals claim they want to end.

A Squirt Away...

The brilliant Salish and Cree poet Lee Maracle closes her poem "Saga of American Truth" with something of a prediction:

> Like an old sick joke American tries to rise
> his worn loins, swollen with misuse
> runs amok to invoke the rage of womanhood.
> His demise is but a squirt away...[67]

Maracle's last stanza in the poem's Epilogue contains another implied prediction:

> Rise Soweto. From my window I see death
> for this America who cannot drown us all.
> Rise Soweto! My turn is coming, 'tis
> just round the corner ... victory.[68]

Maracle undresses the discourse of American imperialism with remarkable skill. She invokes the traditional American perception of foreign land as a virginal body desiring penetration and then transforms that perception into a narrative of empowerment. She suggests, using an image of ejaculation, that the United States will one day collapse in fatigue, a collapse to be initiated by the victims of global American penetration. The earth itself, which the United States is currently damaging irreparably, is given agency as a woman rather than being cast, as American corporations are wont to do, as an expendable commodity to be exploited for profit.

If Maracle uses the racial riots of Soweto as a universal symbol for the aspirations of all colonized people to be liberated, then it is a symbol that works well for Arabs in Iraq and Palestine (as Maracle herself illustrates in other poems). Like South Africa and Australia and North America, the disenfranchisement of indigenous peoples in Iraq and Palestine is justified and sustained by racism, and societies that are racist, as Maracle predicts, are destined to someday fail. As an Arab, I say with confidence and in lockstep with Maracle's verse that our turn is coming; and as an American I say the same thing but for the opposite reason, and I say it with an overwhelming sadness that the nation of my birth is ruining itself. For if anti-Arab racism is allowed to continue flourishing in American society, "death for this America" will one day become more than a poet's rhythmic prediction. The Saga of American Truth. It is indeed like an old sick joke, to which the punchline only grows more and more familiar.

2
Ethnic Identity and Imperative Patriotism: Arab Americans Before and After 9/11

This chapter will examine the effects of 9/11 on Arab Americans and other minorities, with emphasis on pedagogy and literature. It altered nearly all aspects of American life; even the so-called restoration of "the American lifestyle" is a contrived metamorphosis given the deliberate manner in which American leaders urged its convalescence. The events of 9/11 and their aftermath leave social critics with a remarkably broad range of issues to examine, primary among them a more patriotic—some might say more defensive—sensibility among students and educators. This sensibility is especially *apropos* in relation to what are often referred to as ethnic or multicultural studies. (Even though both terms are problematic, I will use the more common designation *ethnic studies* to describe the area studies of non-White American ethnic groups.) Ethnic critics have long invoked and then challenged centers of traditional (White) American power. They also have maintained strong ties to radical politics; ethnic critics, in fact, have been pivotal in unmasking the workings of American imperialism and in turn formulating alternative politics in response to that imperialism, both domestic and international (for instance, Edward Said, Vine Deloria Jr., Robert Warrior, Elizabeth Cook-Lynn, Barbara Christian, Angela Davis, Lisa Suhair Majaj).

Because ethnic critics challenge the production and reproduction of American hegemony, we must explore how those challenges function in a newly reactive—indeed, at times oppressive—American atmosphere. After 9/11, dissent, a cornerstone of ethnic studies, was attacked as unpatriotic, a serious accusation in today's society. In modern American universities, which increasingly are seen as investments that ultimately must pay dividends, dissent—i.e., lack of patriotism—is conceptualized as irresponsible by enraged parents and conservative groups. Since dissent is inherent in ethnic studies, it is usually the target of the attacks (NoIndoctrination.org, for example, is filled with students complaining about professors who utilize minority discourses). An American Indian Studies professor put it to me this way in a recent conversation: "How do we get people to understand the reality of American imperialism in Indian communities when imperialism is such a taboo topic now?". With the appropriate variations, this is a crucial question for any scholar dealing with domestic or international communities that are in some sort of conflict with the United States.

As an Arab American critic, I feel particularly affected by the question enunciated above. If we alter it a bit, we are left with the following: how do instructors of Arab American culture and society comprehend the position of the Arab American community in the aftermath of 9/11? How have Arab American culture and society changed? How, in turn, has the pedagogy of Arab America changed? And how, most important, do we find a viable space to develop Arab American Studies now that Arab Americans receive the sort of attention for which our scholars once clamored?

The last question is resonant, albeit extraordinarily complex. While Arab American critics once lamented a lack of Arab American issues in various disciplines, the sudden inclusion of those issues across the academic spectrum is at best ambivalent. Before 9/11, Arab American scholars were only beginning to theorize the relationship between Arab Americans and the field of ethnic studies (as well as other fields and area studies). We therefore have little prior scholarship with which to work in speculating how to position in the Academy what has become a highly manifold community after 9/11. In the following sections, I will summarize relevant issues in Arab America before and after 9/11; analyze the post-9/11 terminology that shapes mainstream perceptions of Arabs and Arab Americans; discuss theoretical issues that influence both the production and reception of Arab American scholarship; and assess possible relationships among Arab American politics and the politics of other ethnic or minority groups.

Arab Americans Before and After

It perhaps is foolish to discuss the development of a communal scholarship in the aftermath of a particular event. We would like to think, after all, that scholarship—its production and reception—is shaped by more than reaction. Many of us also promote the semi-idealized notion that scholarship shapes events just as much as it is shaped by them. Literary critics, in particular, have attended to questions of influence and resistance for decades, a process that raised more questions with few answers. The recent ascendancy of ethnic literatures has both informed and complicated longstanding debates about the uses and usefulness of literature, which, before the rise of multiculturalism, focused almost exclusively on White authors of the traditional canon. That ascendance is especially resonant after 9/11, an event whose sociopolitical implications scholars and philosophers are only beginning to understand. I mention literature here because it is so often a site where cultural and moral conflicts are invoked and analyzed, indeed encoded. I want to explore those conflicts on their own in the hope that, later, we can better apply them to discussion of literature or the pedagogy of literature. More than anybody, Arab Americans experienced far-reaching sociopolitical implications following 9/11 without, unfortunately, generating a corresponding body of internally constructed—i.e., Arab American-produced—scholarship to examine the rapid transformations occurring in the community. These sociopolitical implications are only now starting to develop into analyzable phenomena. Most important, though, Arab Americans did not have a mature scholarly apparatus before 9/11. It has proved challenging to develop one in response to an event that so drastically affected the make-up of the Arab American community.

The last point warrants some attention because it will be of central concern to this chapter. In the years preceding 9/11, Arab American scholars from a variety of disciplines were discussing Americans of Middle Eastern background as *Arab Americans*—a development whose importance should not be underestimated—and assessing some possibilities of coalescing a distinct area study around that category. Literary critics undertook a majority of the attempts, but were buttressed—sometimes conjointly—by the work of historians, anthropologists, creative writers, psychologists, philosophers, sociologists, lawyers, demographers, pollsters, and others. Although academic circles and American society in total occasionally acknowledged an Arab American entity, the community was largely, in Nadine Naber's words, "the 'invisible' racial/ethnic group" of the United States.[1] But 9/11 dramatically altered this reality. Arab Americans evolved from invisible to glaringly conspicuous (whether or not the conspicuousness was welcomed).

Such a drastic evolution in some cases reinforced the salience of pre-9/11 scholarship, but in other cases rendered it antiquated or, worse, useless. Before 9/11 scholars examined Arab American invisibility or marginality—or whatever other term they employed to denote peripherality—but after 9/11 they were faced with a demand to transmit or translate their culture to mainstream Americans. The demand was matched by an insatiable curiosity about Arabs and Arab Americans; everybody from "everyday" Americans to high-ranking politicians wanted to know about the people who had irrevocably altered American life. Arab Americans suddenly were visible, and because of the pernicious intentions of various law and intelligence agencies, that visibility was not necessarily embraced. Indeed, it was often feared and deplored. These issues suddenly forced Arab Americans into a paradigm shift whose implications are enormous because there was no stable paradigm from which to shift emphasis in the first place. An area study that had been exploratory immediately became too much in demand for its own good.

Another competing but no less relevant factor deals with the political sensibilities of the Arab American community. Michael Suleiman,[2] Alixa Naff,[3] Eric Hooglund,[4] Nabeel Abraham,[5] and Nadine Naber all agree that before the 1967 Arab–Israeli War, Arab Americans, who were overwhelmingly Christian at that point, tended to assimilate even while maintaining cultural features of the so-called Old World (e.g., food, theology, childrearing, family ties—the Arabic language, for the most part, was not passed down from immigrants to children). After 1967, however, many Arab Americans reclaimed a sense of nationalism. The nationalism, sparked in large part by glaring Arab dispossession, was reinforced by a new wave of Muslim Arab immigrants who had been politicized already in the Arab World and had no need, given America's fairly protected civil liberties, to hide their ethnic-religious identities. Newly arrived Christian and Druze Arabs did the same. A steady appearance of "pro-Arab" or "revisionist" historiography on the Near East in the following years helped to instill ethnic pride in Arab Americans, who, prior to 1967, had virtually no representation in popular and political American culture. By the 1990s, a thoroughly *Arab* consciousness existed among Arab immigrants and American-born Arabs, who rapidly were expressing that consciousness intellectually and creatively.

Although no single form of consciousness—or conception of *Arab American*—can be said to have existed during this period, scholars were on the verge of critical breakthroughs in the years directly preceding 9/11. This fact was evident in the publication of Michael Suleiman's edited volume *Arabs in America: Building a New Future*, Khaled Mattawa and Munir Akash's *Post Gibran: Anthology of New Arab American Writing*,[6] and a series of theoretically sophisticated articles by Lisa Suhair Majaj.[7] In the literary arena, Diana Abu-Jaber and Rabih Alameddine received wide acclaim for novels that invoked both Arab American and Near Eastern themes.[8] Vibrant gatherings to celebrate Arab cultures and discuss Arab American concerns occurred across the United States, in large cities and rural towns. College students with half or quarter Arab blood, some three or four generations removed from the Arab World (usually Syria or Lebanon), suddenly found value in being Arab American and reclaimed their ethnicity by visiting the Near East to learn Arabic or work for NGOs in villages and refugee camps. This phenomenon can only be understood if we situate it with similar phenomena occurring with individuals from other ethnic groups—N. Scott Momaday's famous example of his mixedblood mother "choosing" to be Cherokee, for instance.[9] It is no accident that such ethnic valuations, whatever their merits and problems, corresponded with the rise of the Black and Indian power movements of the 1960s and 1970s, as well as the National Association for the Advancement of Colored People (NAACP), the Southern Christian Leadership Conference (SCLC), and various anti-war organizations (even virulently anti-Arab groups like Meir Kahane's Jewish Defense League helped to create an atmosphere in which ethnic identity assumed great importance). While it is difficult to comprehend fully the effects of those movements, they often gave marginalized, lonely, or ambivalent youth (or adults in some cases) the illusion of stable identity or a feeling of belonging to communities distinguishable from mainstream society. The feeling was especially powerful for those displeased with certain American politics. This motivation has been particularly resonant in Arab America.

The reclamation or recovery of an Arab American identity is in many ways analogous to the social trajectories of other ethnic groups, and can therefore be considered typical of modern American acculturation and deculturation. And yet international relations have played a prominent role in the construction and consolidation of Arab America as a social and political unit. Nothing has been of more concern to Arab Americans since 1967 than the Israel–Palestine conflict, although Iraq has also been pivotal since 1990. American support for Israel has long enraged Arab Americans (and others), thereby providing Arab Americans with a tangible rallying cry and political purpose. The support also has been an important binding force for a community that, despite popular perception, is far from homogeneous, containing as it does people with over 20 national backgrounds, a multitude of linguistic dialects, and numerous religions. Therefore, while Palestine may have expedited the coalescence of an Arab American identity, it in no way exclusively dictates or maintains it. Like any other ethnic group, Arab Americans function as a communal entity based on innumerable factors, both cultural and political.

Ultimately, though, it can be said that no single event shaped the destiny of Arab Americans more than 9/11. After 9/11, the Arab American community was thrust into the spotlight. This attention represented a drastic change from the community's previous position, for during the times that Arab Americans attempted to be noticed—times generally related to our flagship issue, Palestinian independence—it was rare for mainstream forums to acknowledge us. When Arab Americans were acknowledged, it was usually in the form of ridicule, dismissal, or an outright racism that had long been considered an unacceptable way to address other ethnic groups. It is a general rule that ambivalence will follow when a once-ignored or outright slandered community is suddenly offered unceasing attention and is asked to define and redefine itself daily. The peculiar nature of the sudden attention after 9/11 only did more to catalyze Arab Americans into serious introspective glances. That attention was simultaneously an outpouring of hostility and kindness. On the day of the attack, Rudy Giuliani and George W. Bush urged Americans not to engage in racial violence and to prevent any that might occur, as did practically every television commentator and politician of significance. For every racist comment and report of harassment, there were ten stories about "average" Americans going out of their way to make their Arab neighbors feel safe and welcome.

But what do those pronouncements actually reveal about the culture from which they were produced and the community at which they were directed? And what were their effects on both? First, while they were in some cases sincere when uttered by politicians and probably sincere in every case when uttered by ordinary citizens, the cultural impulses inspiring them cannot be considered altogether pure since they drew tacitly from a tradition of forced assimilation. (It is also problematic that such pronouncements needed constant repeating to begin with.) While the goodwill of everyday Americans cannot be called into question, one might look upon aspects of the discourse of American leaders with suspicion. They attempted to urge Arab Americans, before 9/11 generally anti-assimilationist and radical, into total assimilation. In this case, it was not a forced assimilation that other ethnic groups, primarily Natives, have experienced. It took the form of the repeated statements: "They're American, too"; "They're American, just like you"; "They also love this country." The suspicion I cite should be drawn out briefly. A community can accept the call, whether or not it was solicited, to be absorbed fully into the politics of its surrounding society only if it assumes that the surrounding society's politics are amenable to the community.

This has never been the case with Arab Americans because the American government has long been involved in the Arab World in a way that most Arab Americans find invasive and unjust. Moreover, draconian legislation like the USA Patriot Act wholly contradicts the occasionally inclusive language of Congress and the Bush administration.

The Patriot Act, however, is only the first legislative initiative of what many legal scholars fear will be a series of federal resolutions that might severely limit civil liberties. In January 2003, Bill Moyers posted on the *NOW* website the text for the Domestic Security Enhancement Act (DSEA) (also known as Patriot Act II), which would further enable federal agents and intelligence officials to intrude in people's private lives and detain them for indefinite periods of time without legal counsel based solely on suspicion. This type of legislation may soon not be limited to visitors, immigrants, aliens, or permanent residents. American citizens also are under scrutiny. In February 2003, *The Nation*'s David Cole revealed the purpose of the DSEA. He writes,

> If the Patriot Act was so named to imply that those who question its sweeping new powers of surveillance, detention and prosecution are traitors, the DSEA takes that theme one giant step further. It provides that any citizen, even native-born, who supports even the lawful activities of an organization the executive branch deems "terrorist" is presumptively stripped of his or her citizenship. To date, the "war on terrorism" has largely been directed at noncitizens, especially Arabs and Muslims. But the DSEA would actually turn citizens associated with "terrorist" groups into aliens.[10]

Cole later notes that suspect citizens "would then be subject to the deportation power, which the DSEA would expand to give the Attorney General the authority to deport any noncitizen whose presence he deems a threat to our 'national defense, foreign policy or economic interests'."[11]

The domestic environment, then, is one that terrifies many Arab Americans and keeps us from politics, especially

Palestinian politics, because the fear of being harassed or arrested is more than mere paranoia. At the same time, numerous Arab Americans feel that we have no real leadership on which we can rely. Nobody genuinely speaks our concerns in the media and nobody has adequate power to protect us from FBI investigations should our names become suspicious to American officials. Arab Americans, and many others, are under the impression that speaking too loudly against the war on terror or American support for Israel is a viable cause for suspicion. In addition, Arab Americans cannot discuss on campus the conditions of Palestinian life in the Occupied Territories without harassment, complaints of anti-Americanism, or, worse, accusations of anti-Semitism.

All the issues enumerated above have appeared in Arab American literature. Directly following 9/11, Palestinian American poet Suheir Hammad penned a widely circulated poem, "First Writing Since," that explored her shared ethnicity with the hijackers and her shared nationality with their victims. The Arab American literary journal *Mizna* has run poems, short stories, and essays that deal with the effects of 9/11 on Arab American identity and on the relationship between Arab Americans and our Arab brethren (the first issue after 9/11 was devoted entirely to the attacks). The themes are constant and usually didactic: the authors feel closer to the American polity and concurrently isolated from it. That sort of theme denotes, as Bill Ashcroft and Pal Ahluwalia have described in relation to Edward Said, the paradox of identity.[12] In the year after 9/11, no critical study of identity in the Arab American community was published in a sociological, psychological, historical, or literary journal, with one exception: a *Middle East Report* devoted to the influence of 9/11 on Arab and Muslim Americans.[13] This lack of critical inquiry is, of course, highly problematic, as the Arab American community continues to enhance our ambivalence by allowing the dominant society to define us and speak on our behalf. Arab Americans seem on the verge of borrowing from the sensibilities common among scholars of other ethnic groups in proclaiming that no matter how well-intentioned the speaker, when it comes to community issues, it should be Arab Americans who have priority in speaking. One often finds this sentiment expressed in literature, since numerous Arab Americans find it the last haven of articulation that still belongs to them. Cultural journals such as *Mizna*, *JUSOOR*, and *al-Jadid* have therefore assumed great importance in the community during the past few years.

"The American Way of Life"

Some years back, I published a column in the *Palestine Chronicle* urging Arab Americans to reformulate a self-image by rejecting the vocabulary of *terrorism* employed so uncritically in today's United States. My columns for the paper usually elicited passionate reactions, but this one provoked outright anger from a few American readers whose vocabulary I had attacked. One reader demanded to know why I "split time between the United States and the Middle East," as my author bio explained. The message claimed that discomfiting motivations were evident in my article: "Apparently your dislike for the American way of life and the [policy of the] current administration to keep it that way, even if it means war, is a problem for you."

This formulation in many ways accurately highlights the relationship between Arab Americans and the larger society in which we live. Often accused of dual sympathies, Arab Americans feel sometimes as if we are removed (of our own accord) from the Arab World, but equally removed (not of our own accord) from the United States. Xenophobia certainly plays a role in the isolation many Arab Americans feel, but it would be foolish to limit our analysis to either xenophobia or racism. While the respondent to my article is most likely

xenophobic and perhaps racist—would she have objected had
I split time between the United States and, say, Britain?—her
sensibilities can be attributed to a more profound phenomenon
dating to the settlement of the New World.

I speak about a particular type of discourse that, with
technical and temporal variations, has existed continuously
in the United States, which I term *imperative patriotism*.
Imperative patriotism assumes (or demands) that dissent in
matters of governance and foreign affairs is unpatriotic and
therefore unsavory. It is drawn from a longstanding sensibility
that nonconformity to whatever at the time is considered to be
"the national interest" is unpatriotic. Imperative patriotism is
most likely to arise in settler societies, which usually need to
create a juridical mentality that professes some sort of divine
mandate to legitimize their presence on indigenous land. The
juridical mentality impresses conformity on the settlers, who
might otherwise demur when being asked to slaughter indigenes
or when absorbing attacks by them. Hilton Obenzinger
demonstrates that this mentality existed in early America, where
settlers "invested New England settlement, and by extension
all of America, with a sense of religious destiny: that the new
society extinguishing the various indigenous peoples' claims
to land and independence was a re-creation of the scriptural
narrative of covenantal, chosen-people identity."[14]

This sensibility has evolved into a detectable feature of
modern American politics. When one hears George W. Bush
present war on Iraq as a "war for civilization" and make
statements such as "either you are for us or against us" and
"God is on America's side," it becomes clear that the early
settler ethos, in which the settlers had a divine mission conferred
upon them, continues to influence American discourse—and,
more important, American morality. Imperative patriotism
arises in this context. I prefer the phrase *imperative patriotism*
to the unmodified *patriotism* because the word *imperative*
insinuates necessity and purpose. It further denotes a particular

set of American desires (enumerated below) that connects to a historical dynamic. In modern America, while imperative patriotism functions at the levels of discourse and philosophy, it generates its strength most consistently at the level of morality. Imperative patriotism manifests itself most explicitly during wartime or domestic unrest. Ethnic nationalist movements, such as the American Indian Movement and Black Panthers, were widely considered to be inimical to American values and therefore also caused the manifestation of imperative patriotism. (Even movements using less nationalist rhetoric, such as the SCLC and Cesar Chavez's United Farm Workers, evoked fear in many Americans.) Moreover, imperative patriotism both informs and is derived from colonial discourse. Politicians frequently speak about the need to occupy Arab countries and "civilize" them by introducing the natives to "democracy." (Like the colonial discourse before it, this one rarely mentions the actual motivation for intervention: the plunder of resources, in this case oil.) Americans today hear so much about the need for their government's "leadership" in all areas of the world that most, like the Europeans before them, automatically equate colonization with generosity and moral strength.

Yet perhaps the most crucial (and discomfiting) feature of imperative patriotism is its relationship with xenophobia. While imperative patriotism has a symbiotic moral association with colonial discourse, it is more disconnected from xenophobia because it does not actually arise from xenophobia, which is a phenomenon that, to a degree, has its roots in European contact with Indians, but more traditionally has resulted from animosity over (perceived or real) economic disparity. On one level, xenophobia is a less vicious form of colonial discourse, but it more often results from a certain type of fear that is generated when people feel that their economic stability (or the possibility of it) is threatened—as, for instance, when laborers battle with immigrants over blue-collar jobs or when middle-to-upper-class Whites complain to city councils about immigrants moving into their neighborhoods. Imperative patriotism, however, tends to inform xenophobia, a fact that is expressed in statements such as, "If you don't like America, go back to where you came from"; "If you don't agree with the United States, why don't you just leave?"; and "A real American works hard and doesn't complain." These statements insinuate that "American" is a stable, fixed identity rooted in a physical and cultural Whiteness for which many immigrants do not qualify. They also indicate that in xenophobia narrow political suppositions often govern social behavior: to dissent from the imagined mores of America is to forfeit identification as American. Leaving the United States then becomes the only logical option.

It is easy to see how these suppositions are played out in the reader's complaint that I "dislike the American way of life." The reader assumes that only one or a few forms of thought and/or behavior constitute "the American way of life." This sensibility has long been common in the United States and has proliferated since 9/11, in no small part because of the colonial discourse arising from hawks in Washington. And yet it would be reductionist to attribute the sensibility to a crude xenophobia informed by imperative patriotism. It is better conceptualized as an articulation of imperative patriotism that appears at first glance to be crude xenophobia, but in reality brings to mind remnants of settler discourse with its rigid juridical undercurrents. One might argue that it is impossible to define "the American way of life" since the United States is a multicultural society with thousands of subcultures (not to mention the fact that numerous Central and South Americans also consider themselves to be "American"). Nevertheless, at the popular level, it is assumed that a "true" American is (or should be) patriotic and capitalistic, and, less explicitly, Christian and White.

Arab Americans exist as a composite of postmodern Americana and American subculture in this complex of issues. To various degrees, our positioning in the United States has been highly complex for some time, but 9/11 exacerbated the complexities by simultaneously endowing the community with sympathetic gestures and amplifying xenophobic outpourings of imperative patriotism, a mindset that is by its very nature antithetical to the Arab American experience. The irony of this positioning became evident when a church in Jacksonville, which has a sizeable Arab American population, posted a sign claiming that Mohammad condoned murder. While Arab Americans protested this stereotype, it was another Christian conservative, radio columnist Andy Martin of Florida, who offered the most vocal response: "I thought we were past that kind of bigotry and ignorance in Florida. But apparently not … . Any religious leader who fosters bigotry is not a religious leader; he or she is espousing evil."

It is difficult to determine whether the discourse seen in the Jacksonville church sign might accurately be construed as racism. *Racism* is a complicated term, and ethnic studies scholars do their communities few favors by applying it loosely and uniformly to a wide range of discursive phenomena. In defining the Jacksonville discourse as racist, one also must contemplate whether all agents of imperative patriotism are racist. We are then left with questions about whether forms of racism expressed unconsciously are as pernicious, in intent and action, as outright racism. The same concern exists with xenophobia. It would be foolish to decontextualize these issues from the founding narratives of the United States. If ethnic cleansing and slavery, among other odious practices, played a salient role in the physical and psychological formation of the United States, then it should be no surprise that various types of racism survive. Indeed, one could claim that the United States has a collective sickness that results from never having officially confronted its destruction of Indian nations, and that this sickness accounts, however abstractly, for many persisting social problems (imperative patriotism, xenophobia, racism, sexism, discrimination). Rather than arguing whether various types of racism exist, we are better served interrogating the actual extent of their existence.

Arab Americans are in a special position to assist in that understanding. First of all, I would argue that the Jacksonville discourse is racist precisely because it cannot be decontextualized from (admittedly more noxious) incidents in the American past. When considering this sort of argument, our analytical framework should include the peculiar amalgam of premillenialism, Messianism, and extremism that marked European settlement of the New World, particularly in New England. Modern American racism developed as a result of the imagery of Indians and Africans promulgated by White settlers—a process that continues into the present—in addition to foreign intervention and biological determinism. Indeed, the covenantal Messianism with which early American settlers invested their identity invents and reinvents itself based on deeply encoded notions of racial superiority. Those notions have been modernized, sometimes disguised as pragmatism, and manage to pervade a surprisingly large portion of mainstream American discourse. The label of *racism* can thus be applied to anti-Arab vitriol independent of the severe dehumanization that occurs by construing a religious group's prophet as a murderer. If, after all, Mohammad is portrayed as subhuman, what does it imply about those who follow his religion?

Obviously, Arab Americans interact with the dominant American culture based on the specifics of Arab immigration and the subsequent development of the Arab American community. But once Arabs formed a distinct communal identity, as do all American ethnic minorities, we inherited a centuries-old history of ethnic-mainstream conflict that has yet to be assessed in detail, either before or after 9/11. Settlement, dispossession, slavery, and overseas imperialism all are included

Denver Public Library

Eugene Field Branch
4/1/2010, 3:33:02 PM

CHARGE RECEIPT

STEC JOA
D03581XXXX

1) Title: Prospector item special loan
Item #: R0903771015
Due Date: 4/22/2010

2) Title: Prospector item special loan
Item #: R0903771007
Due Date: 4/22/2010

Eugene Field Branch
720-865-0240

For information about your library card account or to
renew items, please visit http://mycard.denverlibrary.org
or call 720-865-1133 or any of our 23 locations.

CHECK IT OUT. BRING IT BACK.

in that inheritance. The overseas imperialism has traditionally been most resonant in the Arab American community and is the centerpiece of the community's current reorganization. Like most other minorities, Arab Americans "piggyback" the ethnic tensions that were developed uniquely in the United States based primarily on the oppression of Blacks and Indians. Imperialism, however, is the most immediate issue facing Arab Americans, since much of the imperialism is directed at the Arab World (especially if we consider, as I do, Israel's occupation of the West Bank and Gaza Strip to be an aspect of American imperialism).

Based on this formulation, I reject the notion that anti-Arab racism was formed and has evolved based solely on social features (primarily geopolitics) detectable in the interaction of Arabism and Americana. We are better served looking at that racism as being on a continuum with America's roots in settler colonialism. A correlative settler colonialism in the West Bank, after all, accounts for much of the tension among the United States and Arab nations—and, by extension, Arab Americans. American racism had thrived for years before the first Arab arrived in North America; Arab Americans have faced an evolution of that racism since we began to vocally articulate a Middle Eastern identity after 1967 (which rehashed some of the tensions developed between the Founding Fathers and Muslim pirates off the Barbary Coast 200 years earlier). It is not necessarily a modern racism, but one that has been perpetually reformulated based on contemporary popular and political sentiment and a failure by American leaders to adequately confront the past, in philosophy by apologizing and erecting monuments, or in practice by eliminating colonization and dispossession in other parts of the world.

Thus 9/11, according to this analysis, did not really disrupt anti-Arab racism in any momentous way. Rather, it polarized attitudes that had been in place years before the word *terrorism* entered common parlance. While 9/11 forced most

Americans to confront issues—foreign policy, civil liberties, immigration, minority rights—that had often been muted or ignored, a detectable pre-9/11 trajectory has reasserted itself: Those who were prone to racism or xenophobia before 9/11 (mainly the advocates of imperative patriotism) found a justification for them; conversely, those who were prone to support multiculturalism (mainly left-liberals and liberal arts academics) have used the 9/11 backlash against Arab Americans to argue in favor of cosmopolitanism and the retention of civil liberties. *New Republic* editor Martin Peretz, for example, has consistently conflated Islam and terrorism. In 1995, he proclaimed "that there is a convulsion in Islam, whose particular expression is terror."[15] Alerting Americans to "the very real phenomenon of an international killer jihad," he later wrote, "So much of the spate of terror the world has witnessed [in the past] had been wrought by Arabs."[16]

These sentiments played an enormous role in creating the sort of xenophobic culture that prompted physical attacks—leading, in some cases, to murder—on Arab Americans and those perceived to be Arab American (Sikhs, South Asians, Central Asians, Hispanics) by Americans determined to preserve imperative patriotism. Four years after Peretz's article, in a piece chillingly titled "Terrorism at the Multiplex," Joshua Muravchik echoed Peretz by announcing that "the image of Middle Eastern terrorists wreaking havoc in the streets of America is both compelling and only too plausible."[17] After 9/11, the same set of stereotypes expressed with an almost childish vocabulary—"international killer jihad"?—continued unmolested, only this time with a rhetorical trope the authors considered infallible. Congressman Howard Coble (R-NC) stated on a radio call-in program that internment of Arab Americans is worth discussion because "some of these Arab Americans are probably intent on doing harm to us."[18] Coble's use of the pronoun "us" is noteworthy. It indicates, much like the message I received in response to my *Chronicle* article, that according to the ethnography of imperative patriotism Arab Americans are not actually American. "Us" denotes difference, alterity, even though Coble contradicted his own grammar by adding "American" after "Arab" in juxtaposition with the pronoun "us." Coble's invocation of Japanese Americans also illustrates, with frightening clarity, that negative attitudes about Arab Americans exist in a historical continuum that in many cases led to horrifying behavior.

Unreasonable and Pragmatic

The post-9/11 racism detailed above is not limited to politicians' blunders or marginal and/or jingoistic publications. It made its way, for instance, into what first appeared to be an evenhanded analysis of the Israeli–Palestinian conflict on the op-ed page of the *Washington Post* by former editor Stephen S. Rosenfeld. Displaying a remarkable, if unconscious, propensity for turn-of-the-century anthropological essentialism, Rosenfeld attacks what he dubs "the Palestinians' killing wing" by explaining, "The Palestinians' truest weapon is their high birthrate. It emits a seemingly unstoppable flow of adolescents trained in murder."[19] Rosenfeld's statement is at base no different than that offered in 2002 by prominent writer Daniel Pipes: "In the most elemental terms, we see here [on college campuses] the contrast between the civilized nature of Israel and its friends and the raw barbarism of Israel's enemies."[20] It is worth noting that Pipes, whose moral apparatus exemplifies the very worst facets of imperative patriotism, was generally dismissed as a zealot until 9/11, after which he became popular among media in search of sensationalistic evidence of Islamic aggression or "fifth-column" Arab Americans. (The "fifth-column" charge can be found all over Pipes's website, submitted by enraged readers who deplore the sensibilities of Arab and Arab American scholars.) In fact, Pipes, along with Stanley Kurtz, Martin Kramer, Steve Emerson, and Bill Kristol, as well

as a litany of fundamentalist Protestant leaders, exemplifies
the stereotypical discourse inherent in the post-9/11 backlash
against Arab Americans.

About Pipes, Ian Lustick observes that he "takes views that
no responsible academic would ever articulate. He's so far
outside the pale of mainstream scholarship, yet the [American
news] networks need people to give this view because it's a
popular view. A reasonable position they can get anywhere.
What they're looking for is an unreasonable position."[21] We
can add to Lustick's analysis. What he calls an "unreasonable position" is, after 9/11, perfectly reasonable according to
the pragmatism of a political culture that suddenly found in
Arab Americans an excuse to increase federal interference in
civilian privacy by inducing fear and then working to reduce
that fear through what are justified as practical means, e.g.,
ethnic profiling, surveillance, citizen spying, detention—things
that have occurred recurrently throughout modern American
history (with, most prominently, the American Indian
Movement and Black Panthers). And all these means are, of
course, purportedly used with great regret, in order to preserve
the impossibly abstract but highly compelling "American way
of life" (a phrase Pipes and similar writers use incessantly).
I would replace Lustick's use of the word "unreasonable"
with "pragmatic." Imperative patriotism relies on a perceived
pragmatism in order to command moral legitimacy. Today,
the most conspicuous feature of the pragmatism is the word
terrorism, which is used uncritically to describe anybody (of
the requisite Arab background) who contests either domestic or
international American hegemony. A set of common assumptions must exist between speaker and audience when *terrorism*
is employed without analysis or qualification. Those assumptions, based on the notion that terrorism is a morally repugnant
and inexplicable act exclusive to the East, survive only in the
framework of a corresponding assumption, that Arabs are
inferior in culture and intellect to Americans (read: Whites).

As I mentioned above, 9/11 did not produce these assumptions, although it did provide them with pragmatic legitimacy to advocates of imperative patriotism already predisposed to anti-Arab racism. The stereotypes underlying the assumptions have long existed and have been expressed through popular American culture in, among other media, television and film, as the journal *Cineaste*[22] and media critic Jack Shaheen[23] have recorded. In a detailed study of "the Arab image" in the United States, Ronald Stockton surveyed hundreds of representations of Arabs in numerous media, including negative statements made by presidents and prominent government officials, and concluded that "the generic Arab shares with [the stereotyped] Jews thick lips, evil eyes, unkempt hair, scruffy beard, weak chin, crooked nose, vile look. He also shares with [the stereotyped] Blacks thick lips, heavy brow, stupid expression, stooped shoulders."[24] Stockton advises "that images of Arabs cannot be seen in isolation but are primarily derivative"[25] and illustrates the dangers inherent in negative ethnic imagery:

> It is important to remember that while government policies are not simple outgrowths of public opinion, governments operate within parameters defined by what the public will tolerate. If the public is willing to dehumanize a population—be it domestic or foreign—then exceptional latitude is allowed where human rights are concerned. Slavery, brutal war, mass murder, assassination, and indifference to suffering become more acceptable.[26]

Stockton, whose essay was published in 1994, offers a portentous analysis, especially his caution about depleted human rights and indifference to suffering. In the same year, Nabeel Abraham similarly cautioned that "anti-Arab racism … permeates mainstream cultural and political institutions" in the United States.[27] Stockton's invocation of Jewish stereotypes is noteworthy because, ironically, anti-Arab racism is derived from the same attitudes that produced American anti-Semitism. I dub this situation ironic because one way Americans now marginalize Arabs is by labeling them anti-Semitic when they articulate their (legitimate) political sensibilities. Imperative patriotism, this example illustrates, has the potential to be pervasive.

Turning back to foreign policy, the United States has often fostered hostility with Arabs since the eighteenth-century military engagements off the Barbary Coast and has long had economic interests in the Near East. It has therefore long been in conflict with various Arab nations, and so critics never had the ability—or in some cases the motivation—to assuage the anti-Arab racism Stockton and Abraham describe. More important, since that racism can be identified as analogous to traditional forms of racism in existence since the settlement of North America, the political culture of the United States does not generally inspire a significant oppositional dialectic. Arab Americans, then, occupy a critical, if complicated, position in the modern United States: We connote how, where, and in what conditions a regenerative racism can transmute from tacit to explicit; and we offer ethnic, cultural, and postcolonial studies scholars a remarkable range of social and theoretical questions to analyze, all of them central to the understanding and development of literary theory.

Because Arab Americans have difficulty alleviating an anti-Arab racism sustained partly by attacks by Arabs on the United States and the corresponding American interests in the Arab World, we have an elaborate relationship with the dominant American culture, which is made even more elaborate by the outpourings of sympathy Arab Americans received immediately after 9/11. (Those outpourings have waned considerably four to five years later.) As a result, Arab Americans embody what Jean-François Lyotard calls the *differend*.[28] The differend arises when conflict between two or more groups cannot be resolved because of divergent vocabularies representing incongruous sensibilities. Each side of the conflict subsequently feels as if the language of dialogue precludes it from receiving justice. Lyotard wanted to revolt against both the concept and use of universal language. He believed that to overlook the differend in social analysis is tantamount to the denial of justice because such an omission denies difference. The differences Lyotard discussed are neither primal nor predetermined—that is to say, difference is not an unalterable human feature that prevents rapprochement or unity. Rather, the acknowledgement of difference—in action and language—is a precondition for rapprochement or unity.

With appropriate variations, we can look at the differend to partially elucidate the relationship among Americans and Arab Americans. Much of the tension I have explored exists because of a specific vocabulary directed at Arab Americans. The vocabulary becomes particularly troublesome when it is used to explain Arab culture or, more causally, Arab "behavior" to a curious public. This is where anti-Arab racists, posing as responsible analysts, poison American–Arab American relations. When scholars and commentators denounce Arabs and Arab Americans as "terrorists" and threats to "American national security" and "the American way of life," to borrow from Campus Watch parlance, a profound defensiveness arises in the Arab American community. That defensiveness, coupled with a longstanding ambivalence about an identity that traverses the Atlantic, reinforces the influence of the differend, which in turn reinforces the inability of Arab Americans to fruitfully navigate the metaphorical spaces between center and margin in the United States.

Arab Americans and Ethnic Studies

Ethnic studies scholars have great impetus to invoke these complexities and discuss them to broaden our inquiries into racial and cultural dynamics in post-9/11 America. In a time of such tense politics and furious debate over the government's management of domestic affairs, the United States is a rapidly changing nation. Numerous changes are the result of a small but pivotal community whose origin lies in the region that indirectly kindled many of the domestic transformations enumerated above. As a young Arab American professor, I struggle with the same questions that have occupied countless scholars of other ethnic groups: How can I adequately respond to the racism directed against my community? How does that racism sustain itself and inform various aspects of popular American culture? What can my community do to embolden and empower its youngsters and academics? Where does my community fit in the ever-changing panorama of American multiculturalism? Where should it fit?

These are not easy questions to answer. Entire area studies, after all, have been constructed in the past 40 years in order to explore them. For Arab Americans, one thing is clear. Even if solutions to the questions are difficult to ascertain, it is not difficult to ascertain a starting point: the creation of a vocabulary geared toward eliminating the differend that obstructs productive dialogue with other ethnic groups as well as the American polity in total. In order to create that vocabulary, Arab Americans must successfully challenge individuals who denigrate us, such as Ann Coulter, Don Imus, Jack Cafferty, Joe Scarborough, Mortimer Zuckerman, and various American politicians.

Coulter, for instance, has referred to veteran (and Arab American) journalist Helen Thomas as "that old Arab" and decried the fact that Thomas can "sit within yards of the president."[29] Upon his death, Imus called Yasser Arafat "stinky" and "a rat," and ridiculed his "beady eyes," adding, "all Palestinians look like him [sic]."[30] Scarborough said of Arafat, "This was, after all, the man who invented modern terrorism in the Middle East and by extension was the godfather of September 11."[31] Cafferty has claimed that "the Arab World is where innocent people are kidnapped, blindfolded, tied up, tortured and beheaded, and then videotape of all of this is released to the world as though they're somehow proud of their barbarism. Somehow, I wouldn't be too concerned about the sensitivity of the Arab World." He also has claimed, "They treat women like furniture in [Arab] countries. If I was [sic] a woman, I think I'd rather be in an American jail cell than I would be living with one of those whatever they are over there."[32] In an interview with the McLaughlin Group, Mortimer Zuckerman indicated through a half-joke that there are only two intellectuals in the entire Arab World.[33] In July 2005, Congressman Tom Tancredo (R-CO) suggested that the United States should strike Mecca, the Muslim Holy Land, with nuclear weapons. "You know, you could take out their [Muslims'] holy sites," he told radio host Pat Campbell, later refusing to apologize for his suggestion.[34]

How can this sort of denigration be successfully challenged? This question belongs squarely in the realm of ethnic studies, with the burgeoning Arab American Studies playing a crucial role in an intellectualization of America's popular and political cultures. While many of the issues I have discussed arise because of specific features in the relationship between Arab and non-Arab Americans, they are by no means the exclusive domain of Arab American critics. They existed before Arab Americans raised their voices as a distinct community. Since the racism Arab Americans face is also directed at other minorities, it seems only logical for Arab Americans to demystify stereotype in conjunction with the minorities at whom racism has traditionally been directed. More crucial, given the current deterioration of civil liberties and the precedent created by intense surveillance of the Arab American community, it would appear foolish for other ethnic groups—many of them long suspected of subversion—to ignore Arab America. In any case, it is not necessarily a particular reaction to a particular event (9/11) that is of immense concern to Arab Americans; it is an entire culture of imperative patriotism—and all its attendant manifestations—that existed years before 9/11 and was merely strengthened by the anxiety manufactured in the aftermath of the attacks.

More important, the Arab American community is far from politically and ethnically homogeneous. Not all Arab Americans, for instance, oppose war in Iraq, and some donate large sums of money to the Republican Party. Nor are we in agreement about the Israeli–Palestinian conflict; opinion ranges from the total destruction of Israel, to binational coexistence, to accommodation of Israeli settlements in return for a Palestinian state. Some Muslim Arabs prefer "Muslim" as their primary identification, which places them in a mostly non-Arab community. Similarly, many Lebanese Christians prefer to be identified as "Lebanese," "Maronite," "Christian," or even "Phoenician" rather than as "Arab," even though Middle Eastern ethnicity is apparent in Lebanese Christians culturally and physically. Since they comprise the largest demographic group in Arab America—with luminaries such as Frank Zappa, Danny Thomas, Ralph Nader, Kahlil Gibran, Helen Thomas, and Jamie Farr—the term *Arab American* is anything but trenchant. Some Coptic Egyptians, a growing demographic group in the Detroit area, are likewise apt to call themselves "Copts" before "Arabs." Non-Arab Middle Easterners, as we noted in the introduction, also complicate the Arab American ethnicity, since they are often categorized, of their own accord or according to stereotype, as Arab. These non-Arab Middle Easterners include Iranians, Turks, Kurds, Armenians, Berbers, Circassians, and Central Asians. Certain Mizrahi/Sephardic Jews in the United States also retain an Arab cultural taxonomy, either in addition to or instead of a Jewish identity.

Given these diversities, I am hesitant at this point to theorize new directions in the Arab American community, although it is clear that 9/11 affected to varying degrees every demographic group within Arab America. Because of this fact, all Arab Americans have a stake in examining the community in order to formulate material and academic strategies for awareness, empowerment, and reconciliation. Arab Americans—and, indeed, everybody concerned with the racist undertones of a strengthened imperative patriotism after 9/11—can begin by complicating the simplification of ethnic categories that informs the pragmatism of foreign intervention and depleted civil liberties. I suspect that interethnic dialogue, rather than colloquy with the dominant society that grants credence to anti-Arab racists, is a useful place to begin—and one that will bestow on ethnic studies educators an important material politics to discuss.

Arab Americans After and Beyond

Arab Americans are not without a foundation in undertaking political action and social analysis. Nor are we strangers to hate crimes as a result of American–Arab antagonism. the *Nation*, the *Quill*, the *Progressive*, *School Law News*, *Newsweek*, the *Economist*, and even *Sports Illustrated* and the *New Republic* have published stories in the past few decades about how, as James Abourezk puts it, "when the heat is on, Arab-Americans lose their rights."[35] Neither were we totally silent or invisible before 9/11. Lawrence Davidson has shown that Arab Americans were active in protests against Zionism as early as 1917, the year of the Balfour Declaration.[36] In modern times, Arab Americans were on the verge of viable political influence until it was interrupted by 9/11. In the lead-up to the 2000 presidential election, the *Christian Science Monitor*, *White House Weekly*, *Middle East*, and *Economist* ran articles about the Arab American demographic with titles such as "The Birth of an Arab-American Lobby" and "Arab Americans Emerge as Key Voting Bloc."[37]

Nevertheless, there are a host of unexamined features in Arab America that, if examined, could lead to a more developed understanding of the community's role in the complex of mainstream–ethnic relations. The popularity of hip-hop and the widespread use of urban dialects among young Arab Americans, for instance, indicate that Arab Americans indeed "piggyback" Blacks in expressing their displeasure with a type of oppression they identify with Black history. The Iron Sheik raps about Palestinian liberation, the oppression of Arab Americans, the loss of civil liberties, and Arab American identity, and connects Arab American discourse in remarkable ways with injustices in the Hispanic, Black, and Native communities. Palestinian American poet Suheir Hammad is a performer in Russell Simmons's Broadway show, *Def Poetry Jam*. The late Edward Said, another Palestinian American, was a groundbreaking cultural critic whose reformulation of the term *Orientalism* is employed frequently in Native and African American scholarship.[38] These cross-cultural efforts are not new, however. Lebanese American civil rights activist Ralph Johns encouraged the famous 1960 sit-in at the Woolworth's lunch counter in Greensboro. Palestinian American George Shibley defended innocent Mexican Americans after the Los Angeles Zoot Suit Riots of the 1940s. Based on these examples, it might be said that a common ground among ethnic groups already exists; we simply need to find a language to acknowledge it.

Perhaps, however, the most favorable possibility for Arab Americans to engage in interethnic dialogue lies in our opposition to Zionism. More than any other issue, Palestine mobilized Arab Americans to reject total assimilation and embrace an alternate cultural positioning based on identification with the Near East. By virtue of America's uncritical support for Israel, Palestine necessarily transformed Arab Americans from a rapidly acculturating immigrant group into a radical, anti-mainstream community. By examining how this positioning functions in our interaction with other radical communities of color, Arab Americans can gain the type of recognition we actually seek, rather than unwanted post-9/11 platitudes, and in turn gain more support for reducing American patrimony in the Arab World. If we manage to illustrate through activism and scholarship that Israel's occupation is a classic form of colonization rather than a benign security mechanism, then it is not unthinkable that a broad coalition can be formed to challenge the imperative patriotism that seems now to threaten only domestic Arabs, but in reality endangers all Americans. This possibility is particularly fruitful when we examine the colonization of North America and identify how it continues to influence the discourse of foreign intervention.

Since what has been called decolonization of the mind is so central to the pedagogy of ethnic studies, Arab American concerns reach beyond the Arab American community. Yet the extensive reach of those concerns will not be acknowledged by chance. Arab Americans must force their recognition. Ethnic studies scholars, for their part, can find critical intersections of race, culture, and representation in the Arab American community. Minority scholarship has illustrated in the past 20 years that issues within different ethnic groups are never mutually exclusive, nor are the respective scholarly apparatuses in place to address those issues. If ethnic studies scholars are concerned with community activism in addition to professional work, then America's rapidly changing social dynamics after 9/11 are ripe for assessment with priority on response, especially if we manage to transform "the American way of life" into "American ways of life." It is not by accident that I see ethnic studies as a possible solution to the differend and the pragmatic strength of imperative patriotism, because if there are no solutions to be found in the field, then the field will have failed in its stated mission.

3
Observations on a New Fifth Column: Anti-Arab Racism in the American University

This chapter will focus on anti-Arab racism in the university. More specifically, I will concentrate on the role neoconservative racists play in what often is referred to as the "culture wars" or "PC wars" in American universities. Scholars and other cultural commentators have generally overlooked—foolishly, in my opinion—the manner in which neoconservatives invoke anti-Arab racism as a rallying point for all sorts of proposed restrictions on academic freedom or to pressure university administrators to hire conservative faculty to implement patriotic curricula. If we are to completely understand the intricacies of the debate surrounding political influence on and within universities, then we are impelled to assess how pervasive stereotypes of Arabs and Muslims not only spearhead most of the attacks on universities as hopelessly radical, but also constitute the most common and explicit form of racism in the United States today. I am particularly interested in the assumptions on which neoconservatives rely in degrading academics who dare to conceptualize Arabs (especially Palestinians) as fully human with a legitimate history; these assumptions inevitably perceive Arabs as the source of their own suffering. Finally, I will provide some observations on what type of discourse constitutes anti-Arab racism and explain why it is imperative that scholars of conscience work diligently to alter—or, better still, eliminate—the intellectual culture that allows racism against Arabs to flourish (and indeed that often provides anti-Arab racists with a privileged position of speaking).

It is worth noting here that I don't limit the term *neoconservative* to advisors and secretaries in the Bush II administration; I use it to describe the large community of scholars and political analysts who, rather than interrogating the probity of overseas intervention, seem more interested in colonizing the Arab World, making "preemption" a viable political doctrine, and mystifying Israel's occupation of the West Bank and Gaza Strip. This community, more than any other, poses the greatest threat to hate-free working environments in American universities.

Commiserating around the Camel-dung Fire

Those who believe that racism is largely absent from modern American society—beyond perhaps some scattered incidents undertaken by lunatics—are, of course, blissfully mistaken. Racism has only become more entrenched in the United States since its supposed elimination by the end of the Civil Rights Movement. One needn't go anywhere near the fringe in order to find it. As Michael Berube observes, bestsellers such as Dinesh D'Souza's *The End of Racism* are filled with "ultraconservative and even fascist policy recommendations."[1] From the perspective of those providing the fascist policy recommendations, it would be useless to encourage the government to sanction restrictions on academic discourse without repeatedly invoking minority impudence, since neoconservatives market their racism as a responsible alternative to anti-American propaganda. More important, without the institutionalization of such racism, there would be no way to market the overseas imperialism with which neoconservatives appear obsessed.

Unfortunately, Arabs fit magnificently into this equation. Because Arabs orchestrated the attacks of 9/11, neoconservatives exploited the opportunity to demonize them and then use that demonization to justify further American intervention in the Near East. Whereas it has become unacceptable or professionally risky to explicitly degrade most minorities (although it still happens frequently), it is considered perfectly acceptable to speak about Arabs in the most derogatory and hateful terms imaginable. Such speech rarely provokes outrage beyond the Arab American community and a handful of left-leaning advocacy groups. In fact, speaking hatefully about Arabs often results in applause and promotion, such as, in the case of Daniel Pipes, a government appointee (to the US Institute for Peace).

Let's look at Pipes for a moment to see how anti-Arab racism functions. Although corporate media usually conceptualize Pipes as an important and responsible intellectual, he has sustained his career by creating an atmosphere of fear and paranoia. In 2002, Pipes launched Campus Watch, a group that monitors so-called "anti-Israeli" activity on college campuses. Campus Watch tracks and critiques the speech and classroom pedagogy of academics through profiles of the offending professors. Scholars on the right, center, and left have criticized the enterprise, judging it a serious threat not only to free speech and civil liberties, but also to classroom conduct and the ability of students to learn in an environment free of political tension. If Campus Watch has its way, then, the limits placed on academic speech by political interests in parts of the Arab World, Latin America, and Africa will have pervaded the American Academy, something inimical to the stated mission of American education. Yet philosophers from Jacques Derrida to Noam Chomsky have agreed that American education tacitly reinforces and recreates the United States' dominant values, thereby fulfilling a necessary government function, to preserve the interests of the powerful, any government's most crucial demographic, by convincing all its citizenry that the best interests of the powerful are the best interests of the entire nation. It is no surprise, then, that Pipes can frequently be found testifying in Washington about his findings in Campus Watch; his main goal is to eliminate Title VI funding of Middle East Studies. He often assumes a vitriolic tone in promoting his agenda. In response to accusations that he supports the formation of a government committee to oversee Middle East Studies, Pipes recoiled, claiming that defunding Middle East Studies is a better solution. "My opponents," he threatened, "will then learn what happens when truly I am 'actively pushing' for Congress to adopt a measure."[2]

On the whole, Pipes displays a remarkable propensity for stereotype and generalization.[3] He considers nearly all Muslims to be complicit in terrorism and a threat to American values, both cultural and political (here I have subsumed the Arab American community into a broader Islamic positioning for the sake of clarity). In order to avoid the inevitable charge of racism, Pipes draws a distinction between what he terms "moderate Muslims" and "Islamists." It appears to be a carefully drawn distinction, but Pipes considers any Muslim in any way critical of American policy to be an Islamist and therefore a threat to American security. According to Pipes, all Islamists—i.e., all Muslims, since only silent or subservient Muslims escape his charge of Islamicism—are untrustworthy and must be subjected to special scrutiny including but not limited to ethnic profiling. Pipes claims that Arab and Muslim Americans present a moderate image of themselves in public but secretly plot to transform the United States into an Islamic republic and destroy the country's legal and social foundations. For example, in his weblog, Pipes condemns a section of the Department of State website that celebrates "Muslim Life in America," writing, "It's hard to win a war, you know, when one's foreign ministry publicly endorses the enemy's friends and agents."[4] Here Pipes claims that all foreign Muslims are enemies of the United States and uses this generalization as the basis of a more pressing argument: all American Muslims, intrinsically violent like their overseas brethren, likewise are enemies of the United States. It is clear that Pipes, who derides Arabs for our "conspiracy mentality," himself propagates the same type of conspiracy theories he otherwise ridicules when he imagines Arabs to be their progenitors. (*San Francisco Chronicle* columnist Vlae Kershner humorously but aptly wonders where Pipes acquired his belief that all Islamists endeavor to effect the "Islamization of America": "Where'd he find that, some pseudo-document called the Protocols of the Elders of Mecca?".)[5]

Pipes in no way can be viewed as an isolated crusader. He is part of a network of commentators and scholars (dubbed "failed academics" by Hamid Dabashi) who promote destructive stereotypes of Arabs in the service of political activism. This network includes prominent government officials. When former Attorney General John Ashcroft, for instance, opined in 2002 that "Islam is a religion in which God requires you to send your son to die for him," he neither apologized nor was encouraged by President Bush to apologize. Perhaps former Representative John Cooksey (R-LA) surpassed everybody's idiocy when he proclaimed, "If I see someone who comes in that's got a diaper on his head and a fan belt wrapped around the diaper on his head, that guy needs to be pulled over."[6] What were the consequences of Cooksey's remark? A disingenuous apology obviously crafted by a lawyer that received virtually no attention. In other words, nothing. In mass media, examples of anti-Arab racism also are abundant. The worst example arises from *Tallahassee Democrat* senior writer Bill Cotterell, who proclaimed in an email message, "Except for Jordan and Egypt, no Arab nation has a peace treaty with Israel. They've had 54 years to get over it. They choose not to. OK, they can squat around the camel-dung fire and grumble about it, or they can put their bottoms in the air five times a day and pray for deliverance; that's their business … . And I don't give a damn if Israel kills a few in collateral damage while defending itself. So be it."[7] After some Islamic, Arab American, and progressive groups organized write-in campaigns calling on the *Democrat* to apologize, editor Doug Marlette responded promptly with an article titled "An Apology Is not in Order." (Eventually the *Democrat* issued a formal apology.)

These are only a few of the examples of anti-Arab racism among neoconservative scholars, corporate media, and government officials. Sadly, one could produce an entire tome with examples of mainstream anti-Arab racism after 9/11. One could, for that matter, produce another tome with examples of mainstream anti-Arab racism before 9/11. This fact indicates that 9/11 did not alter in any crucial way the quintessence of anti-Arab racism; it simply altered the way anti-Arab racism is articulated. That is, 9/11 provided legitimacy to heretofore marginal—or, if not marginal, then at least contested—anti-Arab racists, and allowed the large number of Americans who dislike Arabs to express that dislike in the workplace, letters to the editor, dinner parties, and so forth, with little fear of retribution or negative reaction.

The Imperative to Speak

Arabs don't speak, or aren't allowed to speak, very often in print and visual media. Usually when I encounter a discussion about Arabs on the radio or television, whether it's a mainstream or progressive program, the discussants are non-Arab. This situation is alarming for a number of reasons. First of all, it contributes, both directly and indirectly, to the environment in which anti-Arab racism flourishes because it strengthens a culture in which nonacquiescent Arabs are dissuaded, or barred, from articulating their sensibilities. Therefore, even when progressive programs invite non-Arabs to discuss Arab politics or cultures, they inadvertently harm the community they purportedly attempt to help. This isn't to say, to use a nationalist belief common among many in minority communities, that only Arabs have the right to represent themselves. Rather, I would hope for a more inclusive style of discussion in both corporate and nonprofit media when the topics of the Near East, Arab America, civil liberties, immigration, and terrorism arise. Simply stated, Arabs, like other minority or non-Western communities, do not need sympathy or romanticization. Nor do we need reassurance from non-Arabs that we are welcome in the United States, which does little more, as Jürgen Habermas suggests in *Philosophy in a Time of Terror*, than solidify our position as a grudgingly tolerable Other.[8] Instead of what Habermas calls "the act of toleration," Arabs need viable, realistic, and organic solutions to the very real racism that threatens our safety, civil liberties, legal rights, and intellectual autonomy.

I am aware that the previous paragraph appears defensive or even aggressive. The defensiveness arises for a reason. In the six months following 9/11, over 600 violent incidents directed at Arab Americans were reported. Hundreds of cases involving law enforcement profiling also were reported. Students in grade schools and universities reported 45 cases of harassment, in addition to 13 complaints of harassment undertaken by school faculty such as principals and school boards. During the same period, a Yemeni grocer, Abdo Ali Ahmed, was shot to death in his shop in Reedley, California, and Rien Said Ahmed of Fresno was shot and killed while at work. In Cleveland, a Ford Mustang was driven through the entrance of Ohio's largest mosque, causing an estimated $100,000 in damages.[9] Over 20 Arab Americans have been killed in cases described as "hate crimes" since 9/11 and over 50 mosques received some type of damage. According to a May 2005 report published by CAIR, "the number of reported bias crimes and civil rights violations committed against Muslims in the United States soared to its highest level last year since the period immediately after the

Sept. 11, 2001, terrorist attacks." The Associated Press reports that "the council counted 1,522 incidents in which Muslims reported their civil rights had been violated in 2004, a 49 per cent increase over 2003. Another 141 incidents of confirmed or suspected bias crimes were committed against Muslims, a 52 per cent rise."[10]

In addition to the countless examples of personal harassment, thousands of young Arabs have been summoned to FBI offices since 9/11 for what are euphemistically dubbed "voluntary interviews." Likewise, thousands of Arab students have been unjustly deported or denied reentry into the United States. Arab American activists, like the Black and Indian activists before them, are accruing FBI files at a pace that recalls the COINTELPROs of the 1960s and 1970s. Whereas J. Edgar Hoover simply ignored the existing surveillance rules in harassing and ultimately destroying a host of dissident organizations, the FBI no longer needs to resort to extralegal techniques in surveying, incarcerating, and indicting Arabs and Arab Americans, because the rules Hoover once ignored are now all legal.

Other indications of racism are evident. Already the American–Arab Anti-Discrimination Committee (ADC) has filed separate grievances against United, American, and Continental Airlines for institutionalized discrimination against Arab passengers and employees of Arab origin. As Kareem Shora notes, the ADC

> has addressed over 60 incidents of discrimination on the part of airline crew members across the country. Unfortunately, it is now a common expectation in our country for, primarily, men of Middle-Eastern or South Asian origins, to encounter a nervous flight attendant or airline pilot who requests that the man follow them out of the plane after boarding. Once the man is in the jet-way or gate area, he is informed that he is not welcome on the flight because "the crew does not feel comfortable with [him] on board," or "a passenger does not feel safe with [him] on board."[11]

In the workplace, over 688 Arab and Muslim Americans filed discrimination charges; discharge was an issue in 428 charges while the others dealt with various forms of harassment, including stereotyping and racial epithets.[12]

I have yet to meet an Arab who hasn't experienced some form of discrimination or harassment in the United States. One of my closest friends, an Arab student from the Near East, once was the target of a Hollywood-style police sting in his apartment in Norman, Oklahoma, because, according to police, his neighbors were convinced that he and his Arab roommates were trafficking arms. Another friend, a Jordanian Christian, was detained at JFK Airport for hours because his gold cross, something nearly all Arab Christian men wear, invoked suspicion that he was actually a terrorist in disguise (apparently, the customs agents have seen too many movies in which troublemakers escape notice by dressing as priests). A few years ago my wife, whose maiden name is Housein, was refused a promising job because the prospective employer was worried that she might somehow be related to Saddam. Beyond these forms of discrimination, Arabs constantly are subjected to derogatory terms like *raghead*, *towelhead*, *camel jockey*, *dune coon*, and *sand nigger*; Ronald Reagan was noted for his diatribes about Arab "depravity," "ancient tribal rivalries," "irrationality," and "pathological hatred."[13]

Of what relevance are these examples beyond their informational purposes? In order to answer this question, we must revisit the role neoconservatives play in the articulation of anti-Arab racism and the role of universities as a conceptual ground zero in the debate over how Arabs should be treated intellectually. It is acceptable in today's United States to express anti-Arab racism because anti-Arab racism better enables the American government to intervene in Arab nations and because the fear of Arabs (racism is always linked to fear) justifies the imposition of unconstitutional legislation on the American people. Looking at American history, it is clear that American leaders exploit every conceivable pretext to expand their powers over citizen affairs; the American government is provided with a foolproof pretext to expand its domestic authority as long as a large number of Americans either fear or deplore Arabs. Neoconservatives stimulate a cyclical phenomenon in which Arabs, like the Blacks, Indians, and Communists before them, become subjects of a fear that is disseminated to create the very reality that Americans are afraid of.

Moreover, neoconservatives have successfully generated intellectual paradigms in which it is impossible for Arabs to articulate either political or cultural sensibilities without immediately being accused of anti-Americanism or, more likely, anti-Semitism. If, as scholars as early as Louis Althusser have posited, political ideology is a crucial aspect of one's identity, then Arabs exemplify perpetual liminality. And if it is impossible, according to the ethos neoconservatives have managed to engender, to be patriotic and simultaneously oppose American adventurism in the Arab World and Israel's occupation of Palestinian territories, then Arabs are by necessity dissidents, worthy of surveillance, detainment, or deportation. More important, in this formulation Arabs inevitably forfeit individual and collective agency because we are objectified as discursive tropes that signal danger and suspicion. Cultural expression is not exempt from this reality, since Arab cultural objects—headdresses, robes, music, prayer beads—are widely appropriated by mass media and made to signify violence, barbarism, and terror. Mainstream American discourse is constructed in such a way that if Arabs articulate any feature of our identities, we automatically recall the undefined but identifiable terrorist.

Arabs and the American University

The points I detailed above all play a large role in the way Arabs function as students and teachers in American universities. It is, simply stated, extremely difficult to be Arab in today's Academy.

Arabs are subject to an extraordinary amount of racism in society at large, but one might think that on supposedly enlightened college campuses there exists a comfortable environment in which Arab students and professors flourish. In fact the opposite is true. Because of the distinct forms of racism to which Arabs are now subject in American society, I will have to argue that it is actually impossible for numerous students and professors to avoid professing anti-Arab racism because, in part, of the success neoconservatives have had in generating fear and then using pragmatism to render that fear intellectually astute or commonsensical; and, in turn, because of the neoconservative influence on the popular discourse broached by student groups, concerned parents, and activist professors.

Let's focus for a moment on the "distinct forms of racism" to which I alluded above. I hope that by this point I have illustrated that the very existence of Arabs as a cultural and political entity is enough to inspire racism in certain segments of the American populace (doubtless the same segment that finds the existence of, say, Blacks or Hispanics an affront to their national identity). This type of racism is not only common in the United States, but also integral to the biological determinism so crucial to the formation of the overarching American imagination: cultural symbols are visually and then discursively transformed by racists into signs of inferiority, usually with the help of fear-baiting or pseudoscientific manifestos. For instance, when notorious anthropologist Ales Hrdlicka descended upon the Anishinaabe nation in the early twentieth century, he opined that tribal regalia was indicative of underdeveloped minds (which of course implied cultural underdevelopment),[14] just as Representative Cooksey invoked Arab regalia to symbolize moral and cultural depravity. In both cases, Hrdlicka and Cooksey dealt with audiences already predisposed to racist attitudes in need of visual or material justification.

Anti-Arab racism, however, is more distinct (but in no way unique) because it is so greatly influenced by political phenomena, as are, inevitably, the ways in which Arabs respond to racism. More to the point, anti-Arab racism often is connected, both implicitly and explicitly, to imperial adventurism, particularly Israel's settlement of the West Bank and Gaza Strip. When neoconservatives offer their support for Israel's settlement program (which they do often), they are automatically engaged in a pernicious type of racism that causes inconceivable amounts of human suffering, because one cannot justify the theft and plunder of indigenous land without also allocating cultures into value-laden categories (e.g., civilized versus uncivilized, deserving versus undeserving, superior versus inferior, resourceful versus backward). Therefore, while we don't generally hear Daniel Pipes or Stanley Kurtz saying things that might readily be identified as racist—as opposed to Bill Cotterell or John Cooksey, who both have—we are confronted with their racism every time they appear on national media to cheer Israel in its expropriation of Palestinian land. For this reason, anti-Arab racism, like the tacit racism directed against other minorities, is in many ways more dangerous than its cohort, outright racism, because its implicit nature is more difficult to identify and condemn.

Arabs are especially vulnerable to tacit racism because of Israel's close philosophical identification with the United States. To oppose Israel in any way is not only to risk being branded anti-Semitic, but also, neoconservatives have convinced most Americans, to oppose civility, progress, and God Himself. Given America's long and violent history of settlement and land expropriation, Israel's garrison presence in Palestine appears natural to many Americans, to whom Israel's Westernized culture is intelligible (and at times reassuring). Conversely, Israel's settlement is considered necessary by as many as 60 million Americans based strictly on scriptural interpretation. In this case, anti-Arab racism is inscribed in worship. Otherwise, much of the tacit racism Arabs experience is related to what might be called colonialist residue—that is, the survival of the language utilized during the height of European colonialism (which, curiously, was rehashed almost verbatim by the Bush administration in the months leading to the invasion of Iraq).

Based on these realities, most Arabs in American universities exist in contradictory and problematic spaces: for an Arab academic (in, say, the humanities), the simple act of raising one's voice can be controversial. More than that, though, the simple act of instructing students in the history of the Arab World is enough to generate an utter scandal. Junior Arab faculty such as myself know exceedingly well that our tenure is threatened by the simple biological function of speaking. At times, our colleagues and administrators seem to be more concerned with ostensible exercises in diplomacy than with legitimate instruction in the social realities of Arab America and the Near East. Some of these problems have arisen, as Stanley Fish observes, because of the effectiveness of neoconservatives in persuading "the American public to adopt its characterization of the Academy" as a hotbed "of radicalism and pedagogical irresponsibility where dollars are wasted, nonsense is propagated, students are indoctrinated, religion is disrespected, and patriotism is scorned."[15]

Eulogizing Edward Said

Fish's observation is apropos of the way Edward Said's death was received by neoconservative publications (and, unfortunately, purportedly bipartisan ones). When the prominent literary and cultural critic died of leukemia in September 2003, it became more evident than ever how much his vast oeuvre of cultural criticism and political commentary polarized readers along predictable ideological lines. Certainly it is rare for an academic to be widely eulogized in nonacademic publications in an age when most academics have at best limited fame. Yet when the rare American professor known widely outside of the Academy dies, his or her death usually is reported with the type of respect and nostalgia that is afforded any celebrity whose life has ended. Not so with Said. His death occasioned a barrage of polemical attacks by Zionists and neoconservatives, usually ignorant of Said's actual politics and resorting to egregious distortion.

Although Said has been analyzed in scholarly journals such as *boundary 2*, *Alif*, and *Social Text*, I will focus here on how his death was received in a variety of popular media. In those media, Said's death has reinvigorated the longstanding divisions among the pro-Palestinian Left, the ambiguous mainstream, and the Zionist Right. As a result, Said has repeatedly been lionized as an iconic luminary and has even more frequently been demonized as a terrorist. Responses to his death followed consistent patterns: mainstream American media offered generally sympathetic notices but qualified any praise with wariness about Said's vigorous criticism of Israel (the same writers usually forget Said's vigorous criticism of Arab leaders); left-liberal forums such as *Tikkun* differed little from mainstream media, except that some left-liberal authors appeared more disingenuous than, say, the *New York Times*; Arab, Arab American, and pro-Palestinian publications romanticized Said with dynamic nostalgia; neoconservative publications disparaged Said, and in so doing implied that all Arabs are guilty of his failures. The Israeli media followed the same patterns as their American peers, with the mainstream replacing consistency with ambiguity, the Left praising Said's commitment to peace, and the Right vilifying Said with little supporting evidence. The Irish and British press, in my opinion, offered the most fair and nuanced articles available in English.

Mainstream publications—those that purportedly have no ideological agenda—illuminate (and at times inform) the monolithic reactions of Zionists and neoconservatives. The connection between the mainstream and the neoconservative

Right lies primarily in the blurring of reportage and judgment. While obituaries of controversial figures generally mention that those figures were controversial, most obituaries of Said pass judgment on his controversies and in turn evaluate him as having been a flawed, or at times immoral, intellectual.

For example, Richard Bernstein's detailed article in the *New York Times* avoids overt judgment but, through its quote selection, leads readers to believe that Said was incapable of non-polemical scholarship.[16] The *Washington Post* offers a similar, though smaller, announcement under the heading "Palestinian Spokesman Edward Said Dies," a misleading statement that, given the prominence of anti-Arab racism in the United States, surely insinuates to most readers that Said was a vocal advocate of suicide bombing. The *Columbia Spectator*, the leading paper at Said's longtime institution, describes Said as a "profoundly important and imperfect man." This obvious description is revealed as less than benign one paragraph later when the authors criticize Said's "relentless" advocacy of "his chosen cause: the Palestinians," referring to it as "his great flaw," which compelled him to strike "the incorrect balance between his two passions [scholarship and activism]."[17]

More nuanced articles appeared in the Israeli press, which has always had a more direct and, one might say, intimate relationship with Arab nationalism than American media. Rupert Murdoch's *Jerusalem Post*, a longtime forum of Israeli expansionism, ran an interesting opinion piece by Hillel Halkin, who managed to malign and admire Said in the same sentence: "In his books, he was manipulative and pretentious; in person, he seemed natural and intelligent." Of course, the grammar of Halkin's sentence precludes evenhandedness; "was manipulative and pretentious" is a definitive claim beyond the "seemed" appearance of Said's personal beauty. Halkin recalls having brunch at an expensive Manhattan restaurant with Said not long after Said's *The Question of Palestine* was published. Halkin describes that book as "dishonest" and condemns its "usual misrepresentations of Zionism and Israel," but appears to have enjoyed conversing with Said, whom, "to his surprise," he found likeable in person: "Since his views were more moderate in the restaurant than they were in *The Question of Palestine*, we reached an agreement that, had we been the dictators of our two peoples, we could have brought peace to the Middle East."[18]

This paradox illustrates exactly why Said's writings are so misunderstood, in turn allowing neoconservatives to demonize him. Said didn't suddenly become nicer or more moderate simply because he met an Israeli; rather, the Israeli's shortsightedness, cultivated by his devotion to Zionism, never allowed him to believe that a supporter of Palestinian human rights could actually be humane instead of a stereotypically bloodthirsty terrorist. Halkin likely would be averse to using the adjectives "intelligent" and "articulate" to describe a Palestinian activist; he therefore had no ability to comprehend Said's complicated arguments in *The Question of Palestine*, which, I would guess, did not differ from what Said brought up with Halkin in conversation (Said was, if anything, remarkably consistent).

The same type of contradiction appears in a less myopic article by Harvey Blume in the *Jerusalem Report*. Blume, who notes that he "cannot subscribe to the theory of Edward Said as a thug," nevertheless questions Said's unwillingness to endorse a two-state solution to the Israeli–Palestinian conflict until "the second Intifada had made it seem unworkable." Even though Blume admires Said's intellect and political work, his notion that Said rejected a two-state solution until recently evinces remarkable ignorance. Throughout his career, Said's only concern about the two-state solution was the possibility that Israelis and Palestinians would become isolated from one another in separate entities, a possibility he considered untenable. In the years before his death, Said endorsed a binational democratic state, noting that settlements were too entrenched to realistically be dismantled (a point validated by the melodramatic withdrawal of settlers from Gaza). Blume's misreading of Said's politics undermines his admiration, evident at the article's conclusion, where Blume, speaking directly to the deceased Said, explains, "To my mind these weaknesses are no small part of your legacy."[19]

Turning back to the American press, perhaps one of the more troublesome eulogies to Said arose from *Tikkun*, edited by Michael Lerner. Following the mainstream pattern of bestowing praise on Said while simultaneously criticizing positions that Said never actually endorsed, Lerner writes, "We often wished Said could sympathize with the plight of European Jews and the way that their returning to the place they perceived to be their ancient homeland was not an act of Western colonialism." Lerner later claims that "[Said] never took the step of acknowledging that Palestinian resistance to Jewish immigration in the years when Jews were trying to escape the gas chambers of Europe or the displaced persons camps of 1945–48 was immoral."[20] In many ways, Lerner's admonition bespeaks how influential Said was (and still is), because Lerner endows Said with the conceptual apparatus of Palestinian morality. And it is the purported failures of Palestinian morality for which Said, a mere individual, is responsible. Lerner's protest, however, is misguided for different reasons. Said repeatedly expressed sympathy for the Jews of Europe, especially during the Holocaust, and recognized the State of Israel, but never privileged the right of Jews to Palestine. Lerner supports the right of foreign Jews to the Holy Land over indigenous Arabs (in this article and beyond) and thereby obfuscates accurate recognition of Said's moral imperatives.

Other media provided solid accountings of Said's work. As might be expected, the *Irish Times* and various British publications (the *London Review of Books*, the *Guardian Unlimited*, the *Economist*) ran nuanced and sophisticated obituaries. Arab American publications such as *Mizna*, *al-*

Jadid, and the *ElectronicIntifada* printed reverent, nostalgic eulogies. Professional journals like *PMLA* and the *Chronicle of Higher Education* ran gracious notices, although the *Chronicle* later published a slew of angry and inaccurate letters decrying Said's politics. NPR invited a number of responsible scholars to comment on the importance of Said's opus. In one of the shows, Cornel West responded to the obligatory question about terrorism by noting, "The important thing to keep in mind, Edward Said was the last great humanist … . As a humanist, he was critical of all forms of terrorism but he was fundamentally concerned about trying to convince persons to be critical of all forms of authority, all forms of dogma, all forms of system, all forms of orthodoxy."

West reveals perhaps the main reason why neoconservatives so vigorously maligned Said, particularly after his death: his secular humanism. His prominence as a public intellectual who articulated the values of humanism was highly threatening. Moreover, since neoconservatives have long viewed Israel as an indivisible partner in American imperialism, Said was doubly threatening. Just as Michael Lerner forces Said to shoulder the totality of Palestinian history, neoconservatives have transformed him into the (im)moral symbol of Palestinian violence—an unusual Messianic perception that repeatedly articulates a racism that would be unacceptable in any other domestic context. Conversely, supporters of Palestinian self-determination often blindly lionized Said as an icon who emblematized the necessity of Palestinian resistance to occupation.

In other words, Said became a multilayered symbol. As a larger-than-life intellectual, he was made to represent a vast range of opinion that didn't necessarily reflect his own sensibilities, and that frequently distorted his actual political and intellectual pursuits. Hence to neoconservatives Said came to represent incontrovertible Palestinian barbarity. The mere fact that Said refused to submit to either mainstream or neoconservative orthodoxy on the Arab World doomed him to misrepresentation. Said was read by neoconservatives only to identify and then decontextualize passages that supposedly affirm his commitment to terrorism.

In neoconservative forums, David Frum, writing in the *National Review*, contends that Said is not "the great literary critic that his admirers falsely make him out to be," and then levels this accusation: "If the United States was caught unawares on 9/11, Edward Said's name belongs high on the list of those responsible." He continues: "Said served for many years on the Palestinian National Council—the theoretical government of the Palestinian national movement. As such, he was at least formally implicated in Yasser Arafat's three-decade-long terrorist crime spree."[21] Zev Chafets makes similar accusations in the *New York Daily News*, claiming that Said's goal of "eradicating Israel" helped unite "fascists and Communists." Chafets also believes that *Orientalism* "did more for the jihad than a battalion of Osamas."[22] Edward Alexander of the National Association of Scholars invokes the imagery of Russian pogroms; Said's acolytes "found meat and drink in Said's pristinely ignorant and intellectually violent pronouncements about Jews." Claiming that Said considered the Holocaust "a great boon to Jews," Alexander condemns "Said's intense hostility to America" and "his thinly-veiled anti-Semitism" and asserts that Said located sources "in the website of the White Aryan Resistance Movement."[23] Other prominent neoconservatives—Daniel Pipes, David Horowitz, Martin Kramer—published comparable obituaries.

These claims are obviously exaggerated if not malicious, but they hold sway in mainstream American culture because they reinforce the assumptions generated by the fear of terrorism. Those assumptions rely largely on the conceptualization of Arabs as savage or subhuman by popular media and political analysts. The questions mainstream publications like the *Washington Post* and *Columbia Spectator* raise about Said's morality narrow the gap between far Right and mainstream. And Said himself has become a catalyzing figure whose supporters are further isolated from conventional American wisdom because neoconservatives successfully reformulated that wisdom to legitimize the anti-Arab racism that has existed for decades in the United States.

Said will no doubt be analyzed and reanalyzed for decades. Supporters of human rights will continually recall Said's diligence in calling for the humanization of Palestinians, while neoconservatives will isolate passages from Said's work to convince Americans that he advocated the destruction of Israel. Despite this polarization, however, Said's legacy in the popular imagination will transcend these seemingly irreconcilable positions because Said was always correct when he denounced Israel's ethnic cleansing and the unwillingness of Arab tyrants to prevent it. His humanism was too intelligent for colonialists to confront, much less accept. In any event, those who are concerned with the fate of humanity must believe that Said was correct, because if he wasn't, then there is nothing for humans to aspire to but neoconservative realpolitik.

Said is emblematic of the positioning of Arabs in American universities. Since Arab culture is commonly perceived as threatening in American society—and, by extension, within American universities—Arab academics occupy an ambivalent, unnamed space where an escape from politics to culture is unfeasible because, in Fanon's usage of the term, politics is made to pervasively represent culture and, in turn, often prevents Arabs from being perceived as human. I am well aware that it would be problematic to argue that "culture" and "politics" should be examined as mutually exclusive categories since continual interchange between culture and politics defines each. I would argue instead that Arabs are continually *politicized* in the language of the politically obscene; our culture, therefore, inevitably is degraded as something violent and crude. Arabs, in short, are politicized for the political (opposition to Zionism, anti-war activities, disdain of the Patriot Act and immigration regulations) as well as the mundane (cooking *emtabal* and *kibbe*, rubbing prayer beads, wearing beards, speaking Arabic, reading books with Arabic script).

Responding to Anti-Arab Racism

In my professional life, first as a graduate student and now as a professor, I have spent much time with both undergraduate and graduate Arab students. When it comes to their feelings about studying in American universities, their overwhelming sentiment is isolation. Arab students feel isolated because they constantly are anxious about the possibility of hearing contemptuous statements about Arabs from other students and professors (a feeling I encountered repeatedly for ten years as a student, and continue to encounter as a professor). Arab students (especially international students) post-9/11 also feel afraid to respond to contemptuous statements because of the fear of harassment, arrest, or deportation.

While many Americans (mostly, I imagine, White Americans) would likely scoff at these fears, considering them little more than victimology or conspiracy theories, Arab students' suspicion that trouble might ensue if they vocally articulate Arab politics—or, for that matter, openly display symbols of Arab culture—is well-founded. In the months following 9/11 hundreds of Arab students were deported without cause. As for Arab American students, they have been hounded incessantly by the FBI and treated with suspicion by fellow students and educators. The mistreatment has included hundreds of cases of physical abuse or property damage. In any event, the fear of government involvement in universities became more than speculative when, in February 2004, the FBI subpoenaed Drake University in Iowa for information on activists involved in an anti-war conference held on campus. A decidedly apolitical conference called "Islam and the Law: the Question of Sexism" at the University of Texas in February 2004, was disrupted by Army investigators attempting to gather information about organizers and participants. Given the conference's apolitical nature, one can only surmise that the word "Islam" was found to be threatening in and of itself. As a result, one is forced to surmise that all Muslims are in some way threatening to government figures regardless of politics or personal comportment. *Democracy Now*'s Amy Goodman also has reported widespread FBI infiltration into peace groups on campuses across the country, including groups either composed of or concerned with Arabs. It is common knowledge among Arabs that the FBI has monitored and penetrated Arab organizations, on and off campus, for decades. (Brian Glick's *War at Home* is a good primer on FBI infiltration tactics.)[24]

Given that FBI abuse and infiltration are well-documented elsewhere, I would like to focus on the type of racism Arab students often experience and how educators might ameliorate the conditions that allow the racism to exist. In my many discussions with Arab students while gathering stories for this chapter, I heard time and again about racist slurs, uncomfortable classroom environments, misinformation, ignorance, and slander. And this is to say nothing of what Arabs reported about the racist behavior of fellow students. Although the legitimacy of oral testimony is questioned by many in the humanities and social sciences, I cannot ignore the preponderance of incidents relayed to me over the years that bespeak a troubling repetition of anti-Arab racism, nor can I ignore my own experiences, which often corroborate the incidents relayed to me and in turn connote an archetypal racism that transcends disciplinary boundaries.

The most frequent complaint I have heard deals with reading lists. Some courses focused in various capacities on Middle Eastern cultures or politics assign exclusively or overwhelmingly texts written by non-Arabs and non-Muslims. This phenomenon does not connote professorial racism either directly or obliquely (although it certainly does not preclude it). Rather, it is problematic for different reasons, each of which illuminates a social component underlying racism: it delegitimizes Arabs by assuming that they lack the ability to represent their cultures and politics intelligently (an ability apparently innate to Westerners); it shifts emphasis from the region of study to the site of speaking; it results in a false consciousness based on the refusal to adequately confront the very issues supposedly under investigation; and it privileges the Occidental gaze over indigenous sociocultural imperatives. All professors, in any event, who instruct on courses on the Arab World using texts written only by Orientalist Arabs or Westerners come dangerously close to mimicking the infamous Dr. Clarence in Sherman Alexie's *Indian Killer*.

The other main complaint is the abundance of stupid or ignorant comments made about Arabs by both students and instructors. One student, for instance, reported a testimonial from a peer who noted that Bedouin Arabs bury newborns in the desert. Another student observed that her Zionist professor refused to call on her during class discussions. I also heard an alarming number of complaints about negative feedback on papers straying from entrenched Orientalist dogmas. I remember very clearly an undergraduate course in which a conversation on Tayeb Salih descended into exploration of Mustafa Saeed's innate ethical depravity. Other problems include alienation, marginalization, and intimidation. A general pattern of anti-Arab racism in American universities can be discerned with the following features:

- It is sometimes unstated and arises not simply based on what is said, but on what remains unsaid.
- It is tacit, appearing in things like reading lists, maps, and films.
- It appears in racial epithets such as *sand nigger* and *raghead*.

- It encourages professors to avoid or ignore Arab students in the fear that they may challenge the professors' narratives.
- It manifests itself in stories, often presented as facts, of incontrovertible Arab barbarity.
- It relies on uncritical usage of the word *terrorist* (in addition to its overuse).
- It relies, often without the professor's conscious knowledge, on arcane notions of biological determinism.
- It results in sweeping generalizations or simple essentialization.
- It induces patronizing behavior on the part of some professors, who generously strive to better inform the Arab students about the regions and cultures of their origins.
- It isolates Arab students and makes them feel uncomfortable or, if the professor wants a "native" voice for his or her own legitimization, as if they constantly are on display. Or it causes steady anxiety, as Arab students constantly wait for the next zinger about buried babies (always, unfortunately, a possibility).

I imagine that some readers have at this point noticed that the features of anti-Arab racism are comparable, if not identical, to the features of racism directed against Black, Indian, and Hispanic students. The features are indeed analogous, because they arise from the same contexts of misinformation, colonial discourse, and hyperpatriotic chauvinism—all nourished, of course, by the relentless encroachment of neoconservatives and their moralistic supporters on humanities curricula. (The latest assault is David Horowitz's Academic Bill of Rights.) Anti-Arab racism is in no way removed from other, more deeply rooted instances of hate, discrimination, and xenophobia. In fact, as Ronald Stockton has pointed out, anti-Arab racism in the United States primarily is derivative—that is, it exists only because racism existed before the first Arab arrived in North America.

Anti-Arab racism is set apart at this moment because of the strong tendency to summon it as a pragmatic way to support more impartial education. In other words, the rhetoric through which neoconservatives call for less polemical and biased classroom instruction is itself biased and polemical. Anti-Arab racism, therefore, is encoded deeply within the moral structure of today's culture wars. When educators submit in any way to the pressures of outside (neoconservative) influence in preparing reading lists and lectures, there is a good chance that anti-Arab racism will be articulated either tacitly or explicitly because of one ulterior motive, among many, of those applying the pressure: strangulation of any Arab self-determination. Let's look, for instance, at this suggestion from Martin Kramer:

> It is increasingly clear that serious steps must be taken to provide funding for courses in Israel studies. University officials—who should care about their institutions' academic credibility as well as their image in the community—need to know that when they solicit Jewish donors for large gifts, this is an area that should be offered as waiting for support. Members of the Jewish community who are already prepared to make substantial gifts to colleges and universities need to be urged to support Israel studies on campus.[25]

Kramer's logic would likely appear harmless to the educator or casual observer who has little interest in the Arab World. It might even be something that good liberal faculty should support, since area studies are so under attack from the Right. Ironically, however, it is Kramer and fellow neoconservatives who have so harshly attacked any area study that doesn't buttress the interests of the United States.

More crucially, it must be stressed that when Kramer says "Israel studies" he really means *pro*-Israel studies. Moreover, he employs the term as a means to quash not only Middle East Studies, but any discussion of Arabs that doesn't relegate them to utter subservience or reduce them to pithy stereotypes. The only area study Kramer would advocate is Israel studies because it, unlike Native, Chicano/a, and African American Studies, would (or should) match the framework of American foreign policy—i.e., unfettered interventionism and imperialism. Kramer finds Arabs unworthy of study unless a friendly—but occasionally stern—patriarch is in control of their history, lest the rabble develop enough confidence to actually speak for themselves. Furthermore, Kramer advances a rhetorical trope that increasingly is becoming common: the role of universities isn't to foster critical thinking, whatever that is, but to enhance the image of the United States at home and abroad and to work with policymakers to transform students into good citizens. Kramer, like most neoconservatives, repeatedly invokes and then degrades Arabs to justify his agenda, which could never work if he and his audience didn't share the assumption that Arabs are dogmatic and dangerous.[26] Nor would his argument be so compelling to most Americans if they didn't conceptualize Arabs as semi-barbaric or subhuman—a perception continually reinforced by the reductionist categories offered by popular media and political analysts.

If one is comforted to think that Kramer and other neoconservatives will remain marginalized because no good educator would actually listen to them, then he or she needs seriously to rethink the extent of neoconservative influence on the academic mainstream. Consider, for example, a recent *Chronicle of Higher Education* article by Neil Kressel. Condemning what he calls "Muslim Jew-hatred," Kressel argues that "from a psychological perspective, it would be useful to construct a functional typology of anti-Semitism in the Muslim and Arab world. For some people, presumably, the ideology is centrally important, serving some key personality function. For others it is more peripheral, grounded in a social adjustment function. Anti-Semitic ideology involves a wide range of irrational thought processes that might fruitfully be elaborated from a cognitive perspective."[27] This quote, I presume, needs no explanation. Suffice it to say that Arabs might do well to contact the Anishinaabe nation to get advice about how they handled the aftermath of Ales Hrdlicka. It bears mention that Kressel's suggestion would further isolate Arab students, since they probably don't enroll in college classes to have their innate personality disorders and pathological hatred examined by benevolent White men.

From the standpoint of Arab educators, nothing illustrates the preponderance of anti-Arab racism as clearly as the recent controversy surrounding the Department of Middle East and Asian Languages and Cultures (MEALAC) at Columbia University. In late 2004, a shady outfit dubbing itself the David Project released a film titled *Columbia Unbecoming* alleging that MEALAC professors have engaged in intimidating classroom behavior. Jewish students, the film claimed, were targeted by pro-Palestinian instructors, who were accused of numerous ethical violations. *Columbia Unbecoming* inspired national media attention, most of it with varying degrees of sympathy for the students' alleged plight. As of this writing, the response of Columbia President Lee Bollinger has been uninspiring. Bollinger, without evincing strong public support for his embattled faculty, commissioned a panel to investigate the film's claims; the panel's initial findings refuted many of the film's allegations but legitimized many of its concerns, including the notion that Assistant Professor Joseph Massad, the David Project's main target, advances propaganda rather than valid scholarly material. (Massad, I hope, accepted these charges as a compliment given that valid scholarly material generally means the recapitulation, in various scholarly vocabularies, of age-old jingoism.)

I don't find it helpful to linger on the veracity of *Columbia Unbecoming*, for this approach would insinuate that the film transcends categorization as crass propaganda, an unfeasible possibility. It is more fruitful to examine the cultural forces that compel people to engage seriously with its recommendations and in some cases deem them valuable. First of all, like all neoconservative attempts to reduce American higher education to uncritical chauvinism, the David Project mitigates its undemocratic intentions by invoking a desire to encourage balance in classroom instruction. Although "balance" appears to be a noble goal, it is in reality a highly politicized desire because it always seeks to usurp one ideological position and replace it with an alternative. It also assumes, either shrewdly or naively, that knowledge can be created which is external to any ideological vicissitudes.

Thus if "balance," as advocated by organizations like the David Project, were actually implemented, it would do nothing more than replace one set of ideas, in this case formed by decades of research, with a competing set of ideas symbolizing the dogmas of a political movement. The pursuit of truth, which never has had anything to do with balance, is a more appropriate scholarly undertaking, and any survey of, say, Massad's published work reveals a dogged emphasis on that pursuit (the same is true of Massad's MEALAC colleagues Hamid Dabashi and George Saliba). In the framework of the Israel–Palestine conflict, "balance" usually assumes a familiar trajectory: anybody impudent enough to invoke reams of impeccable historiography (or personal experience) to illustrate that Israel is anything other than a Godlike democracy worthy of constant genuflection is accused of bias (as if support for Israel, or, for that matter, any other position, arises without bias). Unbiased crusaders in turn pressure university administrators and politicians to support a balanced curriculum that dehumanizes Palestinians and advances an imperialistic status quo. Most Americans, enamored of the ideal of balance rather than being suspicious of its implications, fail to see the terrifying ironies wrought by these crusaders. (They also are uninformed by corporate media of the moles whom outfits like the David Project enroll in Middle East

Studies courses, the rigorous scholarship that contradicts the intellectual foundations of their alternative curricula, and the longstanding notions of academic freedom inscribed in the institution of tenure.)

"Balance," then, means little more than the ascendancy of false history and the elimination of any narratives that highlight injustices historically in Palestine and currently in the Occupied Territories. Massad, in short, is catching hell for telling the truth, and so he belongs to a venerable tradition of ostensible radicalism that actually intimates destruction of the falsehoods that underlie all manner of nationalistic celebration. Because of the success of the David Project and its many cohorts, it seems unlikely that any truth about Israel/Palestine will be taught systematically in American universities without concurrent pressure from nonacademic interest groups who work to ensure that classrooms retain their traditional function as purveyors of state propaganda. Or, to state it even more clearly: professors interested in truth will become increasingly marginalized despite the fact that it would be much more useful for the David Project and its cohorts to redirect their activism in opposition to Israeli colonization rather than scrambling so desperately to silence those who legitimately condemn with factual accuracy the United States' complicity in Israel's ethnic cleansing.

This situation bespeaks a profound racism, so the question arises of how educators of conscience might respond to it effectively. First of all, it is important to always guard against any sort of argument from the Right—or, in the case of the *Chronicle*, the Center—that wants to effect curricular change. Those arguments invariably rely on tacit racism, if not against Arabs (and it usually is against Arabs), then against any number of minority demographics, particularly African and Native Americans. Although at this point Joseph Massad has not been dismissed from his faculty position, he has been barred from teaching one of his specialized courses on the Israel–Palestine conflict and has thus been limited in his ability to translate his scholarship into instruction. His confinement to less politicized courses is a stark example of how curricular activism on the part of nonacademics can damage the environments in which academics conduct pedagogy and research.

Second, we need to provide a context to simplistic notions of irrational Arab violence. Some violence in the world, I imagine, is irrational, but most of it has a context (whether or not we consider each context justifiable). Arab violence generally is represented in the form of Palestinian suicide bombers, but little mention is usually made of Israel's brutal occupation, which, no matter how hard apologists try to ameliorate it, fosters the misery that induces youngsters to act on their hopelessness. Nor is there much mention of the ethnic cleansing of Palestinians in 1948, 1967, and today. There is even less mention of the systematic violence against Palestinians undertaken by Israeli soldiers and settlers (which has taken far more lives than suicide bombers). That violence includes burying the elderly alive, shooting children at point-blank range, and firing missiles into heavily populated civilian areas. Speaking of Arab violence without mentioning any context is to insinuate, as does Neil Kressel, that the violence is both innate and inexplicable.

Third, we can raise our voices in fury when neoconservatives propose to transform American universities into transit centers that will train students in patriotism (a notion that by its very nature induces anti-Arab racism in the United States). I believe wholeheartedly that academics should, when desired, publish in nonscholarly forums and speak to nonacademic audiences about their research (or political interests). When it comes to neoconservative pressure on university administrators, then we have extra impetus to speak to as many people as possible because, as Stanley Fish notes, although area studies appear to be flourishing, neoconservatives have persuaded the American public that universities are cesspools of radicalism that aim to transform youngsters into anti-American multiculturalists.

Minority professors, it could be argued, are winning the battle over curricula, but neoconservatives know that mass public pressure eventually will compel legislators to coerce university administrators into supporting more nationalistic instruction. Based on this possibility, I would encourage academics to publish op-eds in local newspapers and speak to the public about the PC wars currently in play in universities, because the public overwhelmingly hears only the neoconservative version of university culture (which is ironic since most neoconservatives, including Pipes and Kramer, don't even teach in American universities). I find no aversion to speaking forcefully against any attack on my classroom and the way I interact with my students. As long as the attacks arise from nonacademics and nonteachers who criticize from their perches in neoconservative think tanks, then no professor under attack, directly or indirectly, should hesitate to momentarily abandon esoteric vocabulary and respond using language that almost anybody can understand (Massad has done well in this capacity even though his access to corporate media has been limited).

And finally, it is imperative that educators become aware of the difficulties Arab students experience. Those difficulties certainly deal with racism in American culture at large, but also in university classrooms, as I hope the examples I offered above illustrate. I urge fellow educators not to recreate in the classroom, tacitly or otherwise, the anti-Arab racism that currently pervades so much of the discourse in the United States. If I might speak personally, I never participated in class discussion as an undergraduate. I was always afraid of being accused of extremism if I expressed support for Palestinians or challenged any of the conventional wisdom on the Arab World. And I was driven to both anger and depression when I repeatedly heard my father, a gentle and loving Arab immigrant, characterized, along with all other Arabs, as invariably violent or terroristic. Professors should be aware of how seemingly responsible political discussions about the Arab World can in fact be forums for the articulation of anti-Arab racism because of the very structure of American–Arab relations; since the United States subsumes its interests in the Near East with mystified conceptions of Arab inferiority, support for American policy can in and of itself be racist (as, for instance, when American politicians tell us we should support Israel because it is the only civilized nation in the Middle East). As educators, we are required to ensure the comfort of all our students, which is impossible if Arab students are required to listen to endless discussion about Arab terrorism without any nuance or any intervention on the part of the professor (or when the professor himself or herself is the culprit). Nor can Arab students fully participate in class if they are scared of being branded anti-Semitic or anti-American every time they vocalize their perspectives on the Arab World.

In Conclusion: Ground Zero

Without question, anti-Arab racism is ground zero of the culture wars in American universities. One would never know this fact, however, based on the amount of time academics and political commentators actually spend discussing anti-Arab racism. An entire industry has been created to combat any instruction that grants Arabs agency or that conceptualizes them as worthy of existence outside of Israeli and American patrimony. This industry is well-funded and substantially more vocal in American popular culture than the professoriate. Obviously, neoconservative encroachment on college curricula should concern all professors who aren't neoconservative. More important, though, the neoconservative pundit industry should be of special concern to academics because the influence of its rhetoricians, unlike the influence of most professors, extends outside the university. We are dealing with a nation that already has trampled civil liberties with the Patriot Act and appears to be on the verge of trampling even harder with the DSEA (Patriot II). In addition to the Patriot Act, Americans have been assaulted with the CLEAR Act (H.R. 2671), which allows local law enforcement to enforce civil immigration laws; the SEVIS software that invasively tracks the movement of international students; and H.R. 3077, a bill inspired by neoconservatives that has created government oversight of international area studies. In short, if we remain silent, then it won't be long before we all are required to submit our reading lists to Tom DeLay for approval. That, in short, is what Arabs have to do with the reemergence of the university culture wars. To ignore anti-Arab racism is unethical, but, more immediately, to overlook the role that this racism plays in the politicization of the American classroom would be self-defeating.

4
Is Zionism Racism?

In 1993, Stanley Fish, using his considerable talent for original thought, published an article in the *Atlantic Monthly* dealing with a serious controversy of the day, reverse racism, a paradoxical expression popularized by opponents of welfare and affirmative action and, to a lesser degree, racists who decided to cast themselves as victims of Black discrimination. In both his critical and cultural writings, Fish is unpredictable, a large part of his appeal to readers he frustrates as often as he delights. Fish creates this unpredictability by crafting contradictions in order to infuse his arguments with paradox, irony, and oxymoron. Sometimes, however, Fish simply contradicts himself, particularly when he comments on issues outside his realm of expertise, a shortcoming exemplified by the subject of the Near East.

In his *Atlantic* article, part of his celebrated exchange with Dinesh D'Souza, Fish sets out to illustrate that so-called reverse racism is wholly justified because of historical circumstance. In other words, because Whites have so vigorously discriminated against Blacks throughout American history, Blacks have the right to seize whatever opportunity exists to claim special status and reserve "for themselves privileges they deny to others."[1] To reinforce this controversial argument, Fish references Zionism in the context of a George Bush I speech to the UN in which Bush remarked, "To equate Zionism with the intolerable sin of racism is to twist history and forget the terrible plight of Jews in World War II and indeed throughout history."[2] Fish writes,

> What happened in the Second World War was that six million Jews were exterminated by people who regarded them as racially inferior and a danger to Aryan purity. What happened after the Second World War was that the survivors of that Holocaust established a Jewish state—that is, a state centered on Jewish history, Jewish values, and Jewish traditions: in short, a Jewocentric state. What President Bush objected to was the logical sleight of hand by which these two actions were declared equivalent because they were both expressions of racial exclusiveness. Ignored, as Bush said, was the *historical* difference between them—the difference between a program of genocide and the determination of those who escaped it to establish a community in which they would be the makers, not the victims, of the laws.[3]

Although this version of Zionism is meant simply to be a broad summary running inevitably into a word-count limit, Fish's argument is at best dubious and indeed would appear to most Palestinian readers as hateful. Zionism, first of all, was not created by Holocaust survivors. The impetus to remove the indigenous population from Palestine occurred during a time of great anti-Semitism in Europe but well before Hitler was born. Moreover, I have met only a few Arabs who deem Zionism racist and simultaneously declare it to be the equivalent of German Nazism. Racism is implemented with varying degrees of violence. When a White calls a Black "nigger," nobody dies, but it is no less racist than a lynching—in effect it creates the sort of environment in which a lynching can occur. According to Fish's reasoning, the victim of a racial epithet, as opposed to a slave, deserves no recourse because there is no historical equivalence between the two actions.

Fish continues by summarizing Bush's UN argument:

> Bush was saying to the United Nations, "Look, the Nazis' conviction of racial superiority generated a policy of systematic genocide; the Jews' experience of centuries of persecution in almost every country on earth generated a desire for a homeland of their own. If you manage somehow to convince yourself that these are the same, it

is you, not the Zionists, who are morally confused, and the reason you are morally confused is that you have forgotten history."[4]

Fish's logic here is disastrously myopic. The historical connections he offers between Zionism and reverse racism aren't based on such similarities as he imagines. Blacks were taken from Africa and made into slaves in the New World, and later in the United States. And it remains the United States, the same nation in which they were slaves, where they make claims to socioeconomic reparations. Much as they like to deny it, the descendants of slaveholders benefited enormously from slave labor, in terms of the resources acquired by White America and from the institutionalized privilege granted Whites through the subordination of Blacks. Jews, on the other hand, suffered the Holocaust in Europe, but made their claim to reparations in Palestine.

No concentration camps existed in the Arab World. Jews were never rounded up in Palestine and killed in gas chambers. So how is it that Fish can so nonchalantly dismiss the rights of the indigenous population that was dispossessed via Israel's creation? To Fish, Palestinians apparently don't exist since he scarcely mentions them in glorifying the European conquest of their land, which according to his ludicrous moral index is perfectly acceptable since the conquerors suffered genocide elsewhere. If after slavery ended Black Americans decided they needed a homeland in, say, China (where some Black scholars believe Africans have an origin), and proceeded to displace 700,000 Chinese who had nothing to do with American slavery, it would seem outrageous for Fish to rationalize this displacement based on Black suffering in the United States. Yet he succeeds in rationalizing Palestinian displacement on identical moral grounds because in the United States, Palestinians are tacitly considered to be less human than Israelis (and than the Europeans who committed the atrocities for which the Palestinians somehow are responsible). Fish's argument would work perfectly if Israel were located in Germany.

As it stands, though, that argument descends into apologia for ethnic cleansing. Even if one could justify Fish's argument that European Jews had the moral right to establish a state in a highly populated section of Asia (a questionable proposition), Israel was established in 1948, and even a writer as clever as Fish might have trouble convincing intelligent readers that Israel's current settlement of the West Bank has anything to do with the Holocaust, or can be justified by it. In fact, if his argument is to have any moral authority at all, Fish should note that Palestinians, based on historical circumstance, have legitimate claims to compensation from Israel. He seems to forget that most foreign settlement enterprises have been justified by claims of persecution. Accordingly, the Puritans, suffering in England, had every right to exterminate Indians. And the Boers, marginalized in the Netherlands, were acting reasonably when they displaced Black South Africans in their quest for redemption. Fish's rationale, then, sets a dangerous precedent, as it appears to hierarchize suffering and then delegate that suffering into categories of "deserved," "undeserved," and "unfortunate but inevitable." Palestinian suffering falls into the final category, which, whether or not Fish intended it, lessens their humanity by rendering them expendable, particularly as they are made to endure horrid living circumstances because of European sins, while the nations in which the Holocaust occurred subsist in opulence by comparison.

And we haven't even mentioned the most controversial question Fish raises: Is Zionism racism? His answer is "No." I will have to argue that Fish's answer, like the rest of his article, is thoroughly misguided.

What is Zionism?

Fish, like most media commentators, fails to define Zionism in his article. Zionism is discussed vigorously by both Jews and Arabs without often being defined, most likely because of its complexity and because its supporters and opponents usually assume a universalized notion of what it is (or should be). Yet to discuss whether Zionism is racism without concurrently defining what we mean by *Zionism* is not only untenable, but also an acknowledgement of rhetorical failure.

As for the question, "Is Zionism racism?," my answer also is "No." But if we reformulate the question to ask, "Is there racism inscribed in Zionism?," my answer would be, "Overwhelmingly." It all depends on what type of Zionism is under discussion. I would never make the generic statement "Zionism is racism" because it is too simplistic a formulation to utter with such confidence. *Zionism* in the singular, as we shall see, itself connotes a simplistic philosophical approach. As thinkers concerned with the liberation of Palestine, we are better served by complicating the juxtaposition of Zionism and racism so that we might remove any reductionism in our approaches to Israeli perfidy in the Occupied Territories. I prefer to examine the aspects of Zionism that employ, consciously or not, notions of exclusivity in a racialist context, thereby at least flirting with racism if not advocating it outright.

Definitions of Zionism differ vastly. The Anti-Defamation League (ADL) defines it as "the Jewish national movement of rebirth and renewal in the land of Israel—the historical birthplace of the Jewish people."[5] Zionism, the ADL notes, "continues to be the guiding nationalist movement of the majority of Jews around the world who believe in, support and identify with the State of Israel. Zionism, the national inspiration of the Jewish people to a homeland, is to the Jewish people what the liberation movements of Africa and Asia have been to their peoples."[6] The ADL, forgetting that what is now Iraq is actually the "historical birthplace of the Jewish people," chooses to define Zionism in liberationist terms, although the comparison to Asian and African liberation movements is incorrect. The ADL appears to be confusing Zionism with Palestinian nationalism. Its definition of Zionism purposely omits Palestinians, preferring instead to concentrate on Jewish sovereignty.

Most definitions of Zionism follow this approach. Lisa Katz calls it "the national movement for the return of the Jewish people to and the resumption of Jewish sovereignty in Zion [Palestine]."[7] Katz also notes that "some believe that modern Zionism should focus on attaining worldwide recognition of Israel as the Jewish state and others believe it should be concerned with achieving peace."[8] The liberal Israeli organization Peace Now falls into the latter category, although it, too, seems prone to amnesia about Palestine's indigenous populace. Peace Now member Gidon D. Remba writes, "Zionism is the belief that Israel has a right to exist as a democratic Jewish state—nothing more, nothing less."[9] This definition would be entirely meaningless if Remba's utopian vision didn't evoke propaganda. A democratic state is certainly worthy of worldwide support. Israel, however, is only a democratic state if the 3.5 million Palestinians in the Occupied Territories and the 1.2 million Palestinians in Israel are completely forgotten, an astonishing task that Remba manages to accomplish in one sentence. His reliance on propaganda is further revealed when he mentions progressive Zionism: "[Theodor] Herzl foresaw a Jewish state in which Jews and Arabs enjoyed full equality as citizens."[10] Remba has obviously failed to read Avi Shlaim, Simha Flapan, Zeev Sternhell, Mohamed Heikal, Edward Henderson, Walid Khalidi, Ilan Pappe or the hundreds of other historians who quote Herzl as advocating the removal of Palestinians and transforming the leftovers into menial laborers. This reductionism transforms Zionism into a common, uninspiring form of settler colonialism, replete with the amnesia the settlers institutionalize into their imagination when they become a nation.

Remba's concept of Zionism is better suited for a rightwinger like Gil Mann, who observes, "Zionism is the movement to support a homeland for the Jewish people."[11] Mann expands on this standard definition by subtly playing to Christian support for Israel, an important component of Zionism today:

> Freedom of religion notwithstanding, Israel is primarily a Jewish state, so I think you can safely say that to be a Zionist is, in a sense, being a patriot to the Jewish state. The highest level of dedication or patriotism would probably be to live in Israel, but a person does need not to live in Israel to be a Zionist or be in favor of a Jewish state—nor does a person need to be Jewish to be a Zionist. In fact many non-Jews ... are supportive of the state of Israel and I think they could consider themselves Zionists.[12]

Beyond catering to Christian fundamentalists, Mann's rumination on Zionism attempts to legitimize his contradictory worldview as an outspoken Zionist who hasn't emigrated to Israel. Nearly 30 years ago, Edward Said asked in *The Question of Palestine* what it means to be a Zionist who chooses to stay in the United States, a question that Mann, in his own way, attempts to work through in the passage I cite.[13] The contradiction Said identified and that Mann contemplates is an important feature of Zionism, which highlights its inherent weakness as a liberationist ideology that is tacitly viewed as an inconvenience by many of its advocates (all ethnonationalism, including the Palestinians', contains this weakness).

Other definitions of Zionism reveal its complexity and its inability to ultimately mobilize all Jews as comprehensively as its founders had hoped. In 1975, for instance, Yigal Allon defended Zionism at the UN General Assembly while admitting shortcomings: "Zionism is creating a society, however imperfect it may still be, which tries to implement the highest ideals of democracy—political, social and cultural—for all the inhabitants of Israel, irrespective of religious belief, race or sex."[14] Allon, of course, was well aware that his version of Zionism is romanticized and executed his public relations gambit by failing to mention that the democracy on which he lavishes praise is reserved for Jews—and in 1975, only European Jews, as Sephardic and Black Jews could attest. The fact that Allon extolled Zionism's humanity while allowing that some "imperfections" exist in Israel illustrates that even the most confident definition of Zionism is bound to somehow confront the weight of its interplay with Palestinians, no matter how vehemently the Palestinians are avoided.

It is this interplay with Palestinians that renders Zionism so complicated. As Derek Brown of the *Guardian* notes, "Zionism is all things to all people. To some, it is the noblest of causes. To others, it is a curse."[15] Generally, it has been Arabs who construe Zionism as a curse, as their draft declaration at the 2001 Durban UN Conference Against Racism attests. The Arab delegation moved to reaffirm "that colonization by settlers and foreign occupation constitute sources, causes and forms of racism, racial discrimination, xenophobia and related intolerance." This reaffirmation, problematic because of its ambitious global reach, has traditionally been how Arabs interpret Zionism. While most Zionists omit mention of Palestinians in their paeans to Jewish self-determination, many Arabs remove any human dimension to Zionism and view it instead as a ceaseless encroachment resulting in little more than ethnic cleansing.

A letter writer to the *Ottawa Citizen*, Rana Chreyh, aptly summarizes the Arab perception of Zionism, deeming it "an elitist national movement that is opposed by many Jews."[16] Chreyh's emphasis on the elitism of Zionism is crucial to Arab opposition to Israel's occupation, as the privileges afforded Jewish settlers at the expense of the native populace compel the majority of Arabs to condemn Zionism on moral as well as political grounds. Across the world, elitism in settler projects has long inspired myriad resistance movements, and as long as mainstream versions of Zionism articulate an elitism by ignoring or dehumanizing Arabs, the Arabs will continue to express hostility to even the most benign Zionist ideologies.

Of course, one needn't turn solely to Arabs to find opposition to Zionism. Numerous Europeans, for reasons other than those who are anti-Semitic, oppose it, as does the vast majority of the Southern Hemisphere, viewing it as classic European patrimony. Some progressive Jews, as Arabs like to point out, reject mainstream versions of Zionism, including Uri Avnery, Amy Goodman, Norman Finkelstein, and Baruch Kimmerling. Jewish philosophers have perhaps been the most vocal opponents of Zionism because of its emphasis on ethnic exclusivity and its contrived narrative of national redemption. This philosophical opposition dates to Walter Benjamin, Hannah Arendt, and Martin Buber, and now includes intellectuals like Judith Butler, Noam Chomsky, Ella Shohat, and the late Maxime Rodinson and Jacques Derrida.

Perhaps the most interesting, and vitriolic, Jewish opposition to Zionism can be found among some ultra-Orthodox communities. The American ultra-Orthodox group Neturei Karta claims that "Zionism has for over a century denied Sinaitic revelation. It believes that Jewish exile can be ended by military aggression."[17] Neturei Karta adds some charges more venomous than those found in the statements of Palestinian organizations: "Zionism has spent the past century strategically dispossessing the Palestinian people. It has ignored their just claims and subjected them to persecution, torture and death."[18] Had a non-Jewish group released such a statement, it would likely be deemed anti-Semitic by the Anti-Defamation League (ADL), America Israel Public Affairs Committee (AIPAC), and other mainstream Zionist groups. The fact that Neturei Karta's members are Jewish—the quintessential Jews, they would say—thus complicates the positioning of Zionism in worldwide Jewish communities as well as in the popular debates it induces among Americans of all ethnic and political leanings. Neturei Karta's virulent anti-Zionism indicates that representation is necessarily evasive and incomprehensive. Its members' radical belief that they represent real Judaism is no less ridiculous than mainstream Zionists' assertion that their version of Zionism represents international Jewish interests. Moreover, as Tom Segev and Noah Efron have illustrated, movements like Neturei Karta reveal the ugly truth that some of the worst anti-Semitism in the world arises in intra-Jewish debate.[19]

As the examples above indicate, Zionism is diverse and multifaceted. I have provided a cross-section of various Zionist and anti-Zionist ideologies, which, with a few exceptions, fall into one or more of the following categories: progressive Zionism, as practiced by Peace Now and the Tikkun Community; mainstream Zionism, as practiced by AIPAC and the ADL; messianic Zionism, as practiced by Gush Emunim and the Jewish Defense League (JDL); religious Zionism, as practiced by Israel's National Religious Party; Christian Zionism, as practiced by the Christian Broadcasting Network and numerous American Protestant coalitions; spiritual Zionism, as practiced by numerous Orthodox and conservative synagogues; post-Zionism, as practiced by Gush Shalom as well as some Jewish progressives and intellectuals; and anti-Zionism, as practiced by Neturei Karta.

When we speak of Zionism, therefore, we are hardly dealing with a single entity. In fact, we may well be encountering antagonistic ideologies that exist under the same descriptor. For this reason, it is unfair to say "Zionism is racism," a blanket statement that leaves no room for group or individual nuance. Again, I wish to be clear that I object to this statement not on moral grounds but in the interests of intellectual probity, for I believe without hesitation that the majority of worldviews that arise from Zionism are infused with anti-Arab racism, or directly purvey it. Some revel in it. Others helped create it. In the United States especially, mainstream Zionism has played an enormous role in the proliferation of anti-Arab racism.

Zionism-as-racism has long been a subject of acrimonious debate internationally and in the United States. I will concentrate on three incidents that brought this debate to the front pages of American newspapers: the supposed emergence of a new anti-Semitism; UN General Assembly Resolutions 3379 (1975) and 46/86 (1991); and the Durban UN World Conference Against Racism, Racial Discrimination, Xenophobia, and Related Intolerance.

The New Anti-Semitism

Zionism is now inextricably linked to anti-Semitism. That is to say, people rarely discuss Zionism anymore without somehow incorporating anti-Semitism into the discussion, whether it is done accusingly or skeptically.[20] Mainstream Zionists today are the most vocal theoreticians of what they call a new anti-Semitism, which they generally define as a reemergence of classic anti-Semitism that has evolved to suit today's geopolitical realities. The State of Israel often is a target of this new anti-Semitism and Arabs/Muslims, in addition to Europeans, have increasingly come to purvey it.

Of course, the skeptical observer will note that discussion of this new anti-Semitism inevitably contains an ulterior motive, to increase financial and philosophical support for Israel, thus tying it even more closely to Zionism. We need not dwell on this point, however, because I have yet to find a political position that doesn't contain a financial or philosophical ulterior motive, especially where Arab leaders are concerned. (Palestine has cynically been used as a rhetorical trope by every Arab dictatorship interested in appeasing the populace it systematically exploits.) Nor am I concerned here with either lionizing or demythologizing the new anti-Semitism. I am more interested in examining how Zionist commentators invoke the new anti-Semitism to obscure a corresponding anti-Arab racism. Or, to put it more bluntly, how the new anti-Semitism has institutionalized anti-Arab racism even more firmly in mainstream Zionist thought. This feat has been accomplished by conceptualizing Arabs as remarkably susceptible to propaganda, innately prone to hatred, or unable to transcend violent behavior.

Such dehumanization implicates mainstream Zionism in racism, because if support for Israel is predicated on a theory of anti-Semitism that is itself racist, then mainstream Zionism can demystify settlement by expunging the moral agency of those whose lands are being settled. I would argue that this strategy is merely a reworking of the racism that has always been fundamental to the majority of Zionist projects. From its earliest days, Zionism practiced both exclusion and exclusivity. Indeed, the racism early Zionists expressed toward Arabs was matched only by racism toward Oriental, particularly Yemeni, Jews. Throughout Zionism's history, Zionist leaders, starting with Herzl, have viewed Arabs as expendable, barbaric, threatening, crude, and savage, worthy of removal or subordination as peasants to cleanse the land of snakes and rodents. This fact doesn't make Zionism racism *per se*, but it certainly inculpates a plethora of Zionist leaders as blatant racists.

More important, to this day most versions of Zionism flirt with biological determinism—some voice it directly—by reserving a geographical area for the exclusive use of a particular ethnic group. In fact, an ancient indigenous population was removed in Palestine expressly for this purpose. Beyond the meaningless rhetoric about equal rights for Arabs that Zionist leaders like to vocalize when Israel is criticized or when they endeavor to prove that Israel is more civilized than Arab nations, Arabs are inscribed in the Israeli legal system as second-class citizens and treated accordingly. The Arabs of the Occupied Territories are in much worse shape, since there the exclusivity of Zionist ideology is most apparent: highways are constructed through Palestinian farmland for the sole use of Jewish settlers; 90 per cent of West Bank water is used by Jewish settlers, who comprise roughly 10 per cent of the West Bank population; West Bank and Gaza Palestinians drive vehicles with white license plates, as opposed to the settlers' yellow plates, which severely restricts their movement or eliminates movement altogether; Jewish settlers usually are given community service for murdering Palestinians while Palestinians, guilty or not, have their neighborhoods demolished when anybody is suspected of killing an Israeli.

I am describing, as much as Israel's supporters detest the description, an apartheid system. Few people of conscience in the 1980s would have found the statement "the South African government is racist" to be controversial, but many of the same people find it unconscionable to associate Israel or Zionism with racism in even the loosest of terms. The reality, however, is clear to anybody who has visited the Occupied Territories: Israel practices an apartheid predicated on ethnic exclusivity and much of the Zionism that inspires settlement of Palestinian land is scarcely distinguishable from New World colonization, the conquest of Australia, or the French usurpation of Algeria. To treat Israel's presence in the Occupied Territories as anything other than apartheid not only belies verifiable reality, but amounts to a ludicrous denial inundated with racist delusion.

Israel's exclusionary practices are further demonstrated in its Law of Return, which allows Jews from anywhere in the world to immigrate to Israel and receive citizenship while denying the native Palestinians in both Israel and the Territories any ability to transcend their inferior legal status. The Law of Return also disallows Palestinians displaced in 1948 and after from returning to their homes or receiving just compensation for confiscated properties. Thus an American Jew of European extraction who has never been to the Near East can become a citizen of Israel or receive a resort-like subsidized home in the Territories while an Arab native to Palestine has no legal ability to return to a home from which he or she was displaced (the home having likely been destroyed or occupied by a family from somewhere other than Palestine). This feature of Israeli jurisprudence is troubling, and while it may not bespeak racism the way we have come to identify it in the United States, it tacitly reinforces an attitude of biological determinism and legitimizes Palestinian inferiority based on a racialized model of citizenship.

Many supporters of Israel will find problems with my interpretation of the Law of Return, noting that from the Jewish perspective it is inclusive rather than exclusive, but I believe nonetheless that to claim that no racism exists in such a system evinces the very worst of intellectual sloppiness and ethical depravity. Both progressive and conservative supporters of the Law of Return note that the Law never was intended to be exclusive and was created instead to provide Jews with a perpetual safe haven, something the historical treatment of Jews justifies. They also note that in 1949 the recent horrors of the Holocaust demanded that Israeli leaders implement a safeguard for survivors and Jews who were still in danger in places like the Soviet Union. Although it would require extraordinary insensitivity to claim that Jews deserved no safeguard—in Palestine or anywhere else—the Law of Return leaves no option but to yet again require the Palestinians to atone for sins they never committed. In fact, I see no way to justify the Law of Return without concomitantly dehumanizing Palestinians. I certainly don't wish to underplay the need in the 1940s for Jews to have a safe haven; I simply wish to point out that in creating the legal mechanism for a safe haven, Jews denied the right of Palestinians to one. In so doing, the Zionists of the day set the foundation for the exclusivity that would partly come to define Israel for the ensuing 60 years.[21]

None of the discussion above gives us the ability to say Zionism is racism. Nor, for that matter, have we created an argument foolproof enough to say certain forms of Zionism are racism. We can, however, say that Zionism in nearly all its forms has been infused with racism since the nineteenth century. We can also say that a troublesome number of individual Zionists, from the founders of Israel to some of its defenders today, were or are racist. Furthermore, we can observe that the exclusivity long endemic to Zionism encourages worldviews that delegate people into iniquitous categories. Or we might observe that messianic Zionism and each of its practitioners are racist to the degree of America's Aryan militias. Finally, we have the leeway to condemn the apologism most public American Zionists display toward Zionist racists or the features of modern Zionism that intend to subordinate Palestinians. Indeed, we have the leeway to condemn as racist anybody who supports Israel but refuses to acknowledge that Israel's presence in the Occupied Territories is an unjust enterprise replete with the same philosophical apparatus that provoked the ethnic cleansing of North America's indigenous nations. And we can illustrate how numerous Zionists continue in that racism today by ironically claiming to challenge racism—under, of course, the guise of battling anti-Semitism.

Noting, for example, that anti-Semitism is "a river of poison that runs beneath civilization," Robert Fulford suggests that "ferocious anti-Semitism has become a reigning orthodoxy of the Muslim world."[22] Fulford's article is titled "Anti-Semitism Can't Be Explained or Cured," a title that expresses a fatalism that renders the article's very composition meaningless. If anti-Semitism can't be explained, then why does Fulford explain its supposed pervasiveness in the Arab World, complete with an explanation of why it exists there? And if anti-Semitism can't be cured, then why does Fulford even bother to condemn Arabs as anti-Semitic? His totalized opinion of Arabs compels him to assume that *Arabs*, not anti-Semitism, can't be explained and that their inexplicably savage behavior can't be cured. Israel, therefore, must fortify itself because Arab violence against Jews has existed as long as the two peoples have interacted. Fulford's article provides us with a significant example of how Zionist racism can manifest itself in condemnation of Arab anti-Semitism by portraying all Arabs as incurably hostile. Little mention, of course, is made of Jewish violence against

Arabs, who, according to Fulford, deserve it because they "kill innocent Israelis."[23]

Likewise, Jack Silverstone writes, "anti-Semitism has a new disguise—anti-Zionism or anti-Israelism—and a new principal progenitor, the Muslim world in general and Arabs in particular."[24] This sort of hyperbole is fundamental to deliberations on the new anti-Semitism, which is unfortunate because writers like Silverstone devalue the important issue of anti-Semitism by using it as a smokescreen to articulate anti-Arab racism. Indeed, Silverstone's article is more about Arab barbarism than anything else, and it lacks the nuance that would require one to take it seriously. More crucially, Silverstone, like similar writers, ultimately can't reconcile the invariable contradiction of condemning racism while simultaneously offering uncritical support for a nation that engages continually in racist practices. He therefore presents an image of Israel that is both incomplete and inaccurate. For example,

> Israel is a multicultural and multi-ethnic democratic country. Its citizens and residents come from dozens of differing cultural backgrounds. One million of its six million citizens are Arab Muslims and Christians, with several other smaller minorities, such as Druze, Circassians and Samaritans. There are Arab representatives in Israel's parliament, in the judiciary and in mayoral positions. All Israeli citizens, including Arabs, have full political and civil rights and liberties, far more than they have in any Arab country.[25]

Silverstone's statements, if taken in a vacuum, generally are true, except for his argument that Israeli Palestinians have full civil rights and liberties. Black Americans in the 1960s theoretically had civil rights, but that doesn't mean they actually had access to those rights. The same is true of Israeli Palestinians. They theoretically have civil rights and liberties, but Israel's record of noncompliance with those institutions is repugnant. In any case, Israeli Palestinians are unable to purchase land or serve in the military, which even the most lackadaisical version of civil rights would necessitate.

Silverstone's biggest mistake is forgetting the 3.5 million Palestinians in the Occupied Territories, who have no vote, no right to purchase property (and are often dispossessed of it), no ability to move freely, and no reliable legal recourse in the event of arrest or land confiscation. In maligning Arab barbarism Silverstone inadvertently reveals his support for a barbarism as egregious as the one he maligns—the only difference is that Israeli brutality in the Occupied Territories isn't a myth employed to demystify a pernicious settlement policy. He, like other progenitors of the new anti-Semitism hypothesis, sounds like a conspiracy theorist desperate to deflect attention from the moral cravenness of his political fetish. He directs readers toward "evidence" of Arab inferiority so that his racism might be validated while it simultaneously creates the philosophical conditions for Israel to eternally subjugate the Palestinians. Racism, tacitly or explicitly, always is a central feature of such philosophical conditions. As Aaron Matte writes, "Having recently visited the occupied Palestinian territories, and witnessed the suffering and humiliation of an entire people under military occupation, I cannot stand to hear someone attribute my opposition to what I saw—and the government that carries it out—to anything other than an elementary concern for human well-being."[26]

My arguments here aren't intended to dismiss the very real problem of anti-Semitism around the world. Yet I have trouble on both moral and intellectual grounds supporting a resistance to anti-Semitism that also totalizes Arabs as mindless purveyors of hatred in the service of ethnically cleansing the Palestinians. Like all types of racism, anti-Semitism should be challenged painstakingly but honestly and without malicious ulterior motives. At present, the majority of responses to the new anti-Semitism foment anti-Arab racism and prevent the movement against anti-Semitism from occupying the moral ground it needs to be effective. For if the new anti-Semitism is to be defined as "anti-Zionism and anti-Israelism," to borrow from Silverstone, then not only are honest anti-racists compelled to be anti-Semitic, but the discourse challenging the new anti-Semitism will have merely recycled the canards for which proponents of the old anti-Semitism achieved their well-deserved scorn.

UN General Assembly Resolutions 3379 and 46/86

On 10 November 1975, the UN General Assembly passed its infamous Resolution 3379, which compared Israel to apartheid South Africa and called Zionism "a form of racism and racial discrimination." After much lobbying by the United States, in particular by the late Senator Daniel Patrick Moynihan, the UN General Assembly passed Resolution 46/86 in 1991, rescinding 3379, an Israeli precondition for attending the Madrid Peace Conference organized by George Bush Sr. In both 1975 and 1991, the resolutions sparked great debate, although the virtual consensus in the United States is that 3379 was completely unfair and 46/86 a necessary, if overdue, remedy to the Arab-inspired cynicism of 1975.

Given all the political considerations in play in the 1975 resolution, it would be difficult to argue that it was justified. But if it is assessed in a vacuum, the idea that Zionism is a form of racism and racial discrimination is relatively trenchant, even though the drafters of the resolution should be faulted for their use of totalizing language. Political decisions, however, are never made in a vacuum, so the horror most Israelis felt at having their national liberation movement condemned as racist in an international governing body must be taken into account (even as that horror illustrates why countries that originated as settler societies rely on amnesia to suppress their culpability for horrible crimes). The positive and negative aspects of Resolution 3379 have been debated exhaustively, so I see no need to either summarize those debates or rehash them here. I do, however, consider it beneficial to examine the role anti-Arab racism played in them.

The 16-year period during which Resolution 3379 was in existence saw an extraordinary amount of denial and exaggeration on the part of those working to overturn it. Mortified commentators repeatedly invoked the "Zionism-as-racism" resolution to highlight Israel's plight, forgetting that the resolution never actually called Zionism racism; it dubbed Zionism a form of racism and racial discrimination and condemned the "unholy alliance between South African racism and Zionism," a totally accurate condemnation that can also be found in the work of Israeli scholars such as Benjamin Beit-Hallahmi.[27] Again, I do not intend to argue that the passing of the resolution was justified, but neither should we pretend, as its opponents have done overwhelmingly, that Israel was the guiltless victim of a morbid Arab conspiracy. Zionism, after all, has been responsible for innumerable atrocities, a responsibility shared by nearly all ethnonationalist movements throughout history. And it bordered on racism when commentators dismissed the resolution as typical Arab perfidy, as if the Arabs had no viable claims against Israel to take to the UN.

I fault the Arab states not so much on the content of the resolution, which I don't in the least find shocking or scandalous, but on its timing and the forum in which they chose to articulate their disdain for Israeli crimes against the Palestinians. Theirs was a strategic more than a moral blunder, and one can't help but note the hypocrisy in even purporting to aid the Palestinians in the first place. There is validity to the complaint that with the passing of Resolution 3379, Israel was isolated and then condemned for actions that other nations engage in without public condemnation, but less validity to the corresponding complaint that as a result Resolution 3379 was wholly unjust. This schoolyard "everybody else is doing it" argument long invoked by apologists for Israel's ethnic cleansing is both untrue and foolish, and serves only to highlight the ethical wretchedness required to defend Israel's occupation. Without question, though, Resolution 3379 should have been expanded to include every country that in 1975 was engaged in racist or discriminatory practices against a minority supposedly under its protection (e.g., the United States, Saudi Arabia, Indonesia, and so forth).

Nevertheless, I find it discomfiting that Palestinians had (or have) no legal recourse in response to the suffering Israel has inflicted on them and I don't like the assumptions that arise when Resolution 3379 is attributed to Arab propaganda, which absolves Israel totally of the racism that earned it worldwide condemnation in the first place. Nor does it reflect well on Israel that it has continued to defy dozens of UN resolutions seeking to curtail its brutality in the Occupied Territories. Some of the claims of unfair treatment by the UN made by Israel's supporters are legitimate, but much of that treatment also results from Israel's devastation of Palestinian society and its defiance of applicable international law when the UN references it to inhibit Israel's encroachment on Palestinian territory. Ultimately, neither Resolution 3379 nor 46/86 actually affected the development of the Israel–Palestine conflict, but both resolutions prompted heated debate that saw the Arab inability to acknowledge our own moral and intellectual shortcomings surpassed by the inability of Israel's supporters to even entertain the idea that Israel has ever done anything wrong; instead, they consecrated the idea, used daily three decades later, that any criticism of Israel results from innate Arab anti-Semitism.

The American Left is guilty of this mentality, as indicated in an editorial published upon the passage of Resolution 46/86 in the *Nation*.[28] Condemning the "poison" of Resolution 3379, Philip Green embarks on a deliberation that is worth quoting at length:

It is important to understand just how the "Zionism is racism" resolution was an endorsement of anti-Semitism. Some critics, and victims, of Israel have been confused, because Israel, once it had gained a territorial nation in which many Jews had dwelled since time immemorial, behaved no better (and sometimes worse) than any other nationalist state or movement. Many Zionists, like socialists and liberal democrats and monarchists of the nineteenth and twentieth centuries, have been white racists. The Arab minority of Israel is deprived of civil rights; members of that minority have been expelled from the land of their birth; Israel engages in acts of violence that go beyond a legitimate response to the violence committed against it. All that is true beyond any doubt.

But the Catholics of Northern Ireland (and the Protestants), the Anglophones of Quebec, the Serbs of Croatia and the Croats of Serbia, the Turks of Bulgaria and the Hungarians of Romania, the Armenians of Azerbaijan, the Tamils of Sri Lanka, not to mention the Native Americans of North America—all would be fascinated to learn that there could conceivably be any nationalism free of those aggressions and repressions for which Israel is properly but uniquely condemned. Fascinated, and quite properly skeptical. To have singled out Israeli nationalism for condemnation has been a hypocritical anachronism.[29]

Green's set of historical analogies will not withstand scrutiny and doesn't in turn merit his charge of anti-Semitism. Green seems to be saying two things: that it was ridiculous to single out Israel for condemnation because all nationalist movements engage in violence; and that other nationalist movements—all minorities, such as the Tamils of Sri Lanka and the Native Americans of North America—not only engage in violence that goes uncondemned but that is received with some sympathy internationally.

The final point is true (although North America's indigenous nationalist violence essentially ended in the 1970s), but the comparison with Israel doesn't stand. Nor does Green's claim that the minority groups he mentions would be skeptical about singling out Zionist nationalism for criticism given the similarities among that nationalism and those of the minority groups. In 1975, when Resolution 3379 was passed, Israel was a well-established nation and Jews were in a majority in the Holy Land. Zionism was a foreign settlement movement that had every intention of displacing an indigenous population to fulfill its ethnonationalist objectives. None of the minority groups Green mentions ever has purported to fulfill such objectives, except for the Serbs five years after Green's article, for which they were not only roundly condemned by the UN but attacked by the United States. Moreover, Israel isn't uniquely condemned (although it is unique in the amount of UN resolutions it has flouted or ignored). Hundreds of resolutions sit on the books at the UN condemning nations like South Africa, Iraq, Indonesia, and the United States. Finally, Israel is a nation-state with extraordinary military power as opposed to, say, the Armenians of Azerbaijan, who haven't the means to carry out the brutality for which Israel is criticized.

Green also is incorrect to believe that minority groups such as Native Americans would be skeptical of criticism of Israel. I don't know enough about the literatures of the Turks, Croats, and Tamils, but would argue that Green is incorrect when it comes to Natives. They wouldn't be skeptical about the UN condemnation of Israel. The majority of Indians would support it. Green suggests that the Indians would identify with Zionist nationalism even though it has the same discursive features of the Euro-American nationalism that induced their own displacement and dispossession. This suggestion inadvertently romanticizes Zionism and evinces ignorance about the political sensibilities of Indian communities. Perhaps Green should have consulted Osage Robert Warrior's famous article, "A Native American Perspective: Canaanites, Cowboys, and Indians," where he notes that in the Israeli narrative,

> the obvious characters in the story for Native Americans to identify with are the Canaanites, the people who already lived in the promised land. As a member of the Osage Nation of American Indians who stands in solidarity with other tribal people around the world, I read the Exodus stories with Canaanite eyes. And, it is

the Canaanite side of the story that has been overlooked by those seeking to articulate theologies of liberation. Especially ignored are those parts of the story that describe Yahweh's command to mercilessly annihilate the indigenous population.[30]

Or Green should have consulted the late Choctow-Cherokee Louis Owens, who decries the fact that Indians, "like Palestinians have had to struggle just to have a voice and be acknowledged as 'real'."[31] Cherokee Jace Weaver also would have made a fine source, as when he lambasts the "occupying power" that has "exiled and subjugated" Palestinians and Native Americans.[32] For the type of assault that would certainly make Green squeamish, but that nonetheless arises from the Indian community he imagines to identify with Israel, he should have read Keetoowah Cherokee Ward Churchill, who explains,

> The factors motivating [Holocaust] exclusivists to conduct themselves as they do have been analyzed elsewhere. They concern the agenda of establishing a "truth" which serves to compel permanent maintenance of the privileged political status of Israel, the Jewish state established on Arab land in 1947 as an act of international atonement for the Holocaust; to forge a secular reinforcement, based in the myth of unique suffering, of Judaism's theological belief in itself as comprising a "special" or "chosen" people, entitled to all the prerogatives of such; and to construct a conceptual screen behind which to hide the realities of Israel's ongoing genocide against the Palestinian population whose rights and property were usurped in its very creation.[33]

It is precisely because Indians understand the horror of displacement and foreign settlement that they identify with Palestinian, not Israeli, violence, and why few of them will lament when Zionism is condemned. The fact of the matter is, rightly or wrongly, nearly everybody in the Southern Hemisphere views Zionism as a form of racism, so Green won't get much empathy from those he claims to be in solidarity with Israel.

In any case, Green admits that Israel has engaged in horrendous crimes, "sometimes worse than any other nationalist state or movement." He then admits that the Arab minority in Israel has no civil rights (he might have added human rights) and that Israel's violence is unjustified even when we consider the conditions of Jewish life in Europe. Still he has the state of mind to call UN condemnation anti-Semitic. Thus none of the reasons he has provided supports this conclusion—indeed, all the evidence Green evokes justifies condemnation—so he turns to philosophical questions to persuade what must by now be an incredulous readership: "But much worse was the conflation of nation with race: a conflation to which, again, only Jews were subjected."[34] This "return to 1933," as Green calls it, is entirely the fault of mainstream Zionism, not the UN, as Green himself admits when he says "many Zionists have been white racists." True, we don't talk often about race anymore, as it has largely been replaced by *ethnicity*, and to speak of people today in the humanities as *races* will sometimes result in justifiable scorn. However, the majority of Zionists, especially messianic Zionists, do use a category of race in dealing philosophically with Palestinians—if they didn't, how else could they possibly explain the exclusionary premises on which Jewish settlement is based? Sometimes that category is inscribed unconsciously in the discourse of mainstream Zionists, as when folks like Abraham Foxman and Michael Lerner fret that Jews will become a minority in their own land; at other times, that category is explicit, as when Gush Emunim's members construe Palestinians as members of an inferior and unwanted species.

Other major publications—including the *Washington Post*, under the heading "Taking Out the Trash"—praised Resolution 46/86 while evincing extraordinary disdain for the resolution it rescinded. Morally, I have no problem with this approach, or with the revocation of Resolution 3379. I do find it problematic, though, that in evincing extraordinary disdain for 3379, corporate American media let Zionism off the hook again. While it may be unfair to inscribe the Zionism-as-racism theorem into the books of an international governing body, Zionism (in all its forms) certainly raises moral questions that need not be dismissed in a huff of indignation. In effect, Arabs, Palestinians particularly, were silenced once again, and the crucial issue of Zionism's ethical failings went virtually unexamined.

The Durban UN Conference

By now, most people have forgotten the Durban UN World Conference Against Racism, Racial Discrimination, Xenophobia, and Related Intolerance. In 2001, though, it was the biggest news of the year until it was trumped by September 11. The conference became big news because of a draft declaration presented by the Arab delegation condemning Zionism as racism, which sparked a debate similar to the ones in 1975 and 1991. Unlike UN Resolution 3379, however, the Arab draft declaration at Durban, which was signed by over 400 NGOs, should have been included in the procession (it was, with some revisions) without the controversy it generated, which prompted Israel and the United States to withdraw from the conference.

First, let's look at the problems with the draft declaration. The declaration referred a few times to Zionist practices against Semitism, a ridiculous statement that dehumanizes Jews and seems too nondescript to mean anything. It also referenced a Holocaust against Palestinians, a mistake considering who they claim inflicted it—at the very least, *genocide* would have been a more appropriate term, although *ethnic cleansing* is more accurate. With these emendations, the draft declaration would have been viable. Here are some of its claims:

> 30. We affirm that a foreign occupation founded on settlements, its laws based on racial discrimination, with the aim of continuing domination on the occupied territory, as well as its practices which

consist of reinforcing a total military blockade, isolating towns, cities and villages under occupation from each other, totally contradicts the purposes and principles of the Charter of the United Nations and constitutes a serious violation of international human rights and humanitarian law, a new kind of apartheid, a crime against humanity and a serious threat to international peace and security;

60. We express our deep concern about the practices of racial discrimination against the Palestinians as well as other inhabitants of the Arab occupied territories which have an impact on all aspects of their daily existence such that they prevent the enjoyment of fundamental rights, and call for the cessation of all the practices of racial discrimination to which the Palestinians and the other inhabitants of the Arab territories occupied by Israel are subjected;

102. We recognize that States which pursued policies or practices based on racial or national superiority, such as colonial or other forms of alien domination or foreign occupation, slavery, the slave trade and ethnic cleansing, should assume the responsibility therefore and compensate the victims of such policies and practices;

Everything in these passages, which constitute practically all the controversy, is completely true. Many of Israel's supporters are so in denial, like most inheritors of garrison settlement projects, that they refuse to acknowledge that Palestinians are legally discriminated against by the state. Had this draft declaration been issued by Black South Africans during the 1980s nobody would have generated such controversy, besides perhaps the United States, which dislikes any form of indigenous self-representation, and Israel, whose leaders and arms merchants were known to tool around with apartheid politicians. It's not an accident that the same two countries generated the only real controversy over the Arab draft declaration. The United States had an ulterior motive for withdrawing from the conference: It wanted its delegates home before Black Americans took the floor to discuss the viability of reparations for slavery.

Based on corporate media response to the draft declaration, one would have thought the Arabs had photocopied *The Protocols of the Elders of Zion* and submitted them to the UN. Hysterical columnists bemoaned the Arabs' arrogance, their anti-Semitism, their inappropriate conduct, their bad sense of timing. (One wonders when it is appropriate and good timing to raise legitimate concerns about Israel's treatment of the Palestinians if not at a conference against racism, discrimination, xenophobia, and intolerance—if you answered "never," then you would have correctly identified the response the United States and Israel would give.) A collective "how dare they" seemed to emanate from the editorial offices of all major American newspapers. Again, we see that the onus of moral justification was placed on the Palestinians for vocalizing their disdain at being ethnically cleansed, rather than on the nation responsible for the ethnic cleansing.

Mortimer B. Zuckerman, publisher of *U.S. News and World Report*, accused the Arabs of "openly [fomenting] hatred of Jews."[35] Secretary of State Colin Powell called the Arab draft declaration "hateful."[36] Former Oslo negotiator and Yitzhak Rabin legal advisor Joel Singer complained, "I have now seen a resurrection of an attitude by Arab countries referring to Israel as the 'Zionist entity' rather than the state of Israel."[37] Nowhere in the draft declaration is Israel referred to as *the Zionist entity*. *The Christian Century* reiterated the illogical hypothesis that "the racism conference was the wrong platform and the proposed resolution on Zionism as 'based on racial superiority' was the wrong language with which to address the Middle East conflict. Neither Zionism nor racism determines Israel's current conduct toward Palestinians. It is driven, rather, by Israel's fear that its own security is threatened by a hostile Palestinian people."[38] In a time-honored tradition, created during the mass murder of Indians in the New World, the transatlantic slave trade, the colonization of Africa, and the settlement of Algeria, and then perfected by Teddy Roosevelt,

King Leopold, and Cecil Rhodes, the victim of ethnic cleansing is transformed into a hostile adversary threatening the well-being of the ethnic cleanser.

Michael Lerner, in the *New York Times*, produced perhaps the most disappointing analysis during this period. He writes,

> On its face, the charge against Israel is ludicrous. Anyone visiting Israel is immediately struck by the fact that it is one of the most multiethnic societies in the world. It is, to be sure, a state for those who have accepted Judaism. But that includes black Jews from Ethiopia, Jews from India and China who bear all the racial characteristics of people in those societies, Jews who escaped persecution in Arab lands and are racially indistinguishable from Arab Muslims. The fact is that whatever your racial background, you can convert to Judaism and be accepted with full rights in Israel.[39]

Lerner extols the virtues of Israel's multiracial inclusiveness while slipping in the point that should have been the focus of the article: that Israel grants equal rights only to Jews. He could have also mentioned that non-Israeli Jews have more rights in Israel than indigenous Palestinians, or that the inhabitants of the land before the European incursion have keys and deeds to the homes from which they were displaced but no ability legally to return to them. Any state that offers equal rights only on the precondition of a religious conversion has little to brag about. If Lerner were Palestinian, he would realize how insensitive he sounds.

Moreover, Lerner speaks of "racial characteristics" in nineteenth-century anthropological terms. Going back to Philip Green, we established that to speak of race is anachronistic because *ethnicity* has replaced it as a category. Lerner concentrates on Israel's racial make-up while ignoring its ethnic exclusivity. Religion, as any Israeli Jew, Arab Christian, Pakistani Muslim, Saudi Shiite, or Indian Hindu can attest, is a crucial feature of ethnicity, along with language, geographic origin, spirituality, culture, and ceremonial tradition. In abandoning ethnicity and replacing it with race, Lerner actually recapitulates the racialist dogmas of European colonizers and thus reinforces the exclusionary practices he claims to disdain. Lerner also makes the mistake of reducing all Palestinians to those who live inside the State of Israel, as when he writes, "Moreover, unlike South Africa under apartheid, which targeted anyone born of a certain race, regardless of religion, Israel has given its largest minority, the Israeli Arabs, the vote and the right to representation in the Knesset. Israeli Arabs have an easier time having their votes counted than blacks in some parts of Florida do. Israel has no segregated movie theaters or beaches. And the patterns of segregation in housing are not sanctified by law."[40]

This argument, of course, is a non sequitur. Israel's entire coastline is segregated because the Palestinians of the West Bank, which is landlocked, have no ability to visit it. During the period in which Lerner's article was published, some parts of the Gaza Strip coastline were reserved solely for Jewish settlers; even now, after its ostensible liberation, the Gaza Strip resembles more an outdoor prison than an autonomous nation-state. The sections of the Dead Sea under Israeli authority are open only to Jews and tourists. The Palestinians in the Occupied Territories cannot vote or run for office in Israel. And most Palestinians, who according to *National Geographic* subsist on a per capita income of $1,000 in the West Bank and $600 in the Gaza Strip, can't afford to go to the movies, as opposed to Israeli Jews, who have a per capita income of $20,000, by far the highest in the Near East. Even those who can afford the movies don't often go because they live under curfew or are prevented by Israeli checkpoints from traveling to towns with theaters. About these facts, Lerner says nothing, offering only a generic observation that "Israel has engaged in activities that are morally unacceptable … and deserve to be criticized."[41] Readers are left to wonder where that criticism should occur if not at an international conference dedicated to combating morally unacceptable behavior.

Cherie R. Brown, in an article published in Lerner's magazine, *Tikkun*, equaled his uninspiring performance. Brown proclaims,

> It became clear to me at Durban that anything less than unequivocal support for Israel and the right of Jews to have our own self-determination through a state, even when that state practices oppressive policies, will collude with anti-Jewish oppression. The continued existence of Israel as a nation, as a national homeland for all Jews, as a base for Jewish struggle for survival must be actively supported by all liberation programs. Jews, like every other people, have a right and a need for a state to ensure their self-determination and to provide a base for building unity. No people can be fully liberated without a homeland.
>
> The support for Israel's right to exist does not require ignoring or defending wrong or oppressive policies of the Israeli government, but criticism of such policies should be based on prior unconditional support for Israel's right to exist. We do not have to ignore the grave injustices done to the Palestinian Arabs that accompanied the establishment of Israel, but such injustice does not in itself justify the destruction of Israel. All present homelands on the earth were established by much injury to their previous inhabitants.[42]

The Arab draft declaration at Durban never denied the right of Jews to self-determination. It never questioned the existence of Israel as a nation. It never challenged Israel's right to build unity with anybody. And it never professed any desire to destroy Israel.

Brown's article reveals a paranoia common among Israelis and their supporters based on a perpetual fear that Israel will soon be destroyed (some American leaders after 9/11 began articulating this paranoia about the United States). Quite simply, Brown reads things into the Arab draft declaration and the Arab delegates' statements that aren't there; her critique is therefore little more than a figment of her imagination, fed substantially, no doubt, on the myth that all Arabs are out to get Israel. This fear that all Arabs wish to destroy Israel is problematic in countless ways, one of the most noteworthy being that it is completely racist because it allows ostensible security concerns to inspire reductionist characterizations of the adversary. Brown's attitude devalues a legitimate Palestinian aspiration, liberation from military occupation, and assumes the worst about Palestinians: that they are incapable of rational compromise, that they are unable to live peacefully and peaceably, that they will inevitably choose violence over coexistence. More important, Brown's attitude is quite simply incorrect. If anybody can be implicated in not wanting peace, it is Israel, which has rejected nearly every peaceful overture offered it in the past 50 years, preferring instead to continue plundering Arab land. Writers like Brown and other purveyors of the "they're out to destroy us" myth need to be reminded that Israel has already destroyed the Palestinian nation (yes, it was, on every theoretical definition of the word, a nation). In fact, Israel continues destroying every vestige of Palestinian society. And Israel works actively to prevent the establishment of a Palestinian homeland until it will be too late. In other words, everything Brown fears might happen to Israel (but has little chance of actually occurring) has already happened to the Palestinians and continues happening every day.

Some might object to my argument here by noting that some Palestinians do call for the destruction of Israel. Absolutely true. Some do, just as some Israelis in the Knesset openly call for the deportation of all Arabs from the Holy Land (which stretches into modern Iraq according to some accounts). These calls for the destruction of Israel don't mean that Israel will ever be destroyed; it is much more likely that Palestinians will be deported forcibly. In fact, it is but a minority of Palestinians who make such ludicrous statements, and yet given the airtime they are provided in American and Israeli media, one would think that all Palestinians plot irrationally to kill innocent Jews. As usual, in Brown's article the worst elements of Palestinian society are made to represent all of Palestinian society; as a result, Israel is absolved of doing precisely what the worst elements of Palestinian society merely plot. It would be no different if Gush Emunim were made to represent all of Israel or if Jerry Falwell were made to represent all of the United States (though it doesn't help that he represents the views of its president).

After relaying a nonsensical precondition—criticism of Israeli policies "should be based on prior unconditional support for Israel's right to exist"—Brown announces, "We need to see that our real allies are the Palestinian people."[43] I hope my Palestinian brethren don't find me too presumptuous when I speak as a Palestinian and tell Brown: Thanks, but no thanks. We also have preconditions: those who are to stand with us need first to express prior unconditional support for Palestine's right to exist.

In Conclusion: Beyond Denial

It is worth repeating that one of the worst, and most overlooked, aspects of the "Zionism as racism" debate is the anti-Arab racism the debate engenders and sustains. While Arabs certainly have much work to do in formulating a vocabulary that accurately implicates various forms of Zionism in injustice, defenders of Israel will never earn a sympathetic ear with Arabs (or the majority of peoples on earth) if they continue to construe any attack on Zionism or Israel as an anti-Semitic conspiracy. And as long as mainstream Zionists continue to position Israel as steward of the Occupied Territories, then critics of the occupation have no choice but to at least associate Zionism with racist practices. Ultimately, the exclusivity of Israel's social and judicial institutions bespeak an ethnonationalism that is supposed to be obsolete in the twenty-first century. The popular devotion to that ethnonationalism connotes a version of imperative patriotism in Jewish communities worldwide, which is articulated in the moniker of "self-hating" that is applied to Jews who digress from the mainstream or rightwing Zionist consensus. Such a moniker is not surprising; ideologies that are created and maintained on the mythos of exclusivity are ready-made to develop an outbreak of imperative patriotism.

So, back to the original question: Is Zionism racism? No, but Zionism is, and always has been, an enterprise as racist as each dogma instigated by biological determinism.

5
Why God Hates Me

God hates me for many reasons. I should be more specific: the God of dispensational evangelicals hates me. Detests me. Has ordained that I will die violently and suffer eternally. The God my Nicaraguan mother introduced to me when I was a toddler loved everybody: Muslims, Jews, Hindus, Asians, Natives, Blacks, even the Whites who stole my backpack to search for jumping beans. But mom's God is one of those liberal types, a Commie, really. Mom's God, that multicultural dupe, doesn't even believe in Hell or the rapture. The United States has almost killed mom's God.

The real God, I keep hearing on TV and the radio, is vengeful. He (definitely a He) loves war. *Really* loves war. Loves it when American Jews with piss-poor Hebrew settle the West Bank and take up guns. Loves it even more when they use those guns against Palestinians. Loves it when the president—with whom He communicates daily—fulfills His wishes and takes the United States into a needless war. Loves it when those heathenistic Chinese are spited by His human incarnation, Tom DeLay. More than anything, though, He loves it when His shriveled White emissaries get rich—I mean stinking rich, much richer than their faux alligator shoes would indicate (these emissaries, they need to appear humble, He says). The real God is a hypercapitalist who has infused the human marketplace with a spiritual manifestation of greed and exploitation. The real God loves poor people, but only when they accept their poverty so the rich can increase their wealth. The poor are singled out for special commendation if they give what little they have, or don't have, to the wealthy. Checks and money orders, of course, are accepted.

The real God hates me, though. He hates me because I'm still attached secretly to mom's God. He hates me because I oppose war in Iraq. He hates me because I teach courses in multicultural literatures. He hates me because I imagine China to be a gorgeous country. He hates me because I don't vote Republican. He hates me because I believe theologically that the God of Islam is the same God of Judaism and Christianity. He hates me because I respect the ACLU. He hates me because I love Palestine. But most of all, He hates me because I'm Arab.

The real God, in short, is an asshole.

He needs to once and for all be voted out of American politics before all the enlightened Islamic nations mobilize their armies to stem the tide of radical Christianity and eliminate the threat of violent Christianism that has led to Christian terrorism in Central America, the Middle East, and the Caribbean. Christian terrorists, though, pose the biggest threat to their own government. Radical Christianists, after all, hate our way of life and despise our freedoms; that's why they work so hard to nullify our Constitution.

Excusing Radical Christianism

The ascent in recent years of imperative patriots like Daniel Pipes, Sean Hannity, and Ann Coulter has allowed xenophobia to be an accepted part of mainstream policy debate. Most of the xenophobia is directed against Arabs and Muslims (although *FrontPageMag.com* has a huge section of articles lambasting Hispanic immigration). In particular, it has become orthodoxy in many rightwing circles that Muslims aren't to be trusted because even if they say the right things in public (with White

Republicans, of course, getting to define "right"), they secretly hope to transform the United States into an Islamic republic. All Muslims, therefore, are subject to suspicion because they are unable or unwilling to embrace secularism. This notion is disgraceful intellectually and criminal in its irresponsibility. It is also hypocritical.

I have yet to hear Pipes, Hannity, Coulter or any other imperative patriot mention the community of dispensationalist Christians who want to transform the United States from a secular democracy to a theocracy. The mission statement of Jerry Falwell Ministries, for example, includes "healing the wounds of immorality and godlessness in our nation." Pat Robertson's *The Ten Offenses: Reclaim the Blessings of the Ten Commandments* is little more than a diatribe against secularism and a call to his followers to restore God's proper role in the public sphere. In a recent interview, Tim LaHaye remarked, "We are victims of a secularist society … . And so what we have is a minority of liberal secularists leading our country astray and we have to come back as the conscience of the nation." These sentiments, which clearly contradict the Constitution, are regarded by imperative patriots as laudable nationalistic ideals.

If I were to use Pipes's methodology in challenging evangelical Christians, I would construe all of them as a threat to the American way of life, including those born to evangelical parents but not active in the church. Given their threatening ideology, I would lobby the government to place them under surveillance and arrest any who might in any way endanger American secularism, a fundamental aspect of our freedom, and deny them access to legal counsel. If the government deemed any detainee sufficiently dangerous, I wouldn't complain if that detainee were tortured. I wouldn't worry too much about this position, for I would be confident that corporate media would never criticize it and would continue to utilize me as an expert commentator.

Fortunately, I was taught by mom's God not to totalize, so I know better than to reduce millions of evangelical Christians to the positions expressed by some of their television personalities. The evangelical community, like all Christian communities, is remarkably diverse theologically, although among evangelical communities, the dispensationalists, sometimes called Christian Zionists, receive the most press attention. I will focus on that community in this chapter. Two things will be of particular interest: the influence of dispensationalists on America's political culture and its foreign policy; and the vehement anti-Arab racism articulated by dispensationalist TV personalities that is, according to their theology, not only sanctioned by God but demanded of His followers.

Christian Zionists: a Paradox, not a Contradiction

Dispensationalism first appeared in the United States in the early nineteenth century and is associated with a former minister in the Church of England, John Darby, who traveled frequently to the United States and influenced various Protestant leaders. Dispensationalism acquired its name by dividing the world into seven different eras, or dispensations, each of which is foretold by the Bible. We are now entering the seventh dispensation, which means the end of the world is near. As a result, dispensationalists assume an urgent missionary zeal, hoping to save as many people as possible before the rapture, an event in which God will carry the true believers into heaven before the horrors of the tribulation, when God will unleash His wrath on the sinners and unbelievers. A major precondition of the tribulation is that Israel must be restored to the Chosen People, the Jews, a third of whom will be present for the final battle of Armageddon, having been converted to Christianity by the true Messiah (the other two-thirds will have died in the tribulation).

Dispensationalists thus oppose a Palestinian state in any part of the Holy Land, believing that it would interfere with God's plans for the tribulation and in turn incur His eternal wrath. This God, then, is a weak God, as He relies on humans to fulfill what He should accomplish by divine mandate. Dispensationalists take their calling seriously, viewing the Palestinians as one of the largest impediments to the fulfillment of Scripture. Most believe that Palestinians should be deported to Jordan, where they can form their own state. Others believe that some might possibly remain in the Holy Land, but only if the entire Holy Land is unquestionably under the sovereignty of Israel. Dispensationalists support the settlement of the Occupied Territories and support Israel no matter what its endeavor. They are staunchly opposed to any peace plan, especially those proposed by the Satanic UN. They visit Israel often and donate remarkably large sums of money to the settlements. Hence the moniker of Christian Zionist.

George Bush Jr. received approximately 50 million votes in 2000. Of those 50 million, 30 million came from evangelical Christians, of whom roughly 15 million were dispensationalists. Some 30 per cent of his support, then, came from Christian Zionists. The percentage of Christian Zionists voting for him in his 2004 election victory was similar. Most of the evangelical TV personalities are Christian Zionists, including Tim LaHaye, Pat Robertson, Jerry Falwell, Benny Hinn, Ralph Reed, and Gary Bauer. They have a Capitol Hill lobby group, Christians' Israel Public Action Campaign, led by a former GOP Senate staffer, Richard Hellman. Their advocacy organizations, which all lobby on behalf of Israel, include the International Christian Embassy Jerusalem, Christian Coalition, Southern Baptist Convention, Bridges for Peace, Jerusalem Friendship Fund, Jerusalem Prayer Team, Stand with Israel, Christian Broadcasting Network, International Fellowship of Christians and Jews, Family Research Council, Council for National Policy, and Christians for Israel/USA. One of the oldest and most powerful groups on this list, the International Christian Embassy Jerusalem (ICEJ), is headquartered in Edward Said's family home in West Jerusalem.[1]

Jerry Falwell has lobbied so hard on behalf of Israel that in the 1980s Menachem Begin gifted him a Lear jet.[2] Former Attorney General John Ashcroft was a member of Rabbi Yechiel Eckstein's Jerusalem Prayer Team—in 2001/02, Eckstein's Jerusalem Friendship Fund raised $15 million to help settle the West Bank. In 2002, according to the Associated Press, "American Christians donated $20 million to help Jews resettle in Israel."[3] In January 2004, the Israeli Knesset created a Christian Allies Caucus to better coordinate efforts with Christian Zionists seeking to settle—"resettle" is a preposterous euphemism—Jews in Israel and the Occupied Territories and contribute to public works such as playgrounds and hospitals. All of this influence has been achieved on the strength of religious conviction. As Jerry Falwell says, "Whoever stands against Israel, stands against God."[4] Yet religious conviction never totally inspires policy because religious conviction in the public sphere is symbiotic with cynicism. The Israelis who accept the financial aid offered by Christian Zionists are acting purely out of self-interest, which usually has much to do with religion, but not in this case. The dispensationalist TV personalities who have become wealthy peddling the theology of rapture and tribulation likewise are acting overwhelmingly in their own financial interests. Despite these realities, though, we can say with some certainty that religious conviction is the main factor in the proliferation of Christian Zionism.

Nowhere is the popularity of dispensationalism more evident than in Tim LaHaye and Jerry B. Jenkins's *Left Behind* book series. As of this writing, the series, which has twelve installments, a prequel, and a sequel, has sold more than 62 million copies. The series, which epitomizes the good v. evil worldview, follows its hero, Rayford Steele, an airline pilot, and journalist Buck Williams as they live through the tribulation, having failed to be raptured. Steele and Williams are joined by an Israeli rabbi, Tsion Ben-Judah, who comes to realize that Jesus was actually the real Messiah, as they battle the forces of evil and bring people into God's fold before they are damned eternally. The theological apparatus of the story is provided by LaHaye and each novel is written by Jenkins. The books outsell those by heavyweights such as Stephen King, John Grisham, and J.K. Rowling, but even Jenkins, in a strange show of remorse, admits that they have no literary value: "I know I'm never going to be revered as some classic writer. I don't claim to be C.S. Lewis. The literary-type writers, I admire them. I wish I was smart enough to write a book that's hard to read, you know?"[5]

The series panders to the very worst aspects of American jingoism. Arabs, of course, are standard evildoers who must be slain at all costs. Everything in the novels is delegated into a stock category of "good" or "evil," and the attempt to include multiethnic characters is contrived and stereotyped. Yet the series obviously fills a need among its millions of readers; whether that need is spiritual, emotional, or intellectual, it reveals much about the pathetic state of the political culture from which the novels draw their strength. Make no mistake, the *Left Behind* series is vastly more political than spiritual or theological, and everything that the nonreligious or secular find terrifying about the policy ambitions of Christian Zionists is touted as a prerequisite for satisfying God's wrath and being saved. LaHaye, then, is looking to transform the political culture of the United States with the novels. I worry deeply about the proliferation of anti-Arab racism the novels might inspire, that they portray Arabs as impediments to the fulfillment of God's plan and worthy of annihilation. It appears that anti-Arab racism is a theological requisite of a large portion of the American populace and that blatant anti-Arab racism, rather than causing alarm, allows authors who admit that they can't write to become the United States' bestselling authors. A detailed story in the *Nation* scarcely touched on the novels' dangers to Arabs, and a cover story on LaHaye and Jenkins in *Newsweek* didn't mention Arabs at all.[6] These oversights are horribly irresponsible since the racism it requires to promulgate the dispensationalist theory of tribulation would never be tolerated if it were directed at an ethnic group other than Arabs. At present, though, a theory in which Arabs must first be displaced and then slaughtered *en masse* continues gaining currency in the United States and is usually challenged not on the grounds of its pernicious racism, but on its effects on liberal politics and presidential elections.

Other aspects of dispensationalist politics are equally troubling. The influence of Christian Zionists shouldn't be considered all-encompassing, but it is certainly a force. As William Martin writes,

> Although the Religious Right is not a mainstream movement, it is not a marginal one either. White evangelical Protestants, from whom the movement draws most of its members, comprise nearly 25 per cent of all registered voters—three times the number of African American Christian voters, four times the number of nonreligious voters, and twelve times the number of Jewish voters. Only a fourth to a third of evangelical voters openly identify with the Religious Right, but that segment, on average, is better educated, better paid, and more likely to hold professional jobs than other evangelicals and, indeed, than the American population as a whole. According to a 1994 study by *Campaigns and Elections* magazine, they dominate the Republican Party in at least 18 states and have substantial influence in at least 13 others, a situation many conventional Republicans find incomprehensible and maddening.[7]

One of the ways the dispensationalist movement has grown so rapidly, Martin illustrates, is through its media network:

> The number and reach of such media are truly impressive. The United States alone has more than 200 Christian television stations and nearly 1,500 Christian radio stations, almost all of which are evangelical and most of which carry at least some programs

produced by Religious Right leaders or supporters. Pat Robertson's 700 Club has a daily audience of about 1 million viewers and his Christian Broadcasting Network beams programs to some 90 nations in more than 40 languages. James Dobson's Focus on the Family uses part of its $114 million annual budget to produce eight radio programs, the most important of which—the daily, half-hour Focus on the Family—reaches an estimated 5 million listeners each week. The American Family Association and Concerned Women for America reach hundreds of thousands with their half-hour programs. This insular network not only facilitates mobilization but also fosters a missionary zeal seldom matched by those on the Left and almost never by the more moderate middle.[8]

The most troublesome aspect of this movement is its effect on foreign and domestic policy, beyond the uncritical support of Jewish settlement in the West Bank and the ability to stonewall the implementation of a viable Israeli–Palestinian peace. As *Church and State* notes, "DeLay freely admitted [at a conference] that he filters his political decisions through his 'biblical worldview'."[9] An alarming number of politicians and civilians share DeLay's attitude: "The Bible, one speaker [at the conference] said, provides answers to issues like the minimum wage, the capital gains tax, the 40-hour work week and the estate tax."[10] This sort of prophetic lobbying effort has been in existence for some time. More Americans than the secular care to admit want domestic laws to be changed to include stoning as a form of punishment, as per the Old Testament.[11] And if some dispensationalist TV personalities had their way, "unbelief" would become a law punishable by prison time. Even worse, those who find the dispensationalist influence on the Arab World to be horrifying must certainly be uncomfortable with the fact that

encouraged by special State Department briefings, Christian Right leaders [in the 1980s] offered both ideological and financial support to anticommunist forces in El Salvador, Guatemala, Honduras, and Nicaragua. Most notably, Robertson's Christian Broadcasting Network contributed between $3 million and $7 million to U.S.-backed, anticommunist Contras in Nicaragua and

Honduras. Robertson also lionized Guatemalan military dictator (and Pentecostal Christian) General Ríos Montt, whose brutal regime killed thousands of Indian tribespeople and other civilians regarded as procommunist or, as at least one Guatemalan official charged, as "possessed by demons." Falwell, along with several other TV preachers, defended apartheid forces in South Africa by claiming they had been misportrayed by liberal media and by depicting the African National Congress as a Soviet puppet. More notoriously, Robertson forged strong ties with the late Mobutu Sese Seko, Zaire's corrupt, long-time dictator—an alliance the entrepreneurial broadcaster used to gain forestry and diamond-mining concessions for his African Development Corporation.[12]

The dispensationalists, then, should be of concern to anybody interested in preserving whatever sanity remains in the United States, even if that person is uninterested in the dispensationalists' vicious influence on the Arab World. Robertson's and Falwell's alleged connections to thugs and dictators should further reinforce the truism that oppression never occurs in a vacuum and thus should never be challenged in isolation.

In the remainder of this chapter, however, I will redirect attention to the anti-Arab vitriol engendered by dispensationalist TV personalities and examine how the influence of those TV personalities shouldn't be considered a new phenomenon in the United States. The influence of crooks and rogues is part and parcel of the symbiosis between American Christianity and capitalism.

A Pitched Battle against Evil

Some Christian Zionists have made a career of disparaging Arabs. Dispensationalism derives much of its philosophy from an end-time theory that, like Albert Camus' The Plague, revels in the mass death of faceless Arabs. Not since the days when segregation was justified theologically by its practitioners has a religious tenet been so overwhelmingly racist in the

United States. The God constructed by dispensationalists is a god of hate, vengeful and committed to the survival of White supremacy.

Much of the language Christian Zionists use appropriates Arabs into a tribulationist paradigm that construes them as evil impediments to Jewish repatriation in the Holy Land; in turn, according to this theory, Arabs are both godless and enemies of God. As the *Chattanooga Times Free Press* observes of DeLay, "They may be talking peace and Palestinian statehood in Washington, but DeLay is touring the Holy Land with a message for Israeli hawks: the war is not over, and the United States is Israel's brother in arms in a pitched battle against evil."[13] DeLay spoke with his typical sense of immediacy and exaggeration: "Standing up for good against evil is very hard work; it costs money and blood."[14] It is utterly shocking that an American politician—the recent House Majority Leader, no less—can, in the twenty-first century, refer to a vastly diverse people numbering 300 million as "evil." To be sure, DeLay often is criticized, particularly by liberals and progressives, but rarely for his genocidal attitude toward Arabs. DeLay, in other words, isn't necessarily the scandal here; that he isn't disparaged daily as part of a wide-ranging campaign against his support for ethnic cleansing is the more troublesome scandal.

Nobody, however, is more active than Pat Robertson. Much of his time, when he isn't trying to desecularize American society, is dedicated to procuring the Occupied Territories for the exclusive use of Israel, what he calls "the spiritual capitol of the world."[15] He bases his politics largely on religious interpretation. About the proposed division of Jerusalem, he says, "Now Jerusalem is the capitol of Israel. The Jews took East Jerusalem in fulfillment of the prophecy by Jesus Christ. It was made 2,500 years ago."[16] He continues, invoking fear as his rhetorical strategy:

> I am telling you, ladies and gentlemen, this is suicide. If the United States, and I want you to hear me very clearly, if the United States

takes a role in ripping half of Jerusalem away from Israel and giving it to Yasser Arafat and a group of terrorists, we are going to see the wrath of God fall on this nation that will make tornadoes look like a Sunday school picnic. We have not begun to see how bad it's going to get if we are leading an attempt to do that.[17]

Robertson occasionally engages in some secular observations, as when, decrying "Muslim vandals," he stated, "Of course, we, like all right-thinking people, support Israel because Israel is an island of democracy, an island of individual freedom, an island of the rule of law, and an island of modernity in the midst of a sea of dictatorial regimes, the suppression of individual liberty, and a fanatical religion intent on returning to the feudalism of 8th Century Arabia."[18] I'm relieved after reading Robertson to learn that only Muslims are fanatical, because it would be terrifying if American Christians engaged in the same sort of messianic fanaticism. If that were the case, it wouldn't be long before foreign policy was conducted based not on the national interest but on the basis of a particular interpretation of Scripture. And if that happened, then we'd have absolutely no moral or rhetorical leverage in criticizing Osama bin Laden.

LaHaye also is fond of dehumanizing all Arabs and Muslims and pressing the American government to abandon its secular nonsense in conducting foreign policy. About 9/11, he writes,

We should not be deceived by the well publicized belief in "Allah" as though the Muslim and Arab world truly believe in God. The god they believe in is definitely NOT the God of the Bible, either in the Old or New Testaments. Not only do they practice the unbiblical concept of advancing their beliefs by the sword, they also do not acknowledge Jesus as the Son of God and the Messiah or savior of the world. This act of terrorism is a godless act of rage that is not sanctioned by the God of the Bible. It was a despicable act of hate that can best be described as the ultimate act of a godless man's inhumanity to his fellow man. What could be worse than saying, "If you don't believe as I do, then I have the right to kill you?"[19]

I'm even more relieved after reading LaHaye that Christians don't believe in advancing their beliefs by the sword. I will rush to get the news to the parents of dead Iraqi children and the Palestinians sleeping in tents in squalid refugee camps. In addition, LaHaye is almost correct when he writes, "What could be worse than saying, 'If you don't believe as I do, then I have the right to kill you?'." I can think of only one thing that's worse: saying, "If you don't believe as I do, then God will unleash His eternal wrath on you and slaughter your entire family."

At least Robertson and LaHaye acknowledge, even if it is unintentional, that there is a people called *Palestinians*. LaHaye partner Thomas Ice takes a different approach: "Perhaps the most maddening term that I hear today is related to the term 'Palestinian'."[20] There is no such thing as a Palestinian, Ice argues, referencing Joan Peters's long-discredited *From Time Immemorial* (1984) to prove it. Even if there were Palestinians, according to Ice, they, like all Arabs, would merely be agents of Satan: "As believers in God and His Word, we should not be surprised that Satan and the world system is anti-Israel. We should also not be surprised that in spite of the justice of Israel's cause, the international media echoes [sic] Satan's voice instead of God's. Israel is God's elect nation and He worlds out a major aspect of His plan for history through them."[21] Ice takes conspiracy theory to an unprecedented level here, but the premise of his argument is consistent with other dispensationalist writings: that the Arabs must be stopped at all costs from ruining God's designs for the world.

While it is satisfying emotionally to poke fun at the Christian Zionists, we are better served taking seriously their worldview and its effects on American culture and politics. I am curious, first of all, about how the passages I have cited illustrate a philosophy any different or less dangerous than the one employed by so-called Islamists. The Islamists are Muslim and the dispensationalists are Christian. The differences essentially end there. Leaders of both groups instill fear and fervor in their disciples in order to advance a dangerous political agenda in which random violence is legitimized as the will of God.

Dispensationalists and their apologists will invoke 9/11 to show that Islamists are more dangerous. I would suggest that people check the record of dispensationalists, where they will find not only discursive evidence of equal hatred but also a plethora of violent endeavors either undertaken by dispensationalists or encouraged by them. These endeavors include two invasions of Iraq and a sanctions policy that killed innumerable civilians there; support for apartheid in South Africa; the settlement of Palestine and the ethnic cleansing of Palestinians; financial support to dictators such as Zaire's Mobutu Sese Seko and Guatemala's Ríos Montt; encouragement of genocide against Guatemala's Indians; trade in blood diamonds through dubious corporations; lobbying on behalf of Nicaragua's Contras; and the proliferation of a genocidal racism against Muslims and Arab Orthodox Christians. In fact, it appears that bin Laden could learn a thing or two from the Christianists' efficiency and their ability to affect the decisions of American leaders.

The other main difference between Christianists and Islamists is how they manage to implement their vicious agendas. For the most part, Islamists live in nations where religious fundamentalism is brutally suppressed by dictators fearful that their rule will be undermined. Islamist leaders thus conceive plans underground and recruit people unassociated with any government to carry out their decisions. There is no middleman in this situation. Al-Qaeda, for instance, makes a plan to attack a residential tower in Saudi Arabia and assigns the task to one of its members. Its leaders, then, are directly implicated in the resulting violence.

Christianists, on the other hand, work within an ostensibly democratic system, so they elect politicians to carry out their agendas, or they pressure politicians to make decisions in keeping with their geopolitical desires. Although George Bush Jr. is an evangelical Christian, he is not a dispensationalist, but so much of his electoral and philosophical support comes from dispensationalists that he is hampered by their desires in nearly every decision he makes. He thus curtails criticism of Ariel Sharon when his dispensationalist base threatens to withdraw support if he expresses any unease with Israel's behavior in the Occupied Territories. Likewise, he admits to using God to help him make hard decisions, like whether or not to invade Iraq. According to his messianic schema, he was compelled to execute God's wishes and topple Saddam Hussein. All Christianists supported this unnecessary war by claiming God had willed it. I fail to see how such garbage differs from the Islamism that the Christianists repeatedly condemn as evil.

Just because Christianist leaders don't command their own mercenaries doesn't make them less complicit than the Islamists in unwarranted bloodshed. Their influence on, and support of, all the terrible American foreign policy decisions in the past two decades have been crucial to the formulation of those decisions. Equally important has been their influence on the resurgence of American racism, as well as its evolution as a theological illness that overwhelmingly targets Arabs and Muslims. Messianism has always been present in the United States, dating to the settlement of New England. It has evolved continually throughout the centuries, as do all ideologies, but its fundamental premise that God must command the actions of politicians remains unchanged. Anybody who has illusions about the consequences of this premise should ask forgiveness from the 10 million indigenous people slaughtered during the formation of the United States. Then that person should visit Palestine and work to ensure that a corresponding genocide will not be repeated.

Give a Dollar, Support a Settler

According to the *Washington Post*, 400,000 evangelicals visited
Israel in 2003.[22] The International Fellowship of Christians and
Jews has raised over $100 million for Israel in the past decade.
One dispensationalist church in Arvada, Colorado, contributes
$100,000 annually to Israel. The group Christian Friends for
Israeli Communities funds programs in over a third of the
Jewish settlements in the Occupied Territories.[23] A Christian
Solidarity for Israel rally in Washington in 2002 drew several
thousand participants as well as a number of prominent
politicians. According to Ken Silverstein and Michael Scherer,
"thanks to the top-level connections and grassroots activism
of evangelical Christians, U.S. policy in the Middle East has
never been so closely aligned with Israel as it is under the
administration of George W. Bush."[24] The Israeli Embassy
in Washington "has an 'Office of Interreligious Affairs' that
hosts monthly briefings for evangelicals, welcomes church
bus tours, and organizes breakfasts."[25] There are over 200
Christian Zionist organizations in North America; combined,
those organizations have contributed over $100 million to the
settlement of Jews in the Occupied Territories and millions
more to political campaigns in the United States. About the
Arab opposition to such groups, Franklin Graham proclaimed
that the "Arabs will not be happy until every Jew is dead. They
all hate the Jews. God gave the land to Jews. The Arabs will
never accept that."[26]

Jews of all political persuasions have myriad reactions to
the Christian Zionists. Israeli prime ministers dating back to
Menachem Begin have pandered to them, providing Christianist
leaders with expensive presents (William Blackstone even had
a forest in Galilee named after him). The Israeli Embassy in
Washington receives busloads of Christianists and the Israeli
government lavishes them with attention when they visit
Israel as part of organized tour groups. Numerous Jewish

intellectuals, however, express discomfort with the Christianist–
Israeli alliance, including Robert O. Freedman, Professor
of Political Science at Baltimore Hebrew University, and
Gershom Gorenberg, author of *The End of Days*. Practically
all progressive Jews dislike the alliance, as do a good number
of ultra-Orthodox. Mainstream Zionists have mixed reactions,
although the Zionist Organization of America (ZOA) and the
Anti-Defamation League (ADL) both have encouraged it. Most
mainstream Zionist organizations foster the alliance or refuse
to criticize it. Abraham Foxman of the ADL claims, "Israel is
fighting for security, isolated in a hypocritical world. It's no
time to say [to evangelicals], 'You're not a perfect friend'"[27]
(bracketed addition in original quote).

Foxman, however, has gone beyond neutrality. According
to Silverstein and Scherer, "the ADL has remained silent on
[Jerry] Falwell and in May ran an advertisement in major
newspapers that reprinted an article written by Ralph Reed,
former head of the Christian Coalition, that was titled 'We
People of Faith Stand Firmly with Israel.' And in July, the
Zionist Organization of America honored Pat Robertson for
his work on behalf of Israel."[28] The corrupt political culture
of the United States, cultivated by the ethics of profit, partly
drives groups like the ADL and ZOA to abandon any sense
of decency in the interests of temporary political expediency,
even if they realize (as they should) that their alliance with
Christianists is shallow and bound to fail. Americans are taught
from birth by the political signifiers in popular entertainment
and corporate media to protect their interests even if it requires
the betrayal of friends or some other abandonment of ethics.
Indeed, the ethics of political and financial profit supersedes the
organic values of interpersonal well-being, and so Americans
tacitly are encouraged to seek whatever immediate pay-offs
available even if it means fostering a dangerous political
movement. In accepting Christianist support, then, Foxman
isn't necessarily contravening the interests of his own Zionist

movement; rather, he is supplementing that movement with fundamental American values. He also illustrates quite clearly the desperation it requires to defend Israel in the face of insurmountable evidence of its crimes, a desperation that also is evident in the popularity of *From Time Immemorial* among mainstream Zionists.

Moreover, the ADL and ZOA forget or ignore that most Christianists don't actually support Israel, at least not as Israel currently is recognized by the international community. They support the settlement of the Occupied Territories, which is an entirely different matter that further implicates their versions of Zionism and renders them complicit rhetorically in ethnic cleansing. Foxman should be reminded that there are hundreds of organizations (many of them Palestinian) supporting Israel's right to exist peacefully in the Middle East. Serious questions, therefore, arise about why the ADL has chosen to accept the help of a community that has as its stated aim the removal of all Palestinians from the Holy Land. By aligning themselves with Christianists, the ADL and ZOA render themselves hypocrites every time they claim to support peace in the Middle East. They also have damaged their goal of empowering Jews since the foundation of much Christianist thought is the desire to convert Jews to Christianity (or at least those who remain after God has slaughtered the majority of them).

Christianists also have influenced the conduct of numerous American politicians, as when Senator James Inhofe (R-OK) told the US Senate that he supports Israel "because God said so."[29] A *Newsweek* story illustrates some of the power Christianists exert on American politicians, including the President:

> In April 2002, Christian Zionists were infuriated when the president, in a Rose Garden speech after a particularly heinous suicide bombing in Israel, seemed to equate Palestinian terrorism with the Israeli Army's actions on the West Bank. Not only did he not call for the ouster of Yasir Arafat (a goal of hard-liners for years), Bush sent Secretary of State Colin Powell to the region to

meet with the Palestinian. "That was more than those of us who support Israel could take," said Gary Bauer, a leading Christian Zionist.

A plague of e-mails and letters descended upon the White House. Engineered by Bauer, Falwell, Pat Robertson and others, several hundred thousand messages flooded the administration, urging it to lay off Sharon and jettison Arafat. In their regular conference call with the White House, evangelical leaders made the same case. "Well, let's just say that the Middle East comes up during most of these calls," says Falwell. Other—perhaps more powerful—voices chimed in: congressional leaders and neoconservatives in and out of the administration. White House Press Secretary Ari Fleischer soon was calling Sharon a "man of peace."[30]

The influence of the Christianist community is in many ways a natural progression of American politics, in which the relationship between capitalism and religion has always been strong, as has the power of Messianism in the American imagination. We shouldn't be too surprised that a bizarre religious doctrine helps dictate American foreign policy since the United States was constructed on the bizarre philosophy of divine expansionism that later transmuted into Manifest Destiny. The existence of such a concept in a culture of money-driven political adventurism was bound to induce a religious awakening no less dangerous than the Islamism American leaders constantly denigrate as backward and barbaric. And as long as the United States' product-driven marketplace alienates the majority of its consumers and bolsters a system in which Americans are impoverished financially and spiritually, people will continue to accept crackpot theologies in order to find meaning in a seemingly meaningless world. God can at least explain the unnecessary violence in which the United States is continually engaged by offering Americans the comfort that it is all part of a divinely authorized plan leading to paradise, not more poverty and alienation.

I would be remiss not to reiterate that not all evangelicals are dispensationalists. I have met many evangelicals who support the creation of a Palestinian state and, as with any community that numbers over 50 million, every segment of political opinion in the United States is represented in the evangelical community. Most Black evangelical churches, for instance, are uninterested in LaHaye and Jenkins's *Left Behind* series and take no formal position on the Middle East.[31] Other evangelical congregations find it presumptuous for humans to implement a plan of God's making and thus of His responsibility. At the end of 2003, the Fuller Seminary, a leading evangelical institution in Pasadena, launched a $1 million project to foster dialogue with Muslims. "The Fuller project," according to the *Los Angeles Times*, "is intended to develop practical peacemaking practices for Christians and Muslims, publish a book about them and train local communities in their use. It is the latest of several efforts that Fuller has launched since Sept. 11 to build bridges with Muslims."[32]

Christianists, on the other hand, have done everything possible since 9/11 to create discord among Christians and Muslims. In a sense, they have been the Bush administration's dream come true: Without the uncritical support of Christianist TV personalities and their followers, Bush would have a difficult time justifying the binaristic dementia that has defined his foreign policy. And yet they have caused the Bush administration some headaches, as when they vowed to torpedo the so-called Roadmap to Peace if Bush didn't withdraw his endorsement of it. Only time will tell if the Christianists merely represent a low point, among many, in American history or if their influence will continue to grow. The best we can wish for is the dysfunction we see today, because if the Christianists continue to acquire influence then there won't be any need for the rapture, because they will have destroyed the world before God has time to plan its demise.

In Conclusion: the Reflections of a Christian?

I am a Christian. The fact that this word, *Christian*, is today so often associated with dispensationalists brings me great shame. I've spent much time contemplating what label I might use to describe my religion that doesn't imply such an association. I've created a comfortable enough space for my identity by attempting to reject labels, religious or otherwise, in conceptualizing who I am in the modern United States. I don't go to church, I don't pray, and I don't have much of a relationship with either Jesus or God, so what might possibly compel me to ever self-identify as a *Christian* in the first place? I believe in the existence of a God and I admire Jesus tremendously as a historical figure, but I am highly skeptical of organized religion and have therefore never been religious. Nor do I plan on ever becoming religious.

Yet this rationalization for avoiding labels leaves me a bit uncomfortable. It might work for somebody who was born Christian but not Arab; but for me, an Arab Christian, the word *Christian* is important to who I am, even if it means virtually nothing to me theologically. Perhaps this is true because for Arab Christians, Christianity is our indigenous religion. It is a religion that was created in our backyard and forms an enormous part of our cultural identity. The central figure of our religion is a prophet revered by our Muslim brethren. Our churches have stood for centuries, sometimes millennia. The pictures of Jesus in those churches show him with brown skin and wavy hair, unlike the blond, baby-faced Jesus one finds in American churches. Our Jesus is tough, with Semitic features. Our Jesus looks like an Arab.

There is something special about being part of the world's oldest Christian community, living precisely where all the prophets lived and where the great events taught to us in Sunday school occurred. (Even if these things are mythical, they create great pride, as do the mythical achievements of any community's past.) We are proud to be Christian, even if many of us aren't very religious. It's one of the funny paradoxes of our community that despite our 2,000-year attachment to Christianity, the majority of Arab Christians attend church to socialize—one of the main functions of our gatherings, in fact, is to introduce youngsters of the opposite sex to one another. Ours is not a demanding religion. We are pressured far more by the strictures of our conservative Arab culture. After services we drink and smoke *argeela*. It is the cultural, not religious, aspect of our community that demands we conform to a certain code of behavior. To us, *Christian* means something much different than it does to American Christians. It means being in the minority, among both Arabs and Westerners. It means that our indigenous religion is still in existence. And it means that we can't quite detach ourselves from our religion, a move many of our American friends seem to accomplish so easily.[33]

But I can't totally shake off the discomfort of being *Christian* in the United States when the term has, for me, such negative connotations. After endless hours of research into the dispensationalists, I still don't really understand this new version of Christianity that, like so many things that were created in the United States, is so bold and brash with a great sense of urgency and a reckless devotion to fulfilling its mission. It seems to me that the dispensationalists draw much of their strength from the pioneering ethos of the United States, an ethos inundated with messianistic undertones and a colonialist spirit. I also suspect that this new Christianity was an inevitable consequence of the marriage between leadership and money— corrupt dispensationalists, like many religious figures, have found a way to enrich themselves while teaching subservience to the only people with the power to usurp them.

Either way, it is a version of Christianity that is shocking in its ability to induce hatred of Arabs and in its dedication to ending the world as soon as possible. In this version of Christianity, billions of Muslims, Hindus, Buddhists, and

Taoists exist only to be slaughtered by the forces of Good before being sent to Hell for eternity. In the shameful history of our world's religious intolerance, this new Christianity has managed to achieve a new standard. For this reason, I like to call it Christianism, for if Islamism is to be continually lambasted as a hateful ideology and a threat to world security, then this new Christianity deserves a similar designation. For I am a Christian, a descendant of the first Christians. And I'll be damned if I sacrifice this identity for the benefit of theirs.

6
Redressing Abu Ghraib: the Racism of Denial

When *60 Minutes II* and the *Washington Post* released the gruesome pictures taken by American soldiers in Iraq's Abu Ghraib Prison in May 2004, many Americans knew the military mission in that nation was far from accomplished. Nor, a great many Americans realized, would it ever be accomplished. Those who said from the outset that the invasion had no chance of succeeding may have felt a bittersweet vindication, for the photos of Abu Ghraib not only proved that Americans engage in the sort of behavior for which other nations repeatedly are condemned (and sometimes invaded), but also damaged the moral high ground American leaders reserve for their exclusive use when they wish to grandstand about the degeneracy of others in order to mystify some immoral action (e.g., preemptively invading a sovereign nation). Ultimately, the national outrage over Abu Ghraib proved temporary, as neoconservative media took only a few days to refocus on Arab immorality and corporate media in general stopped short of interesting analysis and eventually let the story disappear.

When the scandal was at its height, public criticism of the soldiers and the administration that sent them to occupy Iraq was so intense that George Bush was forced to appear on Arabic television and apologize. Almost everybody in the days following the release of the photos seemed horrified and condemnation of the abusive soldiers was decidedly nonpartisan. Politicians and media personalities decried the outrage of the abuses, the immorality of them, the aberration they represented, and the failure of military leaders to prevent them. Yet the racism of the abuses was hardly mentioned. I suspect that most politicians and media commentators kept silent about the possibility of a racialist dynamic in Abu Ghraib because it would have meant at least tacitly acknowledging a racialist dynamic in the American decision to invade Iraq. Only the most naive among us, however, would discuss seriously the scandal at Abu Ghraib without examining how the ethnicity of the victims played a critical role in the torture as well as in the American reaction to that torture.

One of the most enduring images from Abu Ghraib is that of Lynddie England holding a leash attached to the neck of a naked Iraqi man, who is lying on the floor in obvious pain. England's expression appears remarkably subdued, even blank, as she stares without emotion at the naked prisoner.

On the Canadian program *Counterspin*, Sherene Razack of the University of Toronto aptly described this image as visual symbolism of a "racial relationship." By using the phrase "racial relationship," Razack identified the overt symbolism of Abu Ghraib that was almost universally overlooked in corporate American media. The brown, bearded man is naked before his White captor. He is subdued on a leash, a device usually reserved for animals, and made to lie on the floor, although the White captor seems to be trying to pull him onto all fours, thus to force the man to emulate a dog and complete the act of dehumanization.

The juxtaposition of England and the prisoner is the perfect metonym for the invasion of Iraq in total, in which the uncivilized brown people were to be subdued for their own good by their enlightened (and benighted) Western liberators. The subjugation also is mental, for much of the reason Bush was able to sell the invasion is because of the longstanding

construction of Arabs as incompetent and therefore dependent
on Western patrimony, whether or not they realize it. The
brown man is to be constrained by the White master and
moved by force in any direction the master chooses. Each
direction invariably results in humiliation. And he is nude
before the master, exposed in all his flaws and having no agency
in the presence of the uniformed captor. In this case, the master
is a woman, offering us further symbolic imagery of colonial
discourse: the invasion was a nurturing expression of concern
for those whose future is too important to leave in their own
hands. In fact, I'm struck most that the picture of England is
symbolic of colonization in general, as it has existed for over
five centuries. The picture captures with painful accuracy the
discursive and physical effects of almost every colonial errand
undertaken in North America, Asia, and Africa. England may
be nothing more than an ignorant backcountry gal who was
seduced by the appeal of power, but the architects of the
Iraq invasion, as I will illustrate later, were well aware of the
symbolic underpinnings to which England and the majority
of the American public appeared oblivious.

A major reason for this obliviousness is the weak analysis of
the Abu Ghraib scandal provided by newspaper columnists and
cable-news talking heads. The columnists and talking heads
who expressed outrage over the behavior of the American
soldiers in Abu Ghraib generally did so by conceptualizing the
torture as an aberration having nothing to do with enlightened
American values. In providing such analyses, they completely
missed the issue of ethnicity and religion and unfairly blamed
the perpetrators of the torture for everything that occurred
in Abu Ghraib. In fact, most rationalizations of Abu Ghraib
insinuated, or stated outright, that the United States is more
civilized than and therefore superior to the Arab World. Better
analyses would have examined the United States' long history of
torture and implicated the racist discourse that led us into Iraq
and thus facilitated the torture of Iraqi civilians. I would go a

step further and argue that, ultimately, Abu Ghraib reveals the inevitable outcome of predicating a nation-state on settlement, genocide, displacement, slavery, apartheid, exceptionalism, and religious messianism. That is to say, the abuse of so-called inferior peoples isn't now an aberration and never has been; there would be no United States if the abuse of countless Others had never happened. To forget this history is tantamount to validating it. As Abu Ghraib shows us, historical amnesia or supercilious denial is never without consequences.

Corporate media response to the Abu Ghraib scandal was infused with both tacit and explicit anti-Arab racism that manifested itself in three main forms (although other racist approaches also were evident in the weeks following the release of the pictures): by dismissing the torture of the Iraqis in Abu Ghraib as little more than "hazing," on par with a fraternity prank; by arguing that the tortured prisoners deserved it; and by justifying the behavior of the soldiers by pointing out that Arabs behave worse than Americans. I take up these points in the three sections which follow.

Just "Hazing"?

Much of the rightwing media responded to the pictures from Abu Ghraib by downplaying their significance, an approach that supplemented the already indisputable dehumanization of Arabs. Rush Limbaugh, with his typical sense of eloquence and propriety, opined, "You know, if you look at—if you, really, if you look at these pictures, I mean, I don't know if it's just me, but it looks just like anything you'd see Madonna or Britney Spears do onstage. Maybe I'm—yeah. And get [a National Endowment for the Arts] grant for something like this. I mean, this is something that you can see onstage at Lincoln Center from an NEA grant, maybe on Sex and the City—the movie."[1] Tom DeLay managed to dehumanize victims of police brutality in addition to Arabs: "I'm sure that

our committees are going to be asking the right questions
… . But a full-fledged congressional investigation—that's
like saying we need an investigation every time there's police
brutality on the street."[2]

Tammy Bruce captures what seems to be the predominant
neoconservative perception of Abu Ghraib, writing, "I consider
the vast majority of what happened at Abu Ghraib to be
hazing—nothing more, nothing less. For weeks, all of us have
been shouted at by the liberal media about how awful the
events were, how having a man stripped naked in front of a
woman was 'torture,' how making a prisoner wear women's
underwear was 'horrific,' and the most recent 'charge' of
forcing men to wear maxi-pads."[3] Yet in her article Bruce
expresses support for torture, thereby making her case for
"hazing" rather unconvincing, and calling into question her
strategy for dealing with Arabs: "Now don't get me wrong—I
believe when it comes to al-Qaeda leadership and operatives,
anything goes. I don't care if you put women's underwear on
their heads, or frankly, even pull out a few fingernails of those
responsible for mass murder, to unmask their continuing plans
for the genocide of civilized peoples. It's called 'torture lite,'
it works, and I'm all for whatever it takes to get information,
and yes, to punish and annihilate terrorist leadership around
the world."[4]

Bruce, who conflates Saudi terrorists with Iraqi civilians,
seems unaware that few of the prisoners in Abu Ghraib were
demonstrably connected to al-Qaeda, implicated in terrorism,
or responsible for mass murder. Indeed, the vast majority of
them were civilians arrested by mistake or in the interests of
serving the colonial authority in its subjugation of a legitimate
Iraqi resistance. Bruce illustrates that the "hazing" argument
is reliant totally on the reduction of all Arabs to potential
terrorists, which is the very reason the prisoners in Abu Ghraib
were arrested. Even in offering a backhanded criticism of the
Abu Ghraib torturers, Bruce manages to articulate an egregious

racism in the service of mystifying American aggression and highlighting Arab barbarity: "It is worth remembering, we are the greatest nation on Earth specifically because acts which are tantamount to hazing are surprising, and unacceptable, to most people."[5]

Other neoconservative analyses similarly downgraded the extent of the crimes in Abu Ghraib or absolved American imperialists of any responsibility for the behavior of the soldiers they dispatched to undertake a preemptive invasion by dehumanizing the people of Iraq. "The majority of American soldiers are professional, disciplined and are risking their lives to win a war," intones the *Wall Street Journal*. "The military has its faults and bad actors, but over the decades it has shown itself to be one of America's most accountable institutions," the *Journal* concludes.[6] Writing in Bill Kristol's *Weekly Standard*, Richard Starr argues that "'sodomizing a detainee with a chemical light' is evidence of a lack of humanity, not a lack of training."[7] The *Journal* and *Weekly Standard* both seem constrained by their support of the invasion in the face of the evidence of torture. In turn, they both end up supporting a failed position that protects the anti-Arab racism both publications are guilty of articulating in the months before the invasion and after the occupation. The soldiers who engaged in torture were acting with the same level of humanity as that illustrated to them by neoconservative politicians, not to mention the neoconservative writers many soldiers are fond of reading.

Any illusions about how neoconservatives perceive Arabs were shattered upon the release of the Abu Ghraib pictures. Neoconservatives overwhelmingly view Arabs as stupid, barbaric, savage, childish, and prone to irrational violence. Once evidence surfaced of the same qualities in the soldiers that neoconservatives continually lionize, the assumptions about Arab inferiority and the natural right of American soldiers to dehumanize them were suddenly given no pretense and, in some cases, were articulated with a nastiness unseen in mainstream American life since George Wallace's presidential candidacy. The notion that American soldiers merely "hazed" the Iraqi prisoners is remarkably mean-spirited, akin to conceptualizing the torture of Abner Louima as mere horseplay that got out of hand because of Louima's physical weakness. And the notion that the soldiers in Abu Ghraib were acting in a manner contrary to American values, military or civilian, evinces stupendous ignorance, akin to dismissing the genocide of Indians as an unfortunate byproduct of the generosity of the American spirit. The fact that Louima's murder was conceptualized as overenthusiastic horseplay and that the genocide of Indians is frequently dismissed as the necessary cost of progress highlights the fundamental problem of Abu Ghraib: that it should not have surprised anybody who is aware of how vigorously politicians, children's textbooks, and corporate media personalities whitewash America's past misadventures.

The *Los Angeles Times*, unbelievably, ran a commentary by Midge Decter that would have been more appropriate in *Soldier of Fortune*. Decter writes, "If war is hell, warfare as currently conducted against mostly unseen bands of enemies in civilian dress hiding among bona fide civilians—and not even faintly comparable to the Civil War or other American wars of recent memory—is its own special kind of nightmare. Added to this nightmare is the knowledge that if we cannot extirpate them in their foreign hiding places, we will have to deal with them on our own shores."[8] Decter forgets that in Iraq the Americans are foreigners, just as she appears unaware that her distinction between "bona fide civilians" and "terrorists" is meaningless when her pronoun usage indicates that she views all Iraqis as terrorists, a prerequisite to finding a moral rationale for torturing them. Noting that during the invasion and occupation "American troops have been almost unbelievably civilized," Decter explains,

Aside from the part this ersatz scandal no doubt will be made to play in the Democratic presidential campaign, this tempest in a teapot about the brutal behavior of a small group of young thugs in wartime says something disturbing about us as a people. This country was assaulted and went to war and may be at war for a long time, for the terrorists who are out to get us have found support and will be provided with ever more dangerous weapons in and by countries beyond Iraq.[9]

Decter is under the illusion that Iraqis have attacked the United States, when, by all available evidence, the opposite is true. In dismissing the torture scandal as "ersatz," she devalues the people of Iraq and constructs a moral context in which they can all be reduced to terrorists poised to "get" the United States. It is this strange mix of confidence and paranoia that underlies the neoconservative response to the Abu Ghraib scandal: faulty evidence of Iraqi aggression is used to validate behavior that was employed in another framework as a pretext to send the nation to war on humanitarian grounds.

Another underlying feature of this neoconservative response is an anger that Arabs refuse to accept the generosity of their American occupiers. This anger inevitably is combined with a condemnation of Arab propaganda, apparently the only means of information to which Arabs are exposed. In this type of argument, Arabs are stripped of their intellectual agency because they are portrayed as mindless dupes who are easily persuaded by the congenital anti-Americanism of their leaders. An article in *FrontPageMag.com* by Lieutenant Colonel Gordon Cucullu exemplifies such a position:

Naturally al-Jazeera and other "Arab Street" propaganda organs have expressed terrible indignation over this incident. The hyperbolic comparisons to the Nazis and, oddly, "Zionists" are popping up everywhere. Arabs, we hear are "outraged and inflamed." "See," leftist academics and Arabist ex-diplomats say, "they are going to hate us even more now."

From a practical standpoint, it is difficult to see *how*. For decades, if not centuries, Arab peoples have been pawns of the mullahs in their mosques. They have been puppets of tyrants and dictators who control all media and most their thoughts and behavior. They danced in the streets in joy when the Twin Towers collapsed. They bounce on the hoods of destroyed Humvees and drag American bodies through the streets.

Until they begin to wise-up to the fact that they are thwarting those who are fighting to liberate them, I worry less about the Arab Street losing its "good will" than I would fret about a recurring Ice Age. For the short term, their hatred is a given. Slowly, methodically, we may be able to change that perception. But it took centuries to mold and may take as long to heal.[10]

The notion that only backward, Third World peoples engage in propaganda has become a truism among most Americans. Cucullu, for instance, is unaware that his entire argument is little more than a recapitulation of American propaganda, more specifically the propaganda generated by the White House and Fox News. Of course, lack of awareness is the primary qualification one needs to repeat propaganda. I would argue that, overwhelmingly, the Arabs Cucullu berates as ignorant consumers of propaganda have a much better understanding of why the invasion occurred than do Cucullu and his enlightened colleagues. In any case, Cucullu is fighting a losing battle, because any strategy of intercultural dialogue that is premised on the explicit superiority of one of the parties will never advance beyond the acrimony the dialogue is constructed to generate.

Outraged by the Outrage

Using the obtuse intellectual context identified above, some neoconservatives simply defended the torture of Iraqi civilians by claiming that they deserved it. The most infamous of these defenses arose from Senator James Inhofe (R-OK), who told a US Senate hearing, "I'm probably not the only one up at this table that is more outraged by the outrage than we are by the treatment. These prisoners, you know they're

not there for traffic violations. If they're in cellblock 1-A or
1-B, these prisoners, they're murderers, they're terrorists,
they're insurgents. Many of them probably have American
blood on their hands and here we're so concerned about the
treatment of those individuals."[11] Inhofe added that "a lot of
the American people don't know what animals those people
are."[12] In an interview with USA Today's Walter Shapiro a
few days after his comments, Inhofe referenced the murder of
Nicolas Berg, claiming that "it shows the kind of people we're
dealing with and why we have to get information from these
cellblock people."[13]

Inhofe, described by the New Republic as "one of the
stupidest" members of Congress, expresses one of the worst
forms of anti-Arab racism imaginable (and one that is too
common, for Palestinians were repeatedly called "filthy
animals" on the Don Imus Show in November of 2004). Like
most types of American racism, his discourse is based wholly
on fantasy (70 to 90 per cent of Iraqi prisoners, according to
coalition military intelligence officers, have been arrested by
mistake). The fantasy on which his discourse is based also
conveniently supplements his broader ideological agendas,
including the convergence of church and state, the annexation
of the Occupied Territories by Israel, and the indefinite
occupation of Iraq. In Inhofe's intellectual schema, all Iraqis
are to be represented by the imaginary dangers posed by the
Abu Ghraib prisoners, who, lest we forget, were tortured,
maimed, and killed, although, according to Inhofe's worldview,
it is they who must justify their behavior to their captors.

More important, Inhofe's presumption that anybody in a
prison must be guilty of something dovetails with a particular
type of racism long at play in the United States. It seems, then,
that the United States has in fact exported some of its values
to Iraq, because by dehumanizing and torturing prisoners,
many of whom were criminalized based solely on a racist
paradigm employed by their captors, the soldiers were engaged

in a longstanding American tradition that can be readily explained by disturbingly large portions of the Black, Native, and Hispanic communities. Likewise, Inhofe is acting all-too-American in excusing the torture by referencing the inhumanity of the victims, who, just as the philosophical apparatus of the prison system encourages, lose all agency once incarcerated.

In Abu Ghraib, we have an example of quintessential colonial behavior: The occupier engages in horrible violence while crafting laws to legitimize that violence and criminalize any violence that might occur in the resistance. The occupier criminalizes actions that it knows will be inevitable, such as looting and stone throwing. The occupier imposes an alien legal structure on the colonized and introduces it by force, without the benefit of education. The occupier rounds up an enormous amount of the colonized and stigmatizes them as criminals and terrorists. Once stigmatized as subhuman the colonized are tortured and humiliated. The occupiers' violence remains legal. If the torture is discovered by the occupiers' populace, a brief scandal will ensue but it won't take long for the occupiers' politicians to rationalize the occupiers' behavior as a minor flaw in an otherwise glorious mission. The legal subjection of the colonized will grow more intense. The prison will continue to symbolize to the occupiers' populace an ideological space in which the colonized necessarily assume the guilt of their existence. The torture of the colonized will continue.

As we saw in previous chapters, much of the discourse of international relations in the United States subordinates Arabs to American sensibilities, so it is nearly impossible to have a fruitful discussion about the "racial relationship" in existence in Abu Ghraib because the discussion will inevitably remain focused on immaterial issues like the guilt of the tortured. A more sophisticated viewpoint might ask who defines guilt and who enforces conformity to that definition. Or, we might note that guilt, in any case, doesn't matter, because torture is unethical regardless of the crimes of the victim. The most important perspective we can raise, however, is that of accountability: what right did the United States have in the first place to invade and occupy a sovereign nation? Who mandated it the right to impose its alien legal structure on Iraqis and then arrest thousands of civilians? And why are some of its politicians claiming that there exists some divine right to extract information by whatever means necessary to enhance the success of an unjust mission? These types of perspectives rarely are heard because Arabs, in Iraq and the United States, usually are confined to the discursive frameworks provided us by the dominant society, the same society that effected the war we wish to question.

In making his outrageous statements, Inhofe reveals to us the invariably violent underside of imperative patriotism. According to his worldview, a worldview enhanced by the ethos of America's divine exceptionalism, no Iraqi is ontologically enough of a human to warrant human rights. Nor is any American ontologically enough of a savage to interact on the basis of intellectual and moral equality with an Iraqi. Inhofe's crude articulation of imperative patriotism would legitimize the hackneyed idea that, according to its newfound preemptive logic, the United States should be invaded, occupied, and subjected to regime change.

They're Worse Than We

One of the more popular responses to the Abu Ghraib scandal is to claim that while the behavior of American soldiers in the prison was unwarranted, or even unsavory, the soldiers weren't acting nearly as badly as Arabs. This claim is supported by the corresponding argument that Americans should be proud that they were so mortified by the Abu Ghraib photos because that mortification is proof of our exceptional values and superior moral credentials. An assumption inevitably arises once this argument is made: That the rest of the world,

Muslims particularly, doesn't have the same moral pedigree as Americans and therefore doesn't so much as flinch when made aware of similar images. Or, the assumption shifts a bit to suggest that the rest of the world, Muslims particularly, has grown so accustomed to mindless violence, as both its recipients and purveyors, that it, unlike Americans, has become desensitized to it.

The *National Review*, for instance, writes,

> Thanks to the involvement of Americans, Abu Ghraib has become synonymous with the abuse and torture of prisoners—one year after the 25 years during which Saddam Hussein used it, and other prisons, to mutilate, not humiliate, and to kill, not torture, thousands upon thousands of Iraqis. Abu Ghraib's late-blooming notoriety is a tribute both to our narcissism and to our sensibilities, in the best sense: America is only interested in the crimes of Americans, and America does consider the brutalizing of prisoners to be a crime.[14]

Beyond the *Review*'s mistaken belief that Iraqis were merely humiliated and tortured in Abu Ghraib, the philosophical underpinnings of its argument are fascinating, as it appears to suggest that Arabs don't consider "the brutalizing of prisoners to be a crime." Yet in the same passage the *Review* argues that "America is only interested in the crimes of Americans," although we can say with certainty that Americans are aware that humiliation, torture, and murder occur across the globe (even if most aren't aware that the United States sometimes helps facilitate such crimes). So, if Americans are aware that these things exist but care only if they are practiced by or on Americans, then the *Review*'s argument is incorrect. According to its logic, Americans patently *don't* consider the brutalizing of prisoners to be a crime because their selective use of moral outrage undermines any potential claim of compassion. The narcissism the *Review* invokes doesn't connote anything resembling moral strength; rather, it connotes a moral inconsistency that exposes the very worst aspect of exceptionalism, the belief that only American life matters. The same narcissism also nurtures the racist perception of Arabs as prone to acquiescence in the presence of violence.

Unlike the *National Review*, Michael Barone of *U.S. News and World Report* approaches exceptionalism without humor or nuance. His version of exceptionalism simultaneously denounces Arab hypocrisy:

> About the Abu Ghraib abuses there is not much divergence of opinion. Almost all Americans are as disgusted as Bush himself. Americans hold themselves to high standards, and if others hold us to those standards even while they excuse or ignore the far more evil acts of others—like the mass murders and torture of Saddam Hussein's regime—that's a price we must pay. It is essential to determine whether these were the isolated acts of a few miscreants or the result of actions of those higher in the chain of command. It is tragic that these abuses, at least for the moment, are overshadowing the bravery, resourcefulness, and generosity of tens of thousands of Americans in uniform in Iraq.[15]

Before Barone lauded the American goodness always under attack by lesser peoples, he might have asked the following questions: Why don't Americans condemn the United States' racialized prison system, which has become little more than a series of expensive buildings constructed with taxpayer money to house the minorities who are incarcerated for corporate profit? Why don't they condemn the School of the Americas? Why don't they condemn the documented torture of those held illegally at Guantanamo Bay? Why was there so little condemnation in the 1980s of the US-supported and US-trained torturers in Central America? Why didn't they decry the support for Hussein's brutality in the 1980s? Why, for that matter, does Barone think nobody will notice that he advocates a theory of exceptional American goodness while concurrently "excusing" and "ignoring" the mass murder of Iraqis in the 1990s and the murder of them in the very prison he discusses?

As an aside, it's interesting that imperative patriots like Barone refer to the soldiers who engaged in the torture in the same terms that they use to describe Arabs: miscreants, thugs, idiots, freaks, scum. Not only did the soldiers engage in behavior that severely contradicted the imperative patriots' exceptionalist worldview, they also acted in a way that imperative patriots would normally associate with Arabs. Thus the racist discourse that usually is reserved for Arabs was applied to those whose actions were considered indicative of Arab, not American, behavior. To the imperative patriots, the torturer and the tortured became one and the same. A disturbing irony follows: the imperative patriots' racist perception of the Arab World helped facilitate the torture of Arabs; so in associating the torturers with Arabs, the imperative patriots also become implicated in the torture. It also makes them weaker morally than the imaginary Arab subjects of their racism.

Later Barone writes, "America's specialness has been its good fortune in asserting and trying to uphold those ideals earlier than others and having the strength, and therefore the obligation, to advance them around the world."[16] Barone evokes one of the most traditional forms of American racism in arguing, despite evidence to the contrary, that the United States is exceptionally brave and resourceful while those the United States subjugates are untrustworthy and vile. This argument is a dull, inane, and unintelligent repetition of age-old colonialist values, and is so troublesome because it feigns ignorance in order to highlight ostensible moral strength. Barone, though, is beating about the bush. His colleague Mortimer B. Zuckerman seems to have a better grasp of what he really is trying to say:

> The video of the beheading of Nicholas Berg adds yet another layer of horror and cruelty to the record of Islamic fanatics. "Pure Evil," headlined the New York Daily News; "Prisoner Abuse, Iraqi Style," wrote the Boston Herald. It reveals a culture in which "hatred trumps bread," to use Cynthia Ozick's phrase from the Wall Street Journal. A culture that glories in the death of innocents thus makes clear whom we are fighting and why. We are up against people who are incited to suppress the most basic human instinct, which is to live, and are willing to kill themselves in their efforts

to destroy as many innocent civilians as they can. Our culture, which celebrates life, is utterly mystified.[17]

More than Bad Apples

Some corporate media managed to look beyond the silly explanation that Abu Ghraib occurred simply because of some bad apples. *Newsweek* describes a picture in which a hooded man stands naked on a box with outstretched arms and wires dangling from his toes, fingers, and penis. The image belies claims that the torturers acted alone "because the practice shown in that photo is an arcane torture method known only to veterans of the interrogation trade."[18] Darius Rejali, a torture expert, explains, "That's a standard torture. It's called 'the Vietnam.' But it's not common knowledge. Ordinary American soldiers did this, but someone taught them."[19]

Newsweek notes that some images from Abu Ghraib show the use of techniques approved officially at the "highest levels of the government" and that, "as a means of pre-empting a repeat of 9/11, Bush, along with Defense Secretary [Donald] Rumsfeld and Attorney General John Ashcroft, signed off on a secret system of detention and interrogation that opened the door to such methods."[20]

Likewise, *Time* reports,

> Here is what the business [of torture] looks like, separate and apart from the brutality documented at Abu Ghraib prison: since 9/11, according to U.S. officials and former prisoners, detainees under U.S. supervision in Iraq, Afghanistan, and Guantanamo Bay, Cuba, and at undisclosed other locations have been stripped naked, covered with hoods, deprived of sleep and light, and made to stand or sit in painful positions for extended periods. Some have been drugged. Sexual humiliation is not unheard of. Even the Federal Bureau of Prisons has lent a hand in this enterprise. According to a Justice Department inspector-general's report, Muslim detainees at the Brooklyn, N.Y., Metropolitan Detention Center after 9/11 were physically and verbally abused by some staff members. Meanwhile, there have been at least 32 suicide attempts

by Guantanamo detainees, and one of those who tried to commit suicide ended up in a coma. In three cases in Iraq and Afghanistan currently under investigation by the Justice Department, detainees died during or after questioning by the CIA.[21]

The reports from *Newsweek* and *Time*, which do well to reveal other instances of torture, don't really move beyond basic reportage to interrogate the context of Abu Ghraib. That context is drawn from a long history of American torture in Asia, Africa, North America, and, especially in recent times, Latin America. Torture also occurs frequently in prisons and police stations across the country. Any notion, then, that Abu Ghraib was merely a shocking aberration is woefully naive or purposely jingoistic. The very existence of the School of the Americas should be proof enough that torture has long been a part of American foreign policy. Moreover, the existence of a deep-seated anti-Arab racism in a nation in which messianism and the fear of terrorists are so prevalent has created the ideal conditions for the ethical justification of torture against Arabs.

The *Time* report's mention of the Brooklyn Detention Center is important because it illustrates that one needn't go to Iraq to find cases of American torture. The torture of Arabs and Muslims has been happening frequently in the United States since 9/11. In Brooklyn, one former inmate alleges that prison guards inserted a flashlight and pencil into his rectum, a technique eerily reminiscent of the Abner Louima torture. In another case, an inmate was slammed repeatedly into a wall for sport. Michael Isikoff of *Newsweek* reveals that there are "more than 300 hours of secret videotapes from a U.S. prison facility in Brooklyn, N.Y., where many Arab and Muslim detainees were incarcerated in the months after 9/11. On the tapes, according to a report by federal investigators, prison guards slam inmates into walls, twist their arms and wrists and subject them to humiliating strip searches in which, in some cases, male prisoners were forced to stand naked in the presence of female guards; in others, prison guards 'laughed, exchanged suggestive looks and made funny noises'."[22]

This type of behavior clearly parallels that of the Abu Ghraib torturers, and is indicative of a longstanding dehumanization of Arabs in the United States nourished by the myth of divine exceptionalism and contextualized by the godly duty to induce the tribulation. Given the abysmal portrayal of Arabs in American media for the better part of a century, it shouldn't have been surprising that young soldiers in a position of power would abuse those under their control. An article by Joe Klein in *Time* eloquently details how Abu Ghraib was anything but an aberration:

> Faith without doubt leads to moral arrogance, the eternal pratfall of the religiously convinced. We are humble before the Lord, Bush insists. We cannot possibly know His will. And yet, we "know" He's on the side of justice—and we define what justice is. Indeed, we can toss around words like justice and evil with impunity, send off mighty armies to "serve the cause of justice" in other lands and be so sure of our righteousness that the merest act of penitence—an apology for an atrocity—becomes a presidential crisis. "This does not represent the America I know," Bush said of the torturers, as if U.S. soldiers were exempt from the temptations of absolute power that have plagued occupying armies from the beginning of time.[23]

Klein later writes, "A distressing, uninflected righteousness has defined this Administration from the start, and it hasn't been limited to the President. Bush's overheated sense of good vs. evil has been reinforced by the intellectual fantasies of neoconservatives like I. Lewis Libby and Paul Wolfowitz, who serve Bush's two most powerful advisors, Dick Cheney and Donald Rumsfeld."[24]

Those who await a scathing column from Michael Barone or Mortimer B. Zuckerman about the documented American torture in Brooklyn, Guantanamo, and Afghanistan will be highly disappointed, for Barone and Zuckerman flawlessly exemplify the pratfall of the religiously convinced.

Victims of High-flown Morality

It has long been an established fact that torture necessarily is preceded by dehumanization. Even the best mainstream commentaries about the Abu Ghraib scandal fail to properly examine the ubiquitous dehumanization of Arabs in the United States. This dehumanization occurs in movies, news broadcasts, television programs, and talk shows. I would argue that it, above all else, created the sort of environment in which torture in Iraq was bound to occur. The endemic racism, imperative patriotism, and religious fundamentalism we discussed in previous chapters all played a role in influencing American youngsters not only to invade an Arab nation, but to reduce the citizens of that nation to a cartoon-like image of bandits and rogues.

It required a strikingly poor intellect to not realize that the torture of Arabs was imminent. A *Newsweek* report on Tim LaHaye and Jerry Jenkins notes in passing that "the [*Left Behind*] books are a favorite with American soldiers in Iraq."[25] Arabs, as we saw in the previous chapter, are portrayed in that series as stock impediments to the fulfillment of God's plan. Arabs can even be read on a secular level in the novels as savages who require the forcible imposition of a Christian government. As Nicholas D. Kristoff of the *New York Times* observes of the novels, "It's disconcerting to find ethnic cleansing celebrated as the height of piety."[26] It's equally disconcerting that soldiers undertaking an ostensibly humanitarian mission are reading books that define humanitarianism as the extermination of Muslims.

Yet other ideologies also create the sort of racist context that rendered the torture of Arabs imminent. A stunning article by Brian Whittaker of the UK's *Guardian* notes that a viciously racist work of pseudoscience, *The Arab Mind*, by the late Rafael Patai, is not only "the bible of neocon headbangers, but it is also the bible on Arab behaviour for the US military."[27] Whittaker explains that "the book is a classic case of Orientalism which, by focusing on what Edward Said called the 'otherness' of Arab culture, sets up barriers that can then be exploited for political purposes."[28] The book describes Arabs in explicit detail as lazy, sexually obsessed, incurably hostile, and irrationally dedicated to an honor-bound culture. As Whittaker notes, "Writing about Arabs, rather than black people, in these terms apparently makes all the difference between a racist smear and an admirable work of scholarship."[29]

The following passages from Whittaker's article illustrate the influence of *The Arab Mind* in the American military:

> According to one professor at a US military college, *The Arab Mind* is "probably the single most popular and widely read book on the Arabs in the US military". It is even used as a textbook for officers at the JFK special warfare school in Fort Bragg.
>
> In some ways, the book's appeal to the military is easy to understand, because it gives a superficially coherent view of the Arab enemy and their supposed personality defects. It is also readily digestible, uncomplicated by nuances and caveats, and has lots of juicy quotes, a generous helping of sex, and no academic jargon.
>
> Patai died in 1996, but his book was revived by Hatherleigh Press in 2002 (nicely timed for the war in Iraq), and reprinted with an enthusiastic introduction by Norvell "Tex" De Atkine, a former US army colonel and the head of Middle East studies at Fort Bragg. "It is essential reading," De Atkine wrote, "At the institution where I teach military officers, *The Arab Mind* forms the basis of my cultural instruction."[30]

The fact that *The Arab Mind* is used so widely in military instruction destroys any illusion that Arabs are approached as human in American foreign policy. It should be added that the demeaning stereotypes to which Arabs are subject in *The Arab Mind* merely reflect the portrayal of Arabs in American society, the same society that produced the soldiers on guard in Abu Ghraib. It is an utter scandal that so few American publications have investigated the military's use of *The Arab Mind* as a bastion of its "cultural instruction." Perhaps if this sort of thing were reported, Americans wouldn't be so shocked when soldiers carry their education to its logical conclusion and apply in the field what they learn in the classroom.

Perhaps nobody has attacked anti-Arab racism more vigorously than London's *Independent* reporter Robert Fisk (yet another Briton excelling in analysis at which most American journalists, with the exception of Seymour Hersh, overwhelmingly fail). About Abu Ghraib, he asks,

> Why are we surprised at their racism, their brutality, their sheer callousness towards Arabs? Those American soldiers in Saddam's old prison at Abu Ghraib, those young British squaddies in Basra came—as soldiers often come—from towns and cities where race hatred has a home: Tennessee [sic] and Lancashire.
>
> How many of "our" lads are ex-jailbirds themselves? How many support the British National Party? Muslims, Arabs, "cloth heads", "rag heads", "terrorists", "evil". You can see how the semantics break down.
>
> Add to that the poisonous, racial dribble of a hundred Hollywood movies that depict Arabs as dirty, lecherous, untrustworthy and violent people—and soldiers are addicted to movies—and it's not difficult to see how some British scumbag will urinate into the face of a hooded man, how some American sadist will stand a hooded Iraqi on a box with wires tied to his hand.[31]

Fisk offers the most appropriate context for assessing the torture at Abu Ghraib. Were it not for the anti-Arab racism endemic in the United States—and, according to Fisk, Britain—it wouldn't have been as easy for young soldiers to so gruesomely abuse their power. Nor would it be so acceptable to torture people in Afghanistan, Guantanamo, Brooklyn, and, doubtlessly, other facilities that house Arab and Muslim detainees. The torturers of these detainees have their own psychological complexities, but the American people have no excuse—other than callous indifference or an unconscious racism—for remaining silent about ghastly human rights abuses. Fisk seems to believe that callous indifference sometimes is informed by an unconscious racism:

We are all victims of our high-flown morality. "They"—the Arabs, Muslims, "cloth heads", "rag heads", "terrorists"—are of a lesser breed, of lower moral standards. They are people to be shouted at. They have to be "liberated" and given "democracy". But we little band of brothers, we dress ourselves up in the uniforms of righteousness. We are marines or military police or a Queen's regiment and we are on the side of good. "They" are on the side of "evil". So we can do no wrong.[32]

It is this "high-flown morality" that contributed to a mentality in which torture of the filthy Other could occur. But this "high-flown morality" also pervaded a major part of the response to the torture. A great number of American commentators expressed shock and outrage once the photos were released and then used that shock and outrage as evidence of the superiority of Americans, thereby reinventing the culture of infallible morality that helped generate the torture in the first place.

In Conclusion: the Permanence of Humiliation

Humiliation is permanent. This isn't to say that once a person is humiliated the humiliation will continue endlessly. Rather, the memory of that humiliation will never dissipate. It will remain with the humiliated person until his or her death. So it is for the Iraqi civilians in Abu Ghraib who were stripped of their dignity by a platoon of soldiers who had the backing of a country whose stock and trade in foreign policy has long been the degradation of Arabs.

While the photos from Abu Ghraib—and only God knows how many others there are from countless locations—indeed are shocking in their depiction of suffering and inhumanity, I find the majority of Americans' response to the photos equally shocking, and almost as disturbing. The notion that Abu Ghraib was merely an anomaly undertaken by an isolated group of misguided soldiers acting solely on their own poor instincts is an insult to anybody with even the slightest intellectual or moral integrity. Abu Ghraib was part of a system of torture and abuse arising from the dehumanization of whomever happens to be the United States' enemy—that is to say, the enemy of corporations who wish to control international markets and don't look kindly on the people who, inadvertently or otherwise, stand in the way. The torture at Abu Ghraib was systematic. This fact certainly doesn't absolve the soldiers guilty of the torture, but the soldiers are only partly to blame. Any progenitor of anti-Arab racism—and there are many in the United States—also shares in the responsibility. And advocates of the anomaly theory will share in the blame the next time torture occurs—and it will occur again.

The photos that so hideously illustrate the humiliation of Arabs are, in a metonymical sense, indicative of the current relationship among Americans and Arabs. The Arabs must continually be subordinated to the Americans physically. More important, though, they must continually be subordinated to the Americans emotionally and intellectually. Iraqi resistance to American occupation thus is deemed *terrorism* regardless of its strategy or origin. Arab disapproval of the invasion becomes a conspiracy theory. Arabic news networks are derided by Fox News as propaganda organs. Any Arab under American patrimony is subject to arrest based on an arbitrary and overtly racist legal apparatus. And the American torture of civilians is transformed into yet another morality play in which the United States grants itself the leading role.

I suppose we could evoke the obvious and say that Arabs have no moral and intellectual agency in the culture of political analysis created and maintained in the United States. But we don't want to miss the larger point. Americans' profound ethos of denial will always lead to behavior that implicates the denial in the sort of crimes only lesser peoples are supposed to undertake. I hope their humiliation at having become what they detest will never go away.

Conclusion:
Stories of a Different Kind

Some advice for aspiring political analysts: expect the very worst from American leaders in relation to the Arab World and they will always exceed your expectations. For that matter, always expect a failed peace process in Israel/ Palestine and you'll seem rather prescient. In fact, expect near-total acquiescence from American liberals in the policies of ethnic cleansing in Palestine and you'll appear downright clairvoyant. That's all the advice I can give. Truth to tell, I have nothing really to say about how to effectively battle racism. I can only say: do something about racism, so others won't define your expectations. And don't, of course, become a political analyst; become instead an active participant in your own destiny and in the destiny of all humans. For that is what the late Louis Owens advised us all over a decade ago, when he announced that North America's indigenous peoples would no longer consent to the "other destinies" endlessly manufactured for them by their oppressors.

The great question that always arises, in fact, in discussions of racism is what to do about it. It is a difficult question to answer because sometimes the pragmatic advice authors offer appears contrived or devalues their analyses. It's probably better to assess racism and let others handle it as individuals, in a way they see as prudent and necessary, or in the framework of a proactive group with an anti-racism agenda. Even here, though, we encounter a tricky situation, because what one person views as prudent and necessary another will inevitably view as foolish and counterproductive. That, I suppose, is why real dialogue in a genuinely democratic system is so important. And as long as anti-Arab racism continues to either silence or dehumanize Arabs, there will be nothing genuine about dialogue or democracy in the United States.

I have problems, for instance, with how some progressive organizations handle issues pertaining to Arabs, so it is problematic for me to suggest that people should counter racism according to their individual or institutional needs when in some cases those needs either promulgate anti-Arab racism or unwittingly reproduce it. Likewise, it seems rather unproductive to posit a strategy for eliminating anti-Arab racism when Arabs are so fiercely ignored by numerous anti-racism activists—in effect, Arabs have ceased to exist even as American imperialism grows more and more reliant on negative images of Arabs to fulfill its ambitious objectives.

I have learned over the years from reading Naomi Shihab Nye, Leslie Silko, Gerald Vizenor, Zora Neale Hurston, Linda Hogan, Mahmoud Darwish, and Audre Lorde that the essence of communication is hearing stories and telling stories. American exceptionalism, however, has all but made this ethic untenable. In the United States' linear worldview, the past is but an inconvenience to the vicious pursuit of an imaginary future deemed necessary to benefit the present. Even the best of us sometimes fall victim to this mentality. Although, for example, the *Nation* provides useful analysis of current events, it, along with a plethora of left-liberal publications (both online and in print), rarely highlights injustices in Indian communities and even more rarely analyzes the genocide of Indians on which the United States was predicated. Its analyses of racism are therefore underdeveloped, albeit usually interesting. Those who are concerned with eliminating American racism need to put its current usage in its historical context, for the dispossession of Indians created the American imperialism that nourishes the Othering of today's geopolitical (read: corporate) enemies. Centuries of slavery also were crucial to the evolution of American exceptionalism. Anybody serious about combating racism should approach American society with a cyclical rather than linear methodology. In short, anti-racism activists need to drop the argument that construes injustice as inimical to American values and confront the American experiment honestly, in its totality.

We need to listen to the so-often silenced Others, whether their voices arise within our own communities or from communities about which we have no knowledge. Americans rarely listen, a byproduct of the colonialist virtues recycled as needed when corporate thieves invent a new scheme to maximize profit. This suggestion doesn't mean we all need to agree with one another; we simply need to hear one another so we can add value to the language we articulate in writing and conversation. By hearing we might accrue invaluable knowledge about unorthodox worldviews and different cultures. Would listening—real listening—actually end racism? No, but it would contribute valuably to any attempted reworking of the past endeavors that brought the United States to its current dysfunction. And without such a reworking, Americans are doomed to the inanity of an unreflective, and uninteresting, political culture.

Only Stories

I learned much about these things years ago during my first visit to Palestine. Any American who travels uncritically to the so-called Third World usually corrupts the value of the experience and contributes to the long tradition of racism in travel narratives, a tradition that, in the case of anti-Arab racism, spans from Mark Twain, with his ironic but Orientalist *Innocents Abroad*, to Geraldine Brooks, with her patronizing *Nine Parts of Desire*.

Yet even constant critical assessment of one's position as a traveler doesn't ensure that one will avoid, tacitly or not, expressing colonial or patronizing values. These things are built into the American consciousness, and I've always felt it better to acknowledge rather than deny them. It is said all over the world that Americans don't know how to listen very well. Understanding such a perception is a good way to avoid imposing alien ethical sensibilities on those who have suffered instead of letting them articulate that suffering themselves.

The dynamics of travel are, of course, complex beyond the limits of written discourse. They come to fruition through the reality of experience, and cannot be contained in any book or essay. I know that, despite my Arab background, I will never comprehend Palestinian life on its own terms. I will always view it through the lens of my American upbringing. This reality needn't be perceived negatively. It is simply a fact that all Americans working abroad on issues of justice should accept. When it is not, colonial dynamics inevitably come into play.

I have spent many hours in Palestine in the mixed company of Westerners and Arabs. More often than not, the Westerners discuss solutions to the Palestine question while the Palestinians remain silent. Sometimes it is not the actions of Americans, but their words, that make them hypocrites. And sometimes it isn't the content underlying the words that invokes hypocrisy, but the act of speaking.

I try and consign myself to what might be considered a journalist's role when in the Near East. The images to which I am subjected in Palestine remain with me throughout the year. I work hard to present those images in American publications, but I am not a journalist by training. I attempt merely to work on instinct by requesting and remembering stories, then recount those stories in the United States.

Even as a foreigner there only for the summer—replete with all the privileges with which an American is endowed—I slowly learned to understand life without freedom. I had lived in a house with other international students, and we would sit on the porch with candles on nights without electricity. In all directions, white elliptical patterns surrounded the pitch darkness, lights from the West Bank's ubiquitous settlements. Our water tanks would be filled at Israel's discretion. It was common for us to go for days without showers—dishes piling high in our sinks—then leave to run errands only to see the settlers washing their cars or watering their lawns.

These were but minor inconveniences, however. It was easy to survive without electricity or running water in the summer, especially when cheap bottled water was available. In fact, some of our greatest memories were created on our porch late at night, chatting and smoking amid the dull flicker of candlelight. Those nights proved to me yet again that no matter what sort of technology humans invent, stories will forever be our greatest resource.

No, it isn't the indignity of apartheid—which, living among the Palestinians, we got to view at close range—that transformed me from would-be academic to aspiring activist. Rather, it is the violence of apartheid and the soothing words of deliverance by which apartheid is framed. It is the constant anger that ensues upon returning to America, the paymaster of this particular apartheid, and finding that nobody is here to listen because blame is placed on the colonized. It is knowing the reality of the situation in Palestine because its images inform and then overtake consciousness, yet being silenced in place of professional experts whose duty is not the abolishment of injustice, but the reinforcement of ideologies that sustain it.

Those who have visited Palestine and return hoping to express the Palestinian narrative to an American audience quickly encounter pervasive frustration. That frustration does not arise entirely in response to generally pro-Israeli political opinion. Quite simply, supporters of Palestinian human rights aren't on equal footing with ideologues of Israeli expansion. They are armed not only with the support of American leaders, but also with a discourse of biblical fulfillment that has gradually become institutionalized in the American imagination. Most important, they cull narratives of divinely inspired national fulfillment that tap into over 500 years of American sensibilities.

We have memories of suffering beyond comprehension: displacement, dispossession, torture, murder, home demolition. We have images of blood, endless blood, staining the lives of civilians living under military occupation. And we have the truth, a truth as impalpable as the emotions in which it is stored, but expressed concretely in human rights ethics and international law.

We have the knowledge that the entire world outside the United States has heard and accepts our story. And we have the knowledge that history will condemn the aggressor and look unkindly on its supporters, as it has in every instance of injustice with unforgiving dedication. But the gaze of history is merely a flight of fancy, for the future cannot ameliorate the present, and a reliance on future history for social justice often inspires apathy. Truth itself can be useless. It took years of graduate school for me to finally rebel against the notion that no truth exists, but whatever form it takes it is usually amorphous or in conflict with other truths. Yes, we have truth, and truth is comforting, but truth has no manifest strategy as do language and power. Truth also comforts the oppressor.

So, how do Arabs express to Americans that Palestinian society has been destroyed and that Israel's military occupation is perpetual destruction?

How do we convey the suffering of Palestinian children, who gather in hordes around visitors and charm them with their gorgeous smiles and undying enthusiasm for life, and who wear prosthetic limbs but carry visions of freedom in their brown glass eyes?

Our lives—ours, the Arab supporters of Palestine—are frustrating in the United States. Our truths are overcome by

500 years of expansion. Our knowledge is construed as the dementia of terrorists. We are left only with stories.

Unending Hypocrisy

I focus so intensely on Palestine because Israel's military occupation dramatizes so explicitly the pervasiveness of anti-Arab racism in the United States and the dangerous cost of whitewashing or ignoring it. For over three decades, the United States has funded an egregious ethnic cleansing, creating regional (and at times international) instability and rendering one of its strongest allies a foreign policy albatross, and yet most Americans support the albatross and the ethnic cleanser. This situation wouldn't be possible if anti-Arab racism weren't a mainstream intellectual consciousness. Nor would it be possible if Arabs weren't so frequently caricatured in American popular culture as bloodthirsty villains or idiotic barbarians.

Other situations replete with anti-Arab racism persist, including the occupation of Iraq, the torture of Muslim detainees, and the profiling of Arab Americans by the Department of Homeland Security. All the situations Arabs now face as citizens or workers in the United States, or in their own countries as victims of an aggressive foreign policy, are neither new nor particularly novel in American history. The pitiful response—or non-response, as it were—of American liberals, the supposed vanguard of decent ethics, to the continuation of American jingoism in the form of anti-Arab racism is currently the shame of the United States and will certainly be approached by future theorists of colonization as another example of the privileged classes remaining quiet when any phenomenon even remotely threatens their privilege. The United States now has a vested interest in propagating anti-Arab racism; those who allow the United States to pursue this interest share in the guilt of its bloody consequences.

Some progressive outlets, of course, have done a wonderful job of both providing Arabs with a voice and discussing anti-Arab racism with insightful clarity. Those outlets include Democracy Now!, *CounterPunch*, *Dissident Voice*, *Isthmus* (Madison), *Z Magazine*, *In These Times*, Free Speech TV, *Clamor Magazine*, and The International Socialist Organization (among others that I am most certainly forgetting). But it was certainly sad in 2004 to see progressive writers like John Nichols, Marc Cooper, David Corn, Katrina vanden Heuvel, Norman Solomon, Todd Gitlin, Ruth Coniff, Michael Moore, Eric Alterman, Eric Schlosser, Medea Benjamin, and Robert Scheer essentially become cheerleaders for the ineffectual Democratic Party. I will go ahead and state the obvious: each of these writers is White, and each has an interest in protecting his or her political privilege. To be sure, that interest is unconscious, the product of a society that has long convinced the dominant class to fight for a social justice that in reality serves the needs of the wealthy—or the writers' own egos.

I have no sympathy for those who identify with a party that professes openly to support the right of the American and Israeli military to occupy Arab lands and impose on Arabs a Western government. It is a situation that illustrates how effectively neoliberal elites are able to appropriate resistance into an empowering corporate agenda. The argument that America's needs are too pressing to embrace a "radical" agenda is astounding in its shortsightedness and stupidity. Whatever rights, liberties, and legal recourse we enjoy in the United States have been achieved through hard work, suffering, and a profound contrarian spirit. If past activists had used the same ethos that the crop of writers above did in 2004 in praising imperialists such as John Kerry, Americans would have no 40-hour workweek, Blacks wouldn't be able to vote, and civil liberties would merely be a fantasy. The fact that each of these things is still in some way true indicates how foolish it is for those interested in real social justice to rely on cowards and capitulators to inspire effective change for the better. Perhaps these folks were merely oblivious, preoccupied as they were with the righteous task of combating racism rather than viewing the world from the perspective of those who continually experience it.

I remember that when I was in graduate school I took a course in Black Critical Theory with the incomparable Catherine John. Professor John has a superb intellect and an unusual ability to articulate complex intellectual points without resorting to diplomacy or jargon. The main theme of her course will forever remain with me: a society predicated on land theft and slavery will, no matter how far its liberal values progress, forever be tainted with the residue of those events. So we are both foolish and self-defeating if we hope to effect just change without dismantling the ethos of dispossession and subjugation that informs the self-image of a nation whose fundamental claim to existence has long been the exceptionalism created by slaveholders and settlers. As the invasion of Iraq attests, no amount of protest in an Americanist context will suppress the propensity of this exceptionalism to buttress the corporatization of American politics. Democrats certainly won't. Nor will White liberals. Nor will minorities who wait for Democrats and White liberals to finally see the light and abandon their privilege to work in the interests of all Americans. There has never been an instance in world history where a ruling class willingly acknowledged the injustices it committed and then quit committing them because it was the right thing to do. Ruling classes must be forced into compliance with a just ethics. If Americans don't vehemently analyze the extent and effects of anti-Arab racism in the United States, I don't see how the United States' current ruling class will ever be forced to do anything more than pretend to respect Arabs while looting their resources.

Unending Stories

The desert near Madaba, Jordan, is a tranquil mixture of pink stones, beige sand, and olive groves. At dusk the view from

Mount Nebo offers a lively patchwork of yellow and green blending finally into the Dead Sea's dark blue water. In this region, small Bedouin communities still wander the landscape with sheep and goats, pitching their tents in the evening to cook *minsaf* and brew coffee. They often are photographed by Western tourists with rental cars and digital cameras.

In Madaba, a traditional Middle Eastern culture has remained intact, although it is grappling with the steady encroachment of cutting-edge technologies and American values. Most of the homes are stacked in narrow alleyways barely wide enough for one car but nonetheless well traveled. The faint smell of roast chicken and *shawarma* is omnipresent. Fruit peels, paper, and cigarette butts litter the streets, for Madaba's residents take out their garbage by throwing it off the balcony every evening. A throng of jewelry stores, their gold samples refracting light in all directions, lines the main thoroughfare, along with watermelon carts, fabrics shops, and tea vendors. Old men, their red *kuffiyeh*s protecting their faces from the sun, sit in small circles to chat, their arms constantly in motion. Gypsies, wearing multicolored scarves and dresses, wander in and out of the fabrics shops, their children always with them. Western dress has become more common in Madaba, but many of its residents still wear the clothes of their ancestors. Most of its residents have cell phones. Some have internet access.

Amman is divided informally into an East and West. East Amman is the lower-class area, a bustling neighborhood with traditional *soug*s, high-density housing, and conservatively dressed women. West Amman is lined with grand boulevards, upscale shopping malls, and mansions constructed with hand-chiseled stone. In West Amman, many young women wear haltertops and miniskirts to dine at the royal-owned Champions and shop at Abdoun Mall, with stores such as Gucci and Dolce and Gabbana. In East Amman, many women wear beige *hejab*s and solid black dresses to visit the fruit stand and butcher shop to purchase groceries to cook dinner.

In its entirety, the city is clean and unbelievably friendly to tourists. It has a remarkable amalgam of East and West and zoning ordinances for smart growth that would be the envy of many American cities. Perhaps its most familiar structure is the American Embassy, an enormous stone compound in ritzy Abdoun enclosed by a wall and guarded with tanks provided by the Jordanian Army.

In the north of Jordan, one can encounter endless olive orchards, their fruit some of the most delicious in the Near East and considerably more delicious than the European olives purchased by Americans. The south of Jordan is mostly desert, with a landscape that rivals the Navajo Nation in its beauty. The landscape is marked by towering red rock formations that rise above the sandbars with breathtaking grandeur. The ancient city of Petra, unrivaled in its splendor, is the area's main attraction. The Bedouin were only recently removed from it by the Jordanian government to make the site more amenable to tourists.

In Beirut, the marriage of East and West is not only a way of life, it has generated its own unique culture. One can sometimes find a woman in a miniskirt walking next to another woman who is covered entirely, only her eyes showing through her black veil. One can also find men wearing the latest French and Italian fashions walking the same street as men dressed in traditional Druze garb or cream *dishdasha*s. For centuries writers have tried unsuccessfully to describe Beirut; one can only comprehend its outrageous but endearing contradictions by traveling there. In order to understand them correctly, though, one has to have been born and raised in Beirut. And even then he or she will be unable to properly explain them. The squalor of Lebanon's Palestinian refugee camps, whose inhabitants have no citizenship or civil rights, seems continents away from the opulent consumer culture of Hamra. In reality, though, less than five miles separate them.

In Palestine, life is much different. Four decades of military occupation have created an extraordinarily inventive culture that has managed to craft a semi-livable lifestyle within an egregious restriction of human and economic movement. The West Bank is small but has a highly diverse topography, from the towering land inclines near the Dead Sea to the relaxing mountains surrounding Ramallah, the once-famous resort town that was destroyed by Israel in 2002. In the north of the West Bank, Nablus's reputation as the sweets capital of the Near East has not been compromised, as a seemingly endless row of bakeries displays huge round pans of orange *kinafe* and *harise* baked perfectly to an amber brown. In the south of the West Bank, Khalil (Hebron) remains famous for its glass factory, where craftsmen design wineglasses in gorgeous patterns of pink and blue. The ancient *soug* in downtown Khalil is incredible not just for its intricate walkways curving into cubbies selling everything from CDs to Persian carpets, but for the wire fencing that covers those walkways to protect pedestrians from the stones heaved into the *soug* by the American settlers who squatted atop the city.

The Gaza Strip has a more consistent topography in its 360 square kilometers, about twice the size of Washington, DC. It is flat and humid, and dangerously overcrowded. Gaza's cities and refugee camps are afflicted with poverty, sometimes awash with open sewage, sometimes filled with tents and piles of rubble. But those cities and camps also are filled with an enviable kindness of spirit, a generosity to visitors that would be difficult to duplicate elsewhere. The constant, hysterical cries in the United States that Gaza is a cesspool for terrorists— yet another demeaning metaphor—severely belies the reality any American without dubious intentions would experience in Gaza. That visitor would see fishermen out at dawn each morning on the Mediterranean shore, having navigated invasive checkpoints, preparing to catch fish to sell at market, under the watchful eye of the Israeli patrol boats monitoring the waters. He or she would see Palestinian children peering through barbed-wire fences at the Jewish children playing on their private beaches. He or she would see people struggling to work because they have been confined to the world's largest outdoor prison. And he or she would see an assortment of strangers who invited him or her for drinks and snacks despite their modest income simply because he or she is a guest in their country. Unless this visitor conceptualized all Arabs as innately violent, he or she would encounter no terrorists.

The stories one absorbs in the Arab World are priceless. When I visited Jordan in the summer after my wedding, my Aunt Loris, Amo Saleem's wife, always wore 21-karat gold earrings, as do most women in the region. One morning as we were dressing, my wife told me that she thought she had heard a salesman in the house that morning. "It seemed like he was selling gold," she told me.

When we joined Martami on the balcony for our morning coffee and cigarettes, surrounded by the bustle of Madaba's Japanese cars and donkey carts, Martami produced a small black box containing beautiful gold earrings. My wife attempted to refuse the gift, but Martami insisted with an Arab's knack for urgency that she take them. When Martami went to refill the coffee, my wife whispered to me, "Did you notice that she's not wearing her earrings?" We never saw Martami's earrings again.

Yet it is the stories from Palestine that I remember most. It was breezy the day our activist delegation visited al-Khader Village in the West Bank in 2001. Beige dust clouds whipped into evanescent funnels. A Jewish-only highway divides the villagers from their farmland. A gray military watchtower protects the rule of law.

The voice of our guide, Husam Jubran, broke the cemetery-like silence. He stood with a small male child in the distance. As we neared, it became evident that the boy's somber expression had little to do with timidity. He had all the markings of a weathered man. He seemed not to notice the relentless camera clicks as our group gathered around him in a semicircle. Dressed in a matching green shirt and shoes, he refused to look at us directly. His left eye drooped lazily atop his cheekbone. Its color did not match his other eye.

His grandmother, wearing a maroon embroidered dress, narrated a tale to us in Arabic. "He wasn't doing anything," Husam translated. "He was just standing on the balcony when they shot out his eye." As she spoke, the grandmother's right arm waved rapidly from ear to thigh. "He's only four," Husam explained. "She had to take him to America for a glass eye." The child took her hand and stared at her, the glassy hue of his pupil reflecting into the cloudless sky.

We were soon joined by a toddler, barely past the point of teetering when standing, with a pink scar above her left eye. She was a miracle survivor, shot in the head as an infant. She couldn't yet speak fluently, but that didn't prevent her from narrating poems about oppression and occupation.

I wandered away from the group, trying to decipher my own perception, attempting to see anything properly with my two healthy eyes. Behind me, two Israeli flags flapped atop a lightpost beyond the watchtower. The verdant agricultural land stared back, empty. Layered barbed wire and M-16s had transformed nature's sustenance into an outdoor prison.

Another evening, we encountered a group of six men hanging around a music store in Bethlehem. They invited us over to smoke *argeela* and listen to the latest dance beats from Lebanon and Egypt. With typical Palestinian hospitality, they offered us their chairs and ignored their own afflictions, urging us instead to tell them about ourselves. When they learned that we had just visited al-Quds, less than five miles away, their merriment gave way to disappointment and silence. Finally, one of them spoke to the only Muslim in our delegation. "Please tell me what al-Aqsa is like."

"You've never been?" she asked with instinctive shock.

"None of us has been."

The scene brought to mind a famous oil painting by Slimon Mansur. It depicts al-Quds as a joyous city filled with peoples from across the world; each nationality displays its national flag. The Palestinians, who helped build the city and who have inhabited it since the days of Canaan, are not allowed inside. Instead, they sit atop the stone wall, hiding their flag behind them lest they get arrested for an illegal display of national culture.

The stories, though, aren't always negative. Once in the Jabalya Refugee Camp in Gaza, for instance, I played an unusual game of soccer. Jabalya is the famous camp where the first Intifada began in 1987. Its 110,000 residents, who are crammed into four square kilometers, are known to support Hamas and have a reputation for courage and bravado. During my first visit the previous year, I had let stereotypical images of militant Palestinians guide my attitude. I was rather surprised (and guilty), therefore, to see that the camp is filled with the same inviting and hospitable people one finds everywhere in Palestine.

On my second visit, groups of curious children followed me everywhere I went, hiding behind walls and giggling every time I turned around. After coaxing some of them from their timidity, we played soccer in the dirt and were soon joined by hundreds of children.

Once the game ended, we sat on mats in the sand to eat. A Palestinian will gladly starve in order that guests will be well fed. Some people in Jabalya have no houses, no freedom, and no money, but they offer food not even the fanciest French bistro can surpass. As I ate, the children climbed all over me, leafing through my backpack and clothes. A chain on my neck caught their attention. A small boy followed the chain to its stopping point on my chest. Inspecting the gold cross, he eyed it with furrowed brows. "*Masiiheh?*" he asked, pointing at the crucifix. "*Aywa, Masiiheh,*" I smiled. "There are *Masiihiyyin,*" he exclaimed, pointing at the ground—meaning there are Christians in Palestine. He pulled me by the arm toward his home, a dilapidated structure without windows and filled with cracks. "*Yula, yula,*" he urged, tugging me inside. As I stood in the sitting area, a plain room with pictures of al-Quds on the walls, I noticed that the bedroom floor was lined with nine mattresses. A kitchen completed the home.

The boy reappeared from the bedroom, a small bar of Cadbury's chocolate in his hand. "You, uh, you ... welcome," he told me, measuring carefully the English words. He unwrapped the chocolate and broke off a third of it. He handed me the larger portion. He took my hand, and as we left the house, uttered proudly, "You, you ... welcome at Palestine."

I realized that the boy, no higher than my waist and generous enough to offer his guest the chocolate he probably worked six months to buy, is the terrorist Israel and America's leaders fear: A child who knows more about the world than most adults, a child who has suffered tenfold beyond his years, a child who dreams of one day going home.

I am shocked continuously when I see the type of Arab World that exists in American media. It isn't in any way the Arab World in which my family lives or the one I so often visit. In fact, I can't think of any instance among hundreds of instances of misrepresentation in the United States in which the image of a people is so starkly different than the actual people being represented. The landscape of the Near East is nothing like the scenes of windy, barren desert ubiquitous in American movies. (A close Lebanese friend of mine has a hell of a time convincing Americans that people ski in Lebanon.) And the peoples of the Arab World aren't the flyting, chanting, flag-burning maniacs that essentially define the Arab image in the United States. Arabs flyt, no doubt—almost always after Israel has bombed a civilian neighborhood. And they chant—usually at church or mosque during prayers. They even burn American flags—but I would venture to guess that, per capita, more

Americans burn American flags than do Arabs. Yet only the Americans who wave flags get to represent the United States on television.

My point is a simple one, and I say it with as much clarity as possible: in discussing Arab violence, you either promulgate the assumption that Arabs are irrationally violent, or you simultaneously examine the context in which that violence arises. There is no other option intellectually: you are either a thoroughgoing racist or you take your responsibilities as a citizen and commentator seriously.

Who, Then, are Arabs?

We are a beautiful people with a brilliant history of achievement in science and philosophy. We have made invaluable contributions to Western civilization in the fields of medicine, astronomy, and mathematics. Coffee is an Arab gift to the West. So are paella, kabobs, hummus, and tabbouli. Arabic words are incorporated widely in both the English and Spanish languages. The world's first civilizations appeared in Africa and the Near East. Our language, Arabic, is extraordinarily complex and profound, and has inspired poetry predating the appearance of English. Arab communities are remarkably diverse in language, religion, ceremony, music, literature, and cultural orientation.

We are—with, of course, the inevitable exceptions—ardently family-oriented and prefer to live near as many relatives as possible. We don't—under any circumstances—put our parents into nursing or retirement homes. We force American guests to eat more than they at first seem willing to do, but they usually confess later that the food was so delicious they were glad to eat thirds without seeming rude. Except for some among us in the West, we don't like immodest dress and immodest behavior in general. If an Arab is told by a guest that his watch is nice, he will take off the watch and give it to the guest. We are taught by our parents to "hit the stones" as passionately as possible. We vigorously protect any visitor to our homes and neighborhoods. We smoke too many cigarettes. We enjoy dancing. We cook almost everything in olive oil. We love our children and siblings and parents with intense dedication.

We are, to put it plainly, no more and no less human than any other people. Our contributions to the world, both positive and negative, are no better or worse than the contributions made by everybody. We certainly have our own ways of doing things, but every culture does so, and there is much to say for relativity in a United States where binaristic categories predominate. I don't believe in Arab exceptionalism, either.

Sometimes, though, it's much easier to say what we aren't rather than trying to explain who we are.

We are not rogues. We are not savages. We are not barbarians. We are not terrorists. And any attempt to totalize Arabs as any of these things merely implicates the speaker in precisely what the speaker claims to abhor in Arabs.

Notes

Introduction

1. Mission statement of Forum Against Islamophobia and Racism (FAIR). Available at www.fairuk.org/introduction.htm
2. Ibid.
3. For instance, the largest Islamic advocacy group in the United States, the Council on American–Islamic Relations (CAIR), uses the word regularly in its press releases and action alerts, but hasn't actually defined it formally on its website for public consumption. The same is true of the Muslim Public Affairs Council (MPAC). In Britain, there appears to be a more conscious—and public—assessment of the word and its implications. In the United States, it is often used on the assumption that readers understand its meaning and, more important, its resonance. This assumption is problematic because it inadvertently delegates the task of representation to the audience and not the speaker.
4. See further Anouar Majid, *Unveiling Traditions*, Durham, NC: Duke University Press, 2000.
5. Lynette Clemetson, "Homeland Security Given Data on Arab Americans," *New York Times*, 30 July 2004, sec. A.
6. See further the Arab American Institute (AAI) website at www.aaiusa.org/demographics.htm. The AAI also notes that many in the Arab American community haven't yet been naturalized.
7. Ibid.
8. Illinois, Texas, Ohio, Massachusetts, and Pennsylvania round out the top ten.
9. See further Haya El Nasser, "U.S. Census Reports on Arab-Americans," *USA Today*, 21 November 2003, sec. A.
10. Ajami, for instance, has claimed that the 9/11 hijackers and Palestinian resistance groups are essentially one and the same: "In hindsight, the terrors visited on Israel by Hamas, Islamic Jihad, and the al-Aqsa Martyrs Brigade were a dress rehearsal for greater terrors to come." In the same article, he also writes, "One day, there may step forth a Palestinian generation that is done with homicide bombers and the cult of violence. In this better vision of things, there

would be no preachers glorifying violence against noncombatants; religion would return to its proper functions. There would be sober acceptance that the Palestine of the imagination is no more, and that partition is the inevitable outcome of this fight for the land. A leader would tell the multitudes that the Jews are there to stay." See further Fouad Ajami, "A Legacy of Pain and Poison," *US News and World Report*, 5 April 2004.

11. For information about Abdel-Muhti's story, see www.democracynow. org/article.pl?sid=04/04/13/1443265&mode=thread&tid=25

12. Robert Jensen, "Stupid White Movie" available at www. counterpunch.org/jensen07052004.html

13. See further Katha Pollitt, "Moore 1, Media 0," *The Nation*, 19 July 2004, and Peter Sussman, "*Fahrenheit 9/11*: Firing up the Choir" available at www.alternet.org/story/19139

Chapter One

1. John O'Sullivan, "Anti-Arab 'Backlash' Just Hype," *Chicago Sun-Times*, 18 June 2002, sec. A.

2. In the same article, O'Sullivan writes, "The kind of 'diversity' enforced on newsrooms by today's media elite is a strictly ethnic and sexual one. It produces a newsroom in which everything looks different but thinks identically. A black conservative reporter has only a slightly better chance of employment than under Jim Crow. One of the strongest sentiments in most newsrooms today is a liberal condescension toward the presumed bigotry of most other people. And when a uniformity of opinion prevails, the errors and prejudices associated with that prevailing opinion will escape detection and influence coverage. In such an atmosphere, Jenin is an accident that is just waiting to be reported."

3. See further David Cole, *Enemy Aliens*, New York: The New Press, 2003.

4. Donna Leinwand, "Muslims See New Opposition to Building Mosques Since 9/11," *USA Today*, 9 March 2004, sec. A.

5. "Survey Shows Sharp Increase in Prosecutions of Arabs, Muslims in US City," Agence France Presse, 21 November 2003.

6. See further Miles Benson, "Jewish Group Departs from Norm, Sponsors Pro-Israel Ads on TV," *Newhouse News Service*, 17 September 2002.

7. Julia Malone, "Group Says Bush Ad 'Profiles' Arabs; Removal of Unidentified Photo Urged," *Atlanta Journal-Constitution*, 13 March 2004, sec. A.

8. Linda Linley, "Arab-American Teens Find Stereotypes Hard to Bear; Terrorism, War Fears Foster Misconceptions, They Say," *Baltimore Sun*, 16 December 2003, sec. B.

9. Ibid.
10. See further Craig Unger, *House of Bush, House of Saud*, New York: Scribner, 2004.
11. John Perazzo, "The Palestinian Culture of Hate," *FrontPageMagazine.com*, 12 January 2004.
12. Ibid.
13. Ibid.
14. Maureen Meehan, "Israeli Textbooks and Children's Literature Promote Racism and Hatred Toward Palestinians and Arabs," *Washington Report on Middle East Affairs*, September 1999, 19.
15. Ibid., 19.
16. Ibid., 19.
17. Ibid., 19.
18. Ibid., 20. See further Elie Podeh, *The Arab–Israeli Conflict in Israeli History Textbooks, 1948–2000*, New York: Bergin and Garvey, 2001.
19. Ibid., 20.
20. Ibid., 20.
21. Ibid., 20.
22. Ibid., 20.
23. Ibid., 20.
24. Greer Fay Cahsman, "Katsav: We'd Never Stoop to Palestinians' Brutality," *Jerusalem Post*, 11 May 2001, sec. A.
25. "Ashcroft Statement on Islam Shows Intolerance, Says Americans United," *Church & State*, March 2002, 15.
26. Tom DeLay, "Resist Until the End in the Path of God," speech delivered on 2 February 2004. Available at www.TomDeLay.house.gov
27. See further Kwame Anthony Appiah, *In My Father's House*, Oxford: Oxford University Press, 1992, 14–15.
28. Tom DeLay, "Israel Resolution Floor Remarks," speech delivered on 25 June 2003. Available at www.TomDeLay.house.gov
29. Steven Plaut, "Pacifism: a Recipe for Suicide," *FrontPageMagazine.com*, 26 March 2004.
30. "Demand Dick Armey Retract Call for Ethnic Cleansing of Palestinians," ADC Action Alert, 2 May 2002. Available at www.adc.org/action/2002/02May2002.htm
31. Steven Vincent, "The War on Arab Tribalism," *FrontPageMagazine.com*, 26 May 2004.
32. Ibid.
33. Ibid.
34. Andrew G. Bostom, "The Sacred Muslim Practice of Beheading," *FrontPageMagazine.com*, 13 May 2004.
35. Ibid.

36. Stephen J. Novakovich, letter *USA Today*, 14 May 2004, sec. A.

37. Terrence P. Jeffrey, "Illegal Immigration: the Terrorist Connection," *Townhall.com*, 29 January 2004.

38. Lawrence Auster, "How to Defeat Jihad in America," *FrontPageMagazine.com*, 26 May 2004.

39. Ibid.

40. Ibid.

41. David Horowitz, "Liberals Hand Terrorists a Victory," *FrontPageMagazine.com*, 17 May 2004.

42. Robert Fisk, "Victims of Our Own High-Flown Morality," *CounterPunch.org*, 1/3 May 2004.

43. Thomas L. Friedman, "Rights in the Real World," *New York Times*, 2 December 2001, sec. A.

44. Ibid.

45. Ibid.

46. Thomas L. Friedman, "Naked Air," *New York Times*, 26 December 2001, sec. A.

47. On 4 March 2003, for example, Dershowitz told CNN's Wolf Blitzer that he supports torture in particular cases on the basis of "a torture warrant, which puts a heavy burden on the government to demonstrate by factual evidence the necessity to administer this horrible, horrible technique of torture. I would talk about nonlethal torture, say, a sterilized needle underneath the nail, which would violate the Geneva Accords, but you know, countries all over the world violate the Geneva Accords. They do it secretly and hypothetically, the way the French did it in Algeria. If we ever came close to doing it, and we don't know whether this is such a case, I think we would want to do it with accountability and openly and not adopt the way of the hypocrite." Available at http://edition. cnn.com/2003/LAW/03/03/cnna.Dershowitz/

Likewise, in a 2004 NPR conversation with Neal Conan, Dershowitz reiterated his support for the concept of torture warrants by referencing what he believes to be successful instances of prevention in Israel: "There are two cases, documented cases, in Israel where buses were going to be blown up, and the use of—they didn't call it torture, but rough interrogation techniques, putting hoods on people and shaking them and putting them in dark, smelly rooms with loud music produced evidence that stopped buses from being exploded. And there was one case where they didn't use it, and a bus was blown up." See further Neal Conan, "Talk of the Nation," *National Public Radio*, 18 November 2004, *LexisNexis*, 18 August 2005.

48. See further Alan M. Dershowitz, *The Case for Israel*, New York: John Wiley & Sons, 2003.

49. In lambasting a 2003 poll in which Europeans considered Israel
    a great threat to peace, for instance, Dershowitz writes, "This is
    all part of a systematic Palestinian effort to supplement a terrorist
    campaign with a propaganda war." See further Alan Dershowitz,
    "Euro Trash," *New York Daily News*, 8 November 2003, sec. A.
    In a 2003 forum at UCLA, Dershowitz criticized the notion of a
    binational democratic state in the Holy Land by saying, "I don't
    want to seem flip about this but there was one leader in the twentieth
    century who tried to create a one-state solution for Europe. His
    name was Adolph Hitler. He tried to end the independent existence
    of France and Italy and Denmark and other countries. No, I think
    that the two-state solution is the only appropriate solution. It's the
    one I have always advocated. It's the one I continue to advocate. It's
    the one that very few Palestinian leaders actually advocate. They are
    not prepared to say two states." Available at www.international.
    ucla.edu/bcir/article.asp?parentid=5071

50. Alan M. Dershowitz, "The Palestinians' Genocide Campaign,"
    Jerusalem Post, 14 April 2004, sec. A.

51. Lerner also has removed individual agency from the participants
    in Israel's occupation, noting, "In the past two thousand years
    we [Jews] have not gone for longer than a period of one hundred
    years before [hatred] erupted again. Given that there's a world of
    oppression, given how that world is structured and how there are
    ruling classes, we have gotten screwed over time and again. This has
    also had the effect of creating a certain kind of personality structure
    that generates more antagonism, because if you're expecting to get
    screwed over you act defensively, which leads other people to be
    angry at you. That behavior reaction, the development of 'offensive'
    traits, is itself part of our victimization. It's part of our history
    of oppression. Israel's policy toward the Palestinians has been the
    tragic consequence of Jewish history, because we are acting out,
    in a paranoid and defensive way, what has been done to us." See
    further Michael Lerner and Cornel West, *Jews and Blacks*, New
    York: Plume, 1996, 124–5.

    His ethic of immoral equivalency was demonstrated in a 2003
    Washingtonpost.com opinion forum in which he made the following
    statements: "I want America to tilt toward Israel. I am strongly
    pro-Israel. That's why I want America to be really pro-Israel, and
    in my view that would mean supporting the peace voices in Israel
    rather than those who are pursuing a self-destructive policy. In
    my view, articulated more fully in my new book *Healing Israel/
    Palestine*, the only way to be pro-Israel is to also be pro-Palestine,
    and the only way to be pro-Palestine is to also be pro-Israel. There
    is no possibility of peace that does not include a deal that is fair

to both sides and recognizes the legitimacy of both sides;" "I do think that the acts of terror against Israeli civilians deserve strong condemnation. At the same time, I believe that acts of violence against Palestinians deserve strong condemnation. But the point is to move beyond this constant blame-game and find solutions;" and "Both Israel and the Palestinians have violated past agreements, and both sides continue to do so. Both sides have acted with bad faith and with overt contempt toward the agreements that they have entered. So to formulate the issue as though one side or the other needs to prove that they are going to be good now is to distort the historical record." One of Lerner's questioners pointed out during the forum that in the op-ed piece that inspired the conversation, Lerner (and his co-author, Cornel West) describes the Palestinians as "having acts of violence" while Israelis have "daily obstacles to the settlement of the conflict." See further "Opinion Focus: Israel and U.S. Politics," *Washingtonpost.com*, 11 November 2003, *LexisNexis*, 18 August 2005.

52. See further Michael Lerner, "Strategize With Us: a Note from Michael Lerner," *Tikkun Mail*, 28 October 2002. Available at www.campus-watch.org/article/id/285

53. Michael Lerner, *Healing Israel/Palestine*, New York: North Atlantic Books, 2003, xi–xii.

54. Ibid.

55. Quoted in Nur Masalha, *Imperial Israel and the Palestinians*, London and Sterling, VA: Pluto, 2000, 56.

56. Ibid., 57, 58.

57. Ibid., 143.

58. Ibid., 142.

59. Avi Shlaim, *The Iron Wall*, New York: Norton, 2001, 12.

60. Ibid., 3.

61. Ibid., 4.

62. Ibid., 4.

63. Ibid., 6.

64. John Kerry, "The Cause of Israel is the Cause of America," April 2001. Available at www.americansforjews.org. Naomi Klein likewise has taken Kerry to task for what she calls his "outrageous (and frankly racist) claim that Americans 'have borne 90 per cent of the casualties in Iraq." See further Naomi Klein, "Kerry and the Gift of Impunity," *Nation*, 13 December 2004.

65. Howard Berman's floor comments for House Debate on pro-Israel Resolution H. Res. 294. Available at www.cmep.org/Alerts/2003June26.htm

66. Quoted in Michael Collins Piper, "New Bill in Congress Targets Teachers Who Dare to Question US Support for Israel," 19 March

2004. Available at www.americanfreepress.net/03_19_04/New_ Bill_/new_bill_.htm

67. Lee Maracle, *Bent Box*, Penticon, British Columbia: Theytus Books, 2000, 44.

68. Ibid., 45.

Chapter Two

1. Nadine Naber, "Ambiguous Insiders: an Investigation of Arab American Invisibility," *Ethnic and Racial Studies*, 23, no. 1, 2000, 37.

2. Michael Suleiman (ed.), *Arabs in America: Building a New Future*, Philadelphia: Temple University Press, 1999.

3. Alixa Naff, *Becoming American: the Early Arab Immigrant Experience*, Carbondale: Southern Illinois University Press, 1993.

4. Eric Hooglund (ed.), *Crossing the Waters: Arabic-Speaking Immigrants to the United States Before 1940*, Washington, D.C.: Smithsonian Institution Press, 1987.

5. Nabeel Abraham, "Anti-Arab Racism and Violence in the United States," in *The Development of Arab-American Identity*, Ernest McCarus (ed.), Ann Arbor: University of Michigan Press, 1994.

6. Khaled Mattawa and Munir Akash (eds), *Post Gibran: Anthology of New Arab American Writing*, Syracuse: Syracuse University Press, 2000.

7. See further Lisa Suhair Majaj, "Arab-American Ethnicity: Location, Coalitions, and Cultural Negotiations," in *Arabs in America: Building a New Future*, Michael W. Suleiman (ed.), Philadelphia: Temple University Press, 1999; Majaj, "Arab American Literature and the Politics of Memory," in *Memory and Cultural Politics*, Amritjit Singh, Joseph T. Skerrett, Jr. and Robert E. Hogan (eds), Boston: Northeastern University Press, 1996; Majaj, "Arab Americans and the Meanings of Race," in *Postcolonial Theory and the United States*, Amritjit Singh and Peter Schmidt (eds), Jackson: University Press of Mississippi, 2000.

8. See further Diana Abu-Jaber, *Arabian Jazz*, New York: Harvest, 1993; Rabih Alameddine, *KOOLAIDS: the Art of War*, New York: Picador, 1998.

9. See further N. Scott Momaday, *The Names*, New York: Harper & Row, 1976.

10. David Cole, "Patriot Act's Big Brother," *Nation*, 27 February 2003, 4.

11. Ibid.

12. See further Bill Ashcroft and Pal Ahluwalia, *Edward Said: the Paradox of Identity*, London and New York: Routledge, 1999.

13. See further *Middle East Report*, 224, 2002.

14. Hilton Obenzinger, *American Palestine*, Princeton: Princeton University Press, 1999, 24.

15. Martin Peretz, "Gift to the World," *New Republic*, June 1995, 47.

16. Ibid.

17. Joshua Muravchik, "Terrorism at the Multiplex," *Commentary*, January 1999, 57.

18. Associated Press, "N.C. Rep.: WWII Internment Camps Were Meant to Help," 5 February 2003. Available at www.foxnews. com/story/0,2933,77677,00.html

19. Stephen S. Rosenfeld, "Beyond Slogans," *Washington Post*, 18 February 2003, sec. A.

20. Daniel Pipes, "The War on Campus," *New York Post*, 13 September 2002, sec. A.

21. Daniel Brook, "Pipes' Dreams," *Philadelphia City Paper*, 18 July 2002, sec. A.

22. See further *Cineaste* 17, 1989, special supplement on the Arab image in American film.

23. See further Jack G. Shaheen, *Reel Bad Arabs*, New York: Olive Branch Press, 2001.

24. Ronald Stockton, "Ethnic Archetypes and the Arab Image," in *The Development of Arab-American Identity*, Ernest McCarus (ed.), Ann Arbor: University of Michigan Press, 1994, 135.

25. Ibid., 120.

26. Ibid., 150.

27. Abraham, "Anti-Arab Racism and Violence," 159.

28. See further Jean-François Lyotard, *The Differend: Phrases in Dispute*, Minneapolis: University of Minnesota Press, 1988.

29. See further Ann Coulter, "Republicans, Bloggers and Gays, Oh My!," 23 February 2005. Available at www.anncoulter.com/cgi-local/printer_friendly.cgi?article=43

30. See further "ADC Press Release and Action Alert: Protest Biased Media Coverage of Palestine and Palestinians," 13 November 2004. Available at www.adc.org/index.php?id=2383

31. Ibid.

32. See further "ADC Action Alert: Jack Cafferty Continues Racist Remarks," 18 November 2004. Available at www.adc.org/index. php?id=2386

33. See further "ADC Reiterates Concerns About Racism Towards Arabs in the Media," 27 January 2005. Available at www.adc. org/index.php?id=2425

34. See further Associated Press, "Tancredo: If They Nuke Us, Bomb Mecca," 18 July 2005. Available at www.foxnews.com/

story/0,2933,162795,00.html. For information about his refusal to apologize, see further M.E. Sprengelmeyer, "Tancredo: No Apology," *Rocky Mountain News*, 19 July 2005, sec. B.

35. See further James Abourezk, "The Arab Scare: When the Heat is on, Arab-Americans Lose Their Rights," *The Progressive*, May 1993, 26–8.

36. See further Lawrence Davidson, *America's Palestine*, Gainsville: University Press of Florida, 2001.

37. See further Guillaume Debre, "Arab Americans Emerge as Key Voting Bloc," *Christian Science Monitor*, 4 April 2000, sec. A; Linda Gasparello, "Arab-Americans Join Ethnic Electoral Wars," *White House Weekly*, 8 November 1999; Leslie Goffe, "Arab-Americans Coming in from the Cold," *The Middle East*, September 1999, 22; "The Birth of an Arab-American Lobby," *Economist*, 14 October 2000, 41.

38. See further Edward Said, *Orientalism*, New York: Vintage, 1979.

Chapter Three

1. Michael Berube, *The Employment of English*, New York: New York University Press, 1998, 207.

2. Daniel Pipes, "Defund Middle East Studies," *New York Sun*, 24 February 2004, sec. A.

3. He has written, for instance, that "the growing Muslim immigration to the West raises a host of disturbing issues—cultural this time, not military—especially in Western Europe. All immigrants bring exotic customs and attitudes, but Muslim customs are more troublesome than most." In the same article, he claims that Muslim "bellicosity spurs anxiety among Westerners, even fears that Muslims will succeed in subverting the liberal tradition." He further states, "And so it is that increasing numbers of Americans and Europeans are turning to a very traditional boogieman—the Muslim. This profound and ancient fear is far from imaginary." See further Daniel Pipes, "The Muslims are Coming! The Muslims are Coming!," 19 November 1990, available at www.danielpipes.org/article/198. In another article, Pipes endorses Michelle Malkin's book, *In Defense of Internment: the Case for Racial Profiling in World War II and the War on Terror*, suggesting that Malkin "correctly concludes that, especially in time of war, governments should take into account nationality, ethnicity, and religious affiliation in their homeland security policies and engage in what she calls 'threat profiling.' These steps may entail bothersome or offensive measures but, she argues, they are preferable to 'being incinerated at your office desk by a flaming hijacked plane'." See further Daniel Pipes, "Why the

Japanese Internment Still Matters," *New York Sun*, 28 December 2004. Available at www.danielpipes.org/article/2309

4. Daniel Pipes, weblog, 25 February 2004. Available at www.danielpipes.org/blog/184

5. Vlae Kershner, "Web Provides Equal Opportunity for Hatred," *San Francisco Chronicle*, 17 August 2000, sec. A.

6. For more information about Cooksey's remark, see further www.sikhnet.com/sikhnet/discussion.nsf/0/720e0e8f1a1ef1a287256acd 005865d0?OpenDocument

7. More information about this development, including information about Cotterell's email, is available at www.cair.com/default.asp? Page=articleView&id=129&theType=AA

8. Giovanna Borradori, *Philosophy in a Time of Terror: Dialogues with Jürgen Habermas and Jacques Derrida*, Chicago: University of Chicago Press, 2003, 40.

9. American–Arab Anti-Discrimination Committee, "The Condition of Arab Americans Post-9/11." Available at www.adc.org

10. Associated Press, "Report: Anti-Muslim Hate Crimes up Sharply," 10 May 2005. Available at http://msnbc.msn.com/id/7809537

11. Kareem Shora, "Guilty of Flying While Brown," *Air and Space Lawyer*, 17, no. 1, 2002.

12. American–Arab Anti-Discrimination Committee, "Equal Employment Fact Sheet." Available at www.adc.org

13. Ronald Stockton, "Ethnic Archetypes and the Arab Image," in *The Development of Arab-American Identity*, Ernest McCarus (ed.), Ann Arbor: University of Michigan Press, 1994, 142.

14. For more information about Hrdlicka and other contemporary cultural anthropologists, see further Melissa L. Meyer, *The White Earth Tragedy: Ethnicity and Dispossession at a Minnesota Anishinaabe Reservation, 1889–1920*, Lincoln, NE: Nebraska University Press, 1999; David Hurst Thomas, *Skull Wars: Kennewick Man, Archaeology, and the Battle for Native American Identity*, New York: Basic Books, 2001.

15. Stanley Fish, "'Intellectual Diversity': the Trojan Horse of a Dark Design," *The Chronicle of Higher Education*, 13 February 2004, sec. B.

16. Bernstein, for example, quotes from a David Shipler review of *The Politics of Dispossession*: "Reading Mr. Said is like being yelled at for hours on end, and it takes a good and willing ear to appreciate his calmer passages of insight, to hear the essential melodies that run beneath the discordant onslaughts." See further Richard Bernstein, "Edward Said, Scholar and Advocate of Palestinian Homeland, Dies at 67," *New York Times*, 26 September 2003, sec. A.

17. Sara Sebrow and Alex Rolfe, "A Mixed Legacy," *Columbia Spectator*, 29 September 2003, sec. A.

18. Hillel Halkin, "My Brunch with Edward Said," *The Jerusalem Post*, 3 October 2003, sec. A.

19. Harvey Blume, "The Mystery of Edward Said," *The Jerusalem Report*, 3 November 2003, sec. A.

20. Michael Lerner, "Edward Said," *Tikkun*, November/December 2003.

21. David Frum, "Edward Said," *National Review*, September 2003.

22. Zev Chafets, "Edward Said Jammed Our View of Arab World," *New York Daily News*, 1 October 2003, sec. A.

23. Edward Alexander, "Edward Said," *National Association of Scholars* Online Forum, 3 October 2003. Available at www.nas.org

24. See further Brian Glick, *War at Home*, Boston: South End Press, 1989.

25. Martin Kramer, weblog, 12 February 2004. Available at www.martinkramer.org

26. He has written, for example, that "today [Muslim fundamentalists] are in thrall to the idea that Jews everywhere, in league with Israel, are behind a sinister plot to destroy Islam. The battleground is anywhere Jews are organized to assist and aid in this plot." See further Martin Kramer, "The Jihad Against the Jews," *Commentary*, October 1994, available at www.martinkramer.org/pages/899528/index.htm. In the same article, Kramer also claims that so-called Arab anti-Semitism, rather than arising from Jewish colonization of Palestine, "came to Muslim lands largely through the translation of anti-Semitic texts into Arabic, and above all *The Protocols of the Elders of Zion*." He also has suggested that "violence has been close to the surface of the Arab experience at all times, not only in politics and war, but in the regulated conduct of social and economic life." See further Martin Kramer, "Giving Order to Despair," *Commentary*, September 1991, available at www.martinkramer.org/pages/899528/index.htm

27. Neil Kressel, "The Urgent Need to Study Islamic anti-Semitism," *The Chronicle of Higher Education*, 12 March 2004, sec. B.

Chapter Four

1. Stanley Fish, "Reverse Racism, or How the Pot Got to Call the Kettle Black," *The Atlantic Monthly*, November 1993, 128.

2. Ibid., 128.

3. Ibid., 129.

4. Ibid., 128, 130.

5. Anti-Defamation League, "What is Zionism?" Available at www. adl.org/durban/zionism.asp

6. Ibid.

7. Lisa Katz, "What is Zionism?" Available at http://judaism.com/cs/ independenceday/f/zionism_p.htm

8. Ibid.

9. Gidon D. Remba, "What is Zionism? A Peace Now Vision." Available at www.chicagopeacenow.org/wiz-short.html

10. Ibid.

11. Gil Mann, "What is Zionism Anyway?" Available at www. beingjewish.org/magazine/fall2002/article1.html

12. Ibid.

13. See further Edward Said, *The Question of Palestine*, New York: Vintage, 1992.

14. Yigal Allon, "What is Zionism?" Available at www.wzo.org

15. Derek Brown, "What is Zionism?" *Guardian*, 4 September 2001, sec. A.

16. Rana Chreyh, letter, *Ottawa Citizen*, 8 September 2001, sec. B.

17. Neturei Karta, "What is Zionism? Judaism Versus Zionism." Available at www.nkusa.org/aboutus/whatzionism.cfm

18. Ibid.

19. See further Tom Segev, *Elvis in Jerusalem*, trans. Haim Watzman, New York: Metropolitan, 2002; Noah Efron, *Real Jews*, New York: Basic Books, 2003.

20. For examples of the most extreme cases of skepticism and accusation, see further Alexander Cockburn and Jeffrey St. Clair (eds), *The Politics of Anti-Semitism*, Petrolia, CA: Counterpunch Press, 2003; Phyllis Chesler, *The New Anti-Semitism*, New York: Jossey-Bass, 2003.

21. For a particularly insidious justification of the Law of Return, see further Letty Cottin Pogrebin, "In Defense of the Law of Return," *Nation*, 22 December 2003. The fact that the *Nation* published Pogrebin's racist defense is unsurprising since it has a history, dating back to its early enthusiastic support for Israel and continuing into the Christopher Hitchens era, of periodically reminding people of color why they should remain wary of White progressives.

22. Robert Fulford, "Anti-Semitism Can't Be Explained or Cured," *National Post*, 27 March 2004, sec. A.

23. Ibid.

24. Jack Silverstone, "How Can We Fight the New (Old) anti-Semitism?," *Canadian Jewish News*, 22 January 2004, sec. A.

25. Jack Silverstone, letter, *The Ottawa Citizen*, 8 September 2001, sec. B.

26. Aaron Matte, "Opposing Israeli Government Doesn't Make You anti-Semitic," *Montreal Gazette*, 29 November 2002, sec. A.

27. See further Benjamin Beit-Hallahmi, *The Israeli Connection: Who Israel Arms and Why*, New York: Random House, 1987.

28. Nearly all of the *Nation*'s staff writers are White, and although the magazine does well to expose various injustices in communities of color, it has little sustained dedication to exploring race and class privilege, from which it has benefited enormously.

29. Philip Green, "Clearing the Air," *Nation*, 6 January 1992, 5.

30. Robert Allen Warrior, "A Native American Perspective: Canaanites, Cowboys, and Indians," in *Voices from the Margin*, R.S. Sugirtharajah (ed.), New York: Orbis, 1991, 279.

31. Louis Owens, *Mixedblood Messages*, Norman: University of Oklahoma Press, 1998, 130.

32. Jace Weaver, *That the People Might Live*, Oxford: Oxford University Press, 1997, 11.

33. Ward Churchill, *A Little Matter of Genocide*, San Francisco: City Lights, 1997, 73–4.

34. Green, "Clearing the Air," 5.

35. Mortimer B. Zuckerman, "Running the Asylum," *U.S. News and World Report*, 17 September 2001, 120.

36. John Donnelly, "US and Israel Quit Racism Conference," *Boston Globe*, 4 September 2001, sec. A.

37. John Donnelly and Anthony Shadid, "Race Talks Point to Palestinian Strategy," *Boston Globe*, 7 September 2001, sec. A.

38. "Debacle in Durban," *Christian Century*, 12 September 2001, 5.

39. Michael Lerner, "The Danger of Walking Out at Durban," *New York Times*, 5 September 2001, sec. A.

40. Ibid.

41. Ibid.

42. Cherie R. Brown, "Lessons Learned in Durban," *Tikkun*, November/December 2001, 23.

43. Ibid., 24.

Chapter Five

1. According to Victoria Clark, "The ICEJ's entrance hall is hung with photographs of Likud leaders who have applauded ICEJ's efforts on Israel's behalf. Notable by his absence is Ehud Barak, the Labour leader who came closest to forging a peace with Arafat. With its 60-strong staff, a budget estimated at $8m a year in 1999 and a membership of some 100,000, the non-profit-making ICEJ devotes the bulk of its resources and energies to helping fulfil prophecies relating to the Jews and their land. Since communism's

collapse in 1991 the ICEJ has funded the transportation of 60,000 Soviet Jews to Israel, 15,000 of them on ICEJ-chartered jumbo jets." See further Victoria Clark, "The Christian Zionists," *Prospect*, 19 June 2003.

2. See further Grace Halsell, *Prophecy and Politics*, Westport: Lawrence Hill, 1986, 74.

3. Malcolm Foster, "Jews have Mixed Reactions to pro-Israel Fervor of 'Christian Zionists'," Associated Press Worldstream, 30 January 2003.

4. William Martin, "The Christian Right and American Foreign Policy," *Foreign Affairs*, 114, 1999, 68.

5. David Gates, "The Pop Prophets," *Newsweek*, 24 May 2004, 49.

6. See further ibid.; Melani McAlister, "An Empire of Their Own," *Nation*, 22 September 2003.

7. Martin, "The Christian Right," 68. Martin also writes, "Leaders of [dispensationalist] groups come together several times a year at meetings of the Council for National Policy (CNP), a low-profile organization whose membership includes heads of various radio, television, and print media organizations: key Congressional figures such as Representatives Dick Armey (R-TX) and Tom DeLay (R-TX) and Senators Trent Lott (R-MS) and Jesse Helms (R-NC); conservative ideologues and operatives such as Oliver North and Paul Weyrich (Free Congress Foundation); and major financial supporters of conservative causes, including members of the wealthy Coors and DeVos (Amway) families. Also playing a role in the CNP are several prominent 'Reconstructionists,' people who seek to reconstitute society on the basis of strict adherence to Biblical law, including stoning and other harsh punishments for violations of Biblical prohibitions against adultery, homosexuality, unbelief, and promulgation of false doctrine."

8. Ibid., 71.

9. "Rep. Tom DeLay and His 'Biblical Worldview': What about the Constitution?" *Church and State*, June 2002, 15.

10. Ibid., 15.

11. Martin, "The Christian Right," 69.

12. Ibid., 71–2.

13. Megan K. Stack, "DeLay Spreads Message of Support for Israel," *Chattanooga Times Free Press*, 31 July 2003, sec. A.

14. Ibid.

15. Pat Robertson, "On Israel and the Road Map to Peace." Available at www.patrobertson.com/Teaching/TeachingonRoadMap.asp

16. Ibid.

17. Ibid. Robertson ends his lesson with more premillenialist threats: "[Jerusalem] is a permanent possession given by God to Abraham,

and all of this territory is the land of Israel. There is no such thing as a Palestine state, nor has there ever been. Now we're going to make something that never happened before in contravention to Scripture. God may love George Bush. God may love America. God [may] love us all, but if we stand in the way of prophecy and try to frustrate what God said in his immutable word, then we're in for a heap of trouble. And I think this is a warning we should all take … . If we ally ourselves with the enemies of Israel, we will be standing against God Almighty. And that's a place I don't want us to be."

18. Pat Robertson, "Why Evangelical Christians Support Israel." Available at www.patrobertson.com

19. Tim LaHaye, "The Prophetic Significance of Sept. 11, 2001," *Pre-trib Perspectives*, September 2001.

20. Thomas Ice, "Myths about Israel and Palestine," *Pre-trib Perspectives*, February 2001. Claiming that "there is no such thing as the ancient land of Palestine," Ice argues that "because of the contemporary use of the term 'Palestine,' I think it is best that Christians refrain from using it to refer to the land of Israel. This is how Israel is usually referred to, even in biblical maps from the time of Christ and before, when the term was not invented until 100 years after the time of Christ."

21. Ibid.

22. Bill Broadway, "The Evangelical–Israeli Connection," *Washington Post*, 27 March 2004, sec. B.

23. Ibid.

24. Ken Silverstein and Michael Scherer, "Born-Again Zionists," *Mother Jones*, September/October 2002, 57.

25. Ibid., 57.

26. Michael Welton, "Unholy Alliance," *Canadian Dimension*, March/April 2003, 19.

27. Broadway, "The Evangelical–Israeli Connection."

28. Silverstein and Scherer, "Born-Again Zionists," 59.

29. Ibid., 58.

30. Howard Fineman et al., "A Very Mixed Message," *Newsweek*, 2 June 2003, 34.

31. According to the *Nation*, Latinos comprise 9 per cent of the *Left Behind* readership and Blacks comprise 7 per cent.

32. Teresa Watanabe, "Seminary is Reaching out to Muslims," *Los Angeles Times*, 6 December 2003, sec. B.

33. The late Edward Said, one of the world's most famous Arab Christians, once noted that "if there's any particular importance to being Christian in Palestine it is obviously that many of us are quite proud of the many centuries, 2,000 years of a Christian presence in Palestine, to which we belong." See further Edward Said, *The Pen*

and the Sword: Conversations with David Barsamian, Monroe: Common Courage Press, 1994, 59.

Chapter Six

1. "Abu Ghraib Idiocy Watch I," *New Republic*, 24 May 2004, 11.
2. "Abu Ghraib Idiocy Watch II," *New Republic*, 24 May 2004, 11.
3. Tammy Bruce, "Why Abu Ghraib Matters," *FrontPageMagazine.com*, 24 May 2004.
4. Ibid.
5. Ibid.
6. "Abuse and the Army," *Wall Street Journal*, 6 May 2004, sec. A.
7. Richard Starr, "A Few Bad Men," *Weekly Standard*, 17 May 2004.
8. Midge Decter, "If Rumsfeld is Driven Out, We All Lose," *Los Angeles Times*, 7 May 2004, sec. A.
9. Ibid.
10. Gordon Cucullu, "The Facts on Abu Ghraib," *FrontPageMagazine.com*, 20 May 2004.
11. "Senator 'Outraged by Outrage' at Prison Abuse," *Reuters*, 11 May 2004.
12. "Tortured Logic," *New Republic*, 24 May 2004, 10.
13. Walter Shapiro, "For Senator, Outrage is more Outrageous Than Abuse," *USA Today*, 12 May 2004, sec. A.
14. "Abuses," *National Review*, 31 May 2004, 14–15.
15. Michael Barone, "No, It's Not the American Way," *U.S. News and World Report*, 17 May 2004, 40.
16. Ibid., 40.
17. Mortimer B. Zuckerman, "A Bit of Perspective, Please," *U.S. News and World Report*, 24 May 2004, 68.
18. John Barry et al., "The Roots of Torture," *Newsweek*, 24 May 2004, 27.
19. Ibid., 27.
20. Ibid., 27.
21. Amanda Ripley et al., "The Rules of Interrogation," *Time*, 17 May 2004, 44.
22. Michael Isikoff, "Brooklyn's Version of Abu Ghraib," *Newsweek*, 24 May 2004, 5.
23. Joe Klein, "The Perils of a Righteous President," *Time*, 17 May 2004, 25.
24. Ibid., 25.
25. David Gates, "The Pop Prophets," *Newsweek*, 24 May 2004, 46.
26. Nicholas Kristoff, "Jesus and Jihad," *New York Times*, 17 July 2004, sec. A.

27. Brian Whittaker, "'Its Best Use Is as a Doorstop,'" *Guardian*, 24 May 2004, sec. A.
28. Ibid.
29. Ibid.
30. Ibid.
31. Fisk, "Victims of Our Own High-Flown Morality."
32. Ibid.

Index